THE JOURNALS OF
GEORGE WHITEFIELD

Also available in the Spiritual Lives series

THE JOURNALS OF
GEORGE WHITEFIELD

Edited by Robert Backhouse

Hodder & Stoughton

LONDON SYDNEY AUCKLAND

British Library Cataloguing in Publication Data.
A catalogue record for this book is available from the British Library.

ISBN 0–340–57777–0

Published by Hodder and Stoughton, a division of Hodder and Stoughton Ltd, Mill Road, Dunton Green, Sevenoaks, Kent TN13 2YA. Editorial Office: 47 Bedford Square, London WC1B 3DP.

Typeset by Watermark, Norfolk House, Hamilton Road, Cromer, Norfolk.

Printed in Great Britain by Cox & Wyman Ltd, Reading, Berks.

Contents

Editor's Introduction

Whitefield's journals began in 1738 when he sent back to England an account of his first visit to America. This became known as Whitefield's *First Journal*. It was received with such enthusiasm, going through four editions in its first year of publication, that Whitefield wrote six further journals which cover his activities in God's service from the end of his *First Journal* up to 1741.

On his second voyage to America Whitefield wrote an account of his life up to his ordination, under the title *A Short Account of God's Dealings with George Whitefield from the Time of his Ordination to his Embarking for Georgia, June 1736 –December 1737*.

In June 1756 Whitefield revised, corrected and abridged all of these writings into a single volume. He felt keenly some of the criticisms that were levelled against his writing and the revised edition gave him the opportunity to take some of these criticisms into account.

The present edition follows the text of Whitefield's own corrected edition of 1756, abridging it and occasionally updating the vocabulary.

Because Whitefield was refused permission to preach in many Church of England churches, he preached in the open air. From the age of 22 until he died at 55 he normally preached two or three times a day, sometimes to crowds of over 20,000 people. It was not unusual for many of his hearers to have tears rolling down their cheeks as they responded to God's voice in their hearts. Whitefield's constant theme was the sinfulness of mankind, the holiness of God and atonement through Jesus Christ. At Whitefield's funeral John Wesley said that history records none 'who called so many myriads of sinners to repentance'.

Robert Backhouse
Crostwight, 1992

Preface

to the 1756 edition, by George Whitefield

Christian Reader,

According to a promise made some time ago, I here present a new edition of the two first parts of my Life, and also of my Journals, in which you will find many mistakes rectified; many passages that were justly exceptionable, erased; and the whole abridged; and yet enough left behind for the natural man (to whom the things of the Spirit of God are but foolishness) to carp at and ridicule.

It was, and is now, my full intention, if God should spare my life and give me freedom, to have added, by way of supplement, a short account of the progress of (what I think may assuredly be styled) the work of God, so far as has come within my cognisance, from the time when the Journals end to this day; but my frequent travelling and preaching oblige me to defer putting such a design in execution to some future opportunity.

Indeed I hoped that long before now I should have entered into rest—but I find we are immortal till our work is done.

However, since it has pleased our heavenly Father to protract my worthless life to such an unexpected length, I desire to thank him from my inmost soul, that he has given me to see the gospel seed that was sown upwards of twenty years ago now grown into a great tree.

9

Glory be to his holy name! Multitudes both in England, Scotland, Wales, Ireland, and various parts of North America, have been brought to lodge under the branches of it. How far it is yet to spread can be known only to him with whom the residue of the Spirit is.

At present, thanks be to God, the prospect is promising. A new set of instruments seem to be rising up, by whom, I trust, those that were first sent forth will not only be succeeded, but eclipsed, as the stars are succeeded and eclipsed by the rising sun. May they go on and prosper; and in the strength of their common Lord, be made happily instrumental to direct a careless unthinking world into a *holy Method* of dying to themselves, and living to God!

This is the only Methodism I desire to know. And that this may meet with a universal flow amongst ministers and people of all denominations I am sure you will join in praying with,

Christian Reader,

Your ready servant for our common master's sake,

G. Whitefield

London,
June 4, 1756

A Short Account of God's Dealings

with the Reverend Mr George Whitefield, AB,
late of Pembroke College, Oxford,
from his infancy to the time of his entering into
Holy Orders (1714–1736)
written by himself, on board the Elizabeth,
Captain Stephenson, bound from London to
Philadelphia, and sent over by him to be published for
the benefit of the orphan-house in Georgia

Introduction

Although the following account of what God has done for my soul will undoubtedly be differently judged by different people, yet, since I believe a single eye to God's glory moves me to write, and I find myself much pressed in spirit to publish it at this time, I am not in the least solicitous about the reception it will meet with in the world.

The benefit I have received from reading the lives of others, the examples we have in scripture of the sacred authors composing their own histories, and more especially the assistance I have had from the Holy Spirit, in bringing many things to my remembrance which otherwise I would have forgotten, seemed to me reasons sufficient to justify my conduct in the sight of God and good men.

Further, as God has been pleased of late to call me to a public work, I thought his children would be glad to know how I was trained up for it.

In the accounts of good men which I have read, I have observed that the writers of them have been partial. They have given us the bright, but not the dark side of their character. This, I think, proceeded from a kind of pious fraud, lest mentioning a person's faults should encourage others in sin. It cannot, I am sure, proceed from the wisdom which comes from above. The sacred writers give an account of their failings as well as their virtues. Peter is not ashamed to confess that with oaths and curses he denied his master three times; nor do the evangelists make any scruple of telling us that out of Mary Magdalene Jesus Christ cast seven devils.

I have therefore endeavoured to follow their good example. I have simply told what I was by nature, as well as what I am by grace.

1 From my infancy until my being for some time at the university

I was born in Gloucester, in the month of December 1714. I can truly say I was contrary from my mother's womb. I was so brutish as to hate instruction, and used purposely to shun all opportunities of receiving it. I can date some very early acts of uncleanness. Lying, filthy talking, and foolish jesting I was much addicted to. Sometimes I used to curse, if not swear. Stealing from my mother I thought no theft at all, and used to make no scruple of taking money out of her pocket before she was up. I have frequently betrayed my trust, and have more than once spent money I took in the house, in buying fruits, tarts, etc., to satisfy my sensual appetite. Numbers of sabbaths have I broken, and generally used to behave myself very irreverently in God's sanctuary. Much money have I spent on plays, and in the common entertainments of the age.

However the young man in the gospel might boast how he had kept the commandments from his youth, with shame and confusion of face I confess that I have broken them all from my youth. Whatever foreseen fitness for salvation others may talk of and glory in, I disclaim any such thing. If I trace myself from my cradle to my manhood, I can see nothing in me but a fitness to be damned. If the Almighty had not gone before me by his grace, and worked most powerfully upon my soul, giving me life by his free Spirit when dead in trespasses and sins, I would now either have been sitting in darkness, and in the shadow of death, or condemned, as the due reward of my crimes, to be for ever lifting up my eyes in torments.

But such was the free grace of God to me, that though corruption worked so strongly in my soul, and produced such early and bitter fruits, yet I can recollect very early movings of the blessed Spirit upon my heart, sufficient to satisfy me that God loved me with an everlasting love, and separated me even from my mother's womb for the work to which he afterwards was pleased to call me.

I had some early convictions of sin; and once, I remember, when some persons (as they frequently did) made it their business to tease me, I immediately retired to my room, and kneeling down, with many tears, prayed over that Psalm wherein David so often repeats these words—'But in the name of the Lord I cut them off.' I was always fond of the idea of being a clergyman, used frequently to imitate the ministers reading prayers, etc. Part of the money I used to steal from my parent I gave to the poor, and some books I privately took from others, for which I have since restored fourfold, I remember were books of devotion.

About the tenth year of my age, it pleased God to permit my mother to marry a second time. It proved what the world would call an unhappy match as for temporals, but God overruled it for good.

When I was about twelve, I was placed at a school called

St Mary de Crypt, in Gloucester—the last grammar school I ever went to. Having a good elocution and memory, I was noted for making speeches before the corporation at their annual visitation. But I cannot say I felt any drawings of God upon my soul for a year or two, saving that I laid out some of the money that was given me on one of those forementioned occasions, in buying Ken's *Manual for Winchester Scholars*—a book that had much affected me when my brother used to read it in my mother's troubles, and which, for some time after I bought it, was of great benefit to my soul.

During my time at school, I was very fond of reading plays, and have kept away from school for days together to prepare myself for acting them. My master seeing how my and my schoolfellows' vein ran, composed something of this kind for us himself, and caused me to dress myself in girls' clothes, which I had often done, to act a part before the corporation.

Before I was fifteen, having, as I thought, made sufficient progress in the classics, and, at the bottom, longing to be set at liberty from the confinement of a school, I one day told my mother that since her circumstances would not permit her to give me a university education, more learning I thought would spoil me for a tradesman; and therefore I judged it best not to learn Latin any longer. She at first refused to consent, but my corruptions soon got the better of her good nature. Hereupon, for some time I went to learn to write only. But my mother's circumstances being much on the decline, and being tractable that way, I from time to time began to assist her occasionally in the public house, till at length I put on my blue apron and my candle-snuffers, washed mops, cleaned rooms, and, in one word, became professed and common barman for nearly a year and a half.

Although I was thus employed in a common inn, and had sometimes the care of the whole house upon my hands, yet I composed two or three sermons, and dedicated one of them in particular to my elder brother. One time, I remember, I was much pressed to self-examination, and found myself very unwilling to look into my heart. Frequently I read the Bible when sitting up at night.

After I had continued about a year in this servile employment, my mother was obliged to leave the inn. My brother, who had been bred up for the business, married; whereupon all was made over to him; and, I being accustomed to the house, it was agreed that I should continue there as an assistant. It happened that my sister-in-law and I could by no means agree.

After continuing for a long while under this burden of mind, I at length resolved, thinking my absence would make all things easy, to go away. Accordingly, by the advice of my brother, and consent of my mother, I went to see my elder brother then settled at Bristol.

Here God was pleased to give me great foretastes of his great devotion, and fill me with such unspeakable raptures, particularly once in St John's church, that I was carried out beyond myself. Thomas a Kempis was my great delight, and I was always impatient till the bell rang to call me to tread the courts of the Lord's house. But in the midst of these illuminations something surely whispered, *This will not last.*

And, indeed, so it happened. For—oh that I could write it in tears of blood!—when I left Bristol, as I did in about two months, and returned to Gloucester, I changed my devotion with my place. Alas! all my fervour went off: I had no inclination to go to church, or draw near to God. In short, my heart, though I had so lately tasted of his love, was far from him.

However, I had so much religion left as to persist in my resolution not to live in the inn; and therefore my mother gave me leave, though she had but a little income, to have a bed on the floor, and live at her house, till providence should point out a place for me.

Having now, as I thought, nothing to do, it was a suitable

time for Satan to tempt me. Much of my time I spent in reading plays, and in sauntering from place to place. I was careful to adorn my body, but took little pains to deck and beautify my soul. Evil communications with my old school-fellows soon corrupted my good manners. By seeing their evil practices, all sense of religion I had experienced wore off my mind, and I at length fell into abominable secret sin, the dismal effects of which I have felt and groaned under ever since.

Having thus lived with my mother for some consider-able time, a young student who was once my schoolfellow and then a servitor of Pembroke College, Oxford, came to pay my mother a visit. Amongst other conversation, he told her how he had discharged all college expenses that quarter, and received a penny. Upon that my mother immediately cried out, 'This will do for my son.' Then turning to me, she said, 'Will you go to Oxford, George?' I replied, 'With all my heart.' Whereupon, having the same friends that this young student had, my mother, without delay, went to see them. They promised their influence to get me a servitor's place in the same college. She then applied to my old master, who much approved of my com-ing to school again.

God was pleased to give me his blessing, and I learned much faster than I did before. But all this while I con-tinued in sin; and, at length, got acquainted with such a set of debauched, abandoned, atheistical youths that if God, by his free, unmerited, and especial grace, had not deli-vered me out of their hands, I should have long since sat in the scorner's chair. By keeping company with them, my thoughts of religion grew more and more like theirs. I went to public service only to make fun and walk about. I took pleasure in their lewd conversation. I began to reason as they did, and was in a fair way of being as infamous as the worst of them.

But, oh stupendous love! God even here stopped me, when running on in a full career to hell. For, just as I was on the brink of ruin, he gave me such a distaste of their principles and practices, that I revealed them to my master, who soon put a stop to their proceedings.

For twelve months, I went on in a round of duties, receiving the sacrament monthly, fasting frequently, attending constantly at public worship, and praying often more than twice a day in private. One of my brothers used to tell me he feared this would not hold long, and that I should forget all when I came to Oxford. This caution did me much service, for it set me upon praying for perseverance; and, under God, the preparation I made in the country was a preservative against the manifold temptations which beset me at my first coming to that seat of learning.

Being now nearly eighteen years old, it was judged proper for me to go to the university. God had prepared my way. The friends before applied to recommended me to the Master of Pembroke College. Another friend took out a bond for £10, which I have since repaid, to defray the first expense of entering; and the Master, contrary to all expectations, admitted me servitor immediately.

This much lessened my expenses; and indeed, God was so gracious that with the profits of my place, and some little presents made me by my kind tutor, for almost the first three years I did not put all my relations together to above £24 expense.

Before I went to the university, I met with Mr Law's *Serious Call to a Devout and Holy Life*, but had not then money to purchase it. Soon after my coming up to the university, seeing a small edition of it in a friend's hand, I soon procured it. God worked powerfully upon my soul, as he has since upon many others, by that and his other excellent treatise upon *Christian Perfection*.

I now began to pray and sing psalms three times every day, besides morning and evening, and to fast every Friday, and to receive the sacrament at a parish church near our college, and at the castle, where the despised Methodists used to receive once a month.

The young men, so called because they lived by rule and method, were then much talked of at Oxford. I had heard of, and loved, them before I came to the university; and so strenuously defended them when I heard them reviled by the students, that they began to think that I also in time would be one of them.

For over a year my soul longed to be acquainted with some of them, and I was strongly pressed to follow their good example, when I saw them go through a ridiculing crowd to receive the holy eucharist at St Mary's. At length, God was pleased to open a door. It happened that a poor woman in one of the workhouses had attempted to cut her throat, but was happily prevented. Upon hearing of this, and knowing that both the Mr Wesleys were very ready to every good work, I sent a poor apple-woman of our college to inform Mr Charles Wesley of it, telling her not to reveal who sent her. She went; but, contrary to my orders, told my name. He having heard of my coming to the castle and a parish-church sacrament, and having met me frequently walking by myself, followed the woman when she was gone away, and sent an invitation to me by her, to come to breakfast with him the next morning.

I thankfully embraced the opportunity. He gave me Professor Francke's treatise *Against the Fear of Man*. In a short time he let me have another book, entitled, *The Life of God in the Soul of Man*. At my first reading it, I wondered what the author meant by saying that some falsely placed religion in going to church, doing hurt to no one, being constant in private devotions, and now and then reaching out their hands to give alms to their poor neighbours. 'Alas!' thought I, 'if this be not true religion, what is?' God soon showed me; for in reading a few lines further, that true religion was union of soul with God, and Christ formed within us, a ray of divine light was instantaneously darted in upon my soul, and from that moment, but not till then, did I know that I must be a new creature.

From time to time Charles Wesley engaged me to come

to him, and introduced me to the rest of the Methodists. They built me up in the knowledge and fear of God, and taught me to endure hardness like a good soldier of Jesus Christ.

I now began, like them, to live by rule, and to pick up the very fragments of my time, that not a moment of it might be lost. Whether I ate or drank, or whatsoever I did, I endeavoured to do all to the glory of God. Like them, having no weekly sacrament, although the rubric required it, at our own college, I received every Sunday at Christ Church. I joined with them in keeping the stations by fasting on Wednesdays and Fridays, engaged to visit the sick and the prisoners, and to read to poor people, till I made it a custom, as most of us did, to spend an hour every day in doing acts of charity.

The course of my studies soon entirely changed. Whereas, before, I was busied in studying the dry science, and books that went no farther than the surface, I now resolved to read only such as entered into the heart of religion, and which led me directly into an experimental knowledge of Jesus Christ, and him crucified.

2 A brief and summary account of my temptations

The first thing I was called to give up for God was what the world calls my fair reputation. I had no sooner received the sacrament publicly on a week-day at St Mary's, but I was set up as a mark for all the polite students that knew me to shoot at. Soon after this, I incurred the displeasure of the Master of the college, who frequently chid, and once threatened to expel me, if I ever visited the poor again. Being surprised at this treatment, and overawed by his authority, I spoke inadvisedly with my lips, and said, if it displeased him I would not. My conscience soon pricked me for this sinful compliance. I immediately repented, and visited the poor at the first opportunity. My worthy tutor, being a moderate man, did not oppose me. I daily underwent some contempt at college. Some have thrown dirt at me; others, by degrees, took away their pay from me; and two friends, that were dear to me, grew shy of and forsook me.

My inward sufferings were of a more uncommon nature. All power of meditating, or even thinking, was taken from me. My memory quite failed me. My whole soul was barren and dry, and I could fancy myself to be like nothing so much as a man locked up in iron armour.

Whenever I kneeled down, I felt great pressures both in soul and body, and have often prayed under the weight of them till the sweat came through me. God only knows how many nights I have lain upon my bed groaning under the weight I felt. Whole days and weeks have I spent in lying prostrate on the ground in silent or vocal prayer; and, having nobody to show me a better way, I thought to get peace and purity by outward austerities. Accordingly, by degrees, I began to leave off eating fruits and such like, and gave the money I usually spent in that way to the poor. Afterward, I always chose the worst sort of food, though my place furnished me with variety. I fasted twice a week. My apparel was mean. I thought it unbecoming a penitent to have his hair powdered. I wore woollen gloves, a patched gown and dirty shoes and therefore looked upon myself as very humble.

For many months, I went on in this legal state, but finding pride creeping in at the end of almost every thought, word, and action, and meeting with Castaniza's *Spiritual Combat*, in which he says that he that is employed in mortifying his will is as well employed as though he were converting Indians, Satan so imposed upon my understanding that he persuaded me to shut myself up in my study, till I could do good without feeling any mixture of corruption, lest, in endeavouring to save others, as I did now, I should at last by pride and self-complacency lose myself.

About five or six weeks I had now spent in my study, except when college business obliged me to go down. During this time I was fighting with my corruptions, and did little else besides kneeling down by my bedside, feeling, as it were, a heavy pressure upon my body, as well as an unspeakable oppression of mind, yet offering up my soul to God, to do with me as he pleased. It was now suggested to me that Jesus Christ was among the wild beasts when he was tempted, and that I ought to follow his example; and being willing, as I thought, to imitate Jesus Christ, after supper I went into Christ Church Walk, near our college, and continued in silent prayer under one of the trees, kneeling upon my knees, till the great bell rang for retirement to the college, not without finding some reluctance in the natural man against staying so long in the cold.

By this time, I had left off keeping my diary, using my set prayers, or scarce my voice in prayer, visiting the prisoners, etc. Nothing remained for me to leave, unless I forsook public worship, except my religious friends. Now it was suggested that I must leave them also for Christ's sake. This was a sore trial; but rather than not be, as I fancied, Christ's disciple, I resolved to renounce them, though as dear to me as my own soul. Accordingly, the next day being Wednesday, when we kept one of our weekly fasts, instead of meeting with my brethren as usual, I went out into the fields, and prayed silently by myself. Our evening meeting I neglected also, and did not go to breakfast, according to appointment, with Mr Charles Wesley the day following. This, with many other concurring circumstances, made my honoured friend, Mr Charles Wesley, suspect something more than ordinary was the matter. He came to my room, apprised me of my danger if I would not take advice, and recommended me to his brother John, Fellow of Lincoln College, as more experienced than himself. God gave me a teachable temper, I went to see his brother, with whom from that time I had the honour of growing intimate. He advised me to resume all my externals, though not to depend on them in the least. From time to time he gave me directions as my pitiable state required.

During this and all other seasons of temptation my soul

was inwardly supported with great courage and resolution from above. Every day God made me willing to renew the combat, and though my soul, when quite empty of God, was very prone to seek satisfaction in the creature, and sometimes I fell into sensuality, yet I was generally enabled to wait in silence for the salvation of God, or to persist in prayer, till some beams of spiritual light and comfort were vouchsafed me from on high. Thomas a Kempis (since translated and published by Mr John Wesley), Castaniza's *Spiritual Combat*, and the Greek Testament, every reading of which I endeavoured to turn into a prayer, were of great help and furtherance to me. On receiving the holy sacrament, especially before trials, I have found grace in a very affecting manner, and in abundant measure, sometimes imparted to my soul—an irrefragable proof to me of the miserable delusion of the author of that work called *The Plain Account of the Sacrament*, which sinks that holy ordinance into a bare memorial.

To proceed—I had now taken up my externals again and began to visit the poor. A few days after, as I was walking along, I met with a poor woman, whose husband was then in Bocardo, or Oxford Town Gaol. Seeing her much upset, I enquired the cause. She told me, not being able to bear the crying of her children, ready to perish for hunger, and having nothing to relieve them, she had been to drown herself, but was mercifully prevented, and said she was coming to my room to inform me of it. I gave her some immediate relief, and desired her to meet me at the prison with her husband in the afternoon. She came, and there God visited them both by his free grace. She was powerfully given life from above; and when I had finished reading, he also came to me like the trembling gaoler, and, grasping my hand, cried out, 'I am upon the brink of hell!' From this time forward, both of them grew in grace. God, by his providence, soon delivered him from his confinement. Though notorious offenders against God and one another before, yet now they became help-meet for each other in the great work of their salvation.

Soon after this, Lent came on, which our friends kept very strictly, eating no flesh during the six weeks, except on Saturdays also, and ate nothing on the other days, except on Sunday, but sage tea without sugar, and coarse bread. I constantly walked out in the cold mornings till part of one of my hands was quite black. This, with my continued abstinence, and inward conflicts, at length so emaciated my body that, at Passion week, finding I could scarce creep upstairs, I was obliged to inform my kind tutor of my condition, who immediately sent for a physician.

This caused no small triumph amongst the collegians, who began to cry out, 'What is his fasting come to now?' But, although my fit of sickness continued for six or seven weeks, I trust I shall have reason to thank God for it, through the endless ages of eternity, for about the end of the seven weeks, after having undergone innumerable buffetings of Satan, and many months inexpressible trials by night and day under the spirit of bondage, God was pleased at length to remove the heavy load, to enable me to lay hold on his dear Son by a living faith, and, by giving me the spirit of adoption, to seal me, as I humbly hope, even to the day of everlasting redemption. But oh! with what joy—joy unspeakable—even joy that was full of, and big with glory, was my soul filled, when the weight of sin went off, and an abiding sense of the pardoning love of God, and a full assurance of faith broke in upon my disconsolate soul! Surely it was my wedding day—a day to be had in everlasting remembrance. At first my joys were like a spring tide, and, as it were, overflowed the banks. Go where I would, I could not avoid singing of psalms aloud; afterwards it became more settled—and, blessed be God, saving a few casual intervals, has remained and increased in my soul ever since. But to proceed.

3 From the time of my first leaving the university to go to Gloucester, till the time of my ordination

'I will endeavour either to find or make a friend,' had been my resolution now for some time; and therefore, immediately upon my coming down, after importunate prayer one day, I resolved to go to the house of one Mrs W., to whom I had formerly read plays, the *Spectator*, Pope's Homer, and such-like books—hoping the alteration she would now find in my sentiments might, under God, influence her soul. She soon became a fool for Christ's sake. Not long after, God made me instrumental to awaken several more young persons, who soon formed themselves into a little Society, and quickly had the honour of being despised at Gloucester, as we had been before them at Oxford. Thus *all* that will live godly in Christ Jesus must suffer persecution.

My mind being now more open and enlarged, I began to read the holy scriptures upon my knees, laying aside all other books, and praying over, if possible, every line and word. This proved meat indeed, and drink indeed, to my soul. I daily walked with God, and going to visit a relation, then in one of the almshouses, God brought in my way a young woman who was hungering and thirsting after righteousness. She received the word into an honest and good heart, and since has proved a true follower of Jesus Christ.

God enabled me to give a public testimony of my repentance as to seeing and acting plays. For, hearing the Strollers were coming to town, and knowing what an egregious offender I had been that way, I made extracts from Mr Law's excellent treatise *The Absolute Unlawfulness of the Stage Entertainment*. This was put into the *Gloucester Journal* for six weeks successively, and God was pleased to give it his blessing.

4 Of my preparation for Holy Orders

Being now about twenty-one years of age, some began to enquire when I was to take Orders; but the saying of the apostle, 'He must not be a recent convert, or he may become conceited and fall under same judgement as the devil'; and that first question of our excellent ordination service, 'Do you trust that you are *inwardly* moved by the Holy Ghost to take upon you this office and administration?' used even to make me tremble whenever I thought of entering into the ministry. With strong cryings and tears I have often said, 'Lord, I am a youth of uncircumcised lips; Lord, send me not into your vineyard yet!'

I still continued instant in prayer against going into Holy Orders, and was not thoroughly convinced it was the divine will till God, by his providence, brought me acquainted with Dr Benson, the late worthy Bishop of Gloucester. One afternoon as I was coming from the cathedral prayers, one of the vergers was sent to inform me that his lordship desired to speak with me. And imagining it was to chide me, I began to consider within myself what I had done to deserve his lordship's displeasure. But to my great surprise, when I came to the top of the palace stairs, the bishop took me by the hand, told me he was glad to see me, and bid me to wait a little till he had put off his habit, and he would return to me again.

At his coming into the room, the bishop told me he had heard of my character, liked my behaviour at church, and enquired my age. 'Although,' said he, 'I have declared I would not ordain anyone under twenty-three, yet I shall think it my duty to ordain you whenever you come for Holy Orders.'

At length I came to a resolution, by God's leave, to offer myself for Holy Orders the next Ember Days.

My friends urged several reasons for my continuing at the university. The Mr Wesleys had not long been gone abroad, and now no one was left to take care of the prison affairs, they said. They further urged that God had blessed my endeavours *there* as well as at Gloucester; that the university was the fountain-head; that every gownsman's name was Legion; and that if I should be made instrumental in converting one of *them*, it would be as much as converting a whole parish. At the same time, unknown to me, some of them sent to that great and good man, the late Sir John Philips, who was a great encourager of the Oxford Methodists; and, though he had never seen, but only heard of, me, yet he sent word he would allow me £30 a year if I would continue at the university. Upon this, finding the care of the prisoners would be no more than, under God, I could undertake with pleasure, and knowing the university was the best place to prosecute my studies, I resolved, God willing, to await at Oxford a blessing on the first-fruits of my ministerial labours.

About three days before the time appointed for ordination, the bishop came to town. The next evening, I sent his lordship an abstract of my private examination on these two questions. 'Do you trust that you are inwardly moved by the Holy Ghost to take upon you this office and administration?' and 'Are you called according to the will of our Lord Jesus Christ, and the laws of this realm?' The next morning I went to see the bishop. He received me with much love, telling me he was glad I had come; that he was satisfied with the allowance given me by Sir John Philips. 'I had myself,' said he, 'made provision for you of two little parishes; but since you choose to be at Oxford, I am very well pleased.'

On Sunday morning, I rose early, and prayed over St Paul's letter to Timothy, and more particularly over that precept, 'Don't let anyone look down on you because you are young' (1 Timothy 4:12). When I went up to the altar, I could think of nothing but Samuel's standing a little child before the Lord with a linen ephod. When the bishop laid his hands upon my head, I offered up my whole spirit, soul and body to the service of God's sanctuary. I read the gospel, at the bishop's command, with power, and afterwards sealed the good confession I had made before many witnesses, by partaking of the holy sacrament of our Lord's most blessed body and blood.

The next morning, waiting upon God in prayer to know

what he would have me to do, these words, 'Speak out, Paul,' came with great power to my soul. Immediately my heart was enlarged. God spoke to me by his Spirit, and I was no longer dumb. I finished a sermon I had in hand some time before, and began another; and preached the Sunday following to a very crowded audience, with as much freedom as though I had been a preacher for some years.

Oh, the unspeakable benefit of reading to the poor, and exercising our talents while students at the university! Such prior acts are very proper to prepare us for the work of our Lord, and make us not unapt to teach in a more public manner. It is remarkable that our Lord sent out his disciples on short missions before they were so solemnly authorised at the day of Pentecost. Would the Heads and Tutors of our universities but follow his example, and, instead of discouraging their pupils from doing anything of this nature, send them to visit the sick and the prisoners, and to pray with and read practical books of religion to the poor, they would find such exercises of more service to them, and to the church of God, than all their private and public lectures put together.

Thus God dealt with my soul. At the same time, by his gracious providence, he supplied me with all things needful for my body also.

I shall hereafter relate God's further dealings with my soul, and how he led me into my present way of acting. Meanwhile, dear reader, whoever you are, I pray God what I have now written may not prove a savour of death unto death, but a savour of life unto life unto your soul. Many, I fear, through ignorance, and unbelief, when they read this, will contradict and blaspheme. Be not of this number; but if you are as yet unaffected with the contagion of the world, I pray God to keep you so; for, believe me, innocence is better than repentance; and though sin may afford you some brutish present pleasure, yet the remembrance of it afterwards is exceedingly bitter. If you are immersed in sin as I was, take no encouragement from me to continue in it on the one hand, nor despair of mercy on the other. Let God's goodness to me lead you also to repentance. The same Lord is rich to all who call on him through faith in Christ Jesus. If through divine grace I have done anything praiseworthy, not unto me, not unto me, but unto God give all the glory! If you are awakened to a sense of the divine life, and are hungering and thirsting after that righteousness which is by faith only in Jesus Christ, and the indwelling of his blessed Spirit in your heart, think it not absolutely necessary to pass through all the temptations that have beset me round about on every side. It is in the spiritual as in the natural life—some feel more, others less, but all experience some pangs and travails of the soul, before the man Christ Jesus is formed within them, and brought forth and arrived at the measure of his fullness, who fills all in all. If God deals with you in a more gentle way, yet so that a thorough work of conversion is effected in your heart, you ought to be exceedingly thankful. Or, if he should lead you through a longer wilderness than I have passed through, you need not complain. The more you are humbled now, the more you will be exalted afterwards. One taste of Christ's love in the heart will make amends for everything. And, if you have felt the powers of the world to come, and been made a partaker of the Holy Ghost, I know you will rejoice, and give thanks for what God has done for my soul.

To conclude—may all who peruse these few pages be as much affected alternately with grief and joy in reading, as I have been in writing them; they will then have the desired effect, and cause many thanksgivings to be offered on my behalf to that God who has called me out of darkness into his marvellous light! And that you, dear reader, whoever you are, may experience the like and greater blessings, is the hearty prayer of your soul's friend and servant.

George Whitefield

A Further Account of God's Dealings

with the Reverend Mr George Whitefield,
from the time of his ordination
to his embarking for Georgia
(June 1736—December 1737)

Having been ordained at Gloucester on Trinity Sunday, 1736, and preached my sermon on the *Necessity and Benefit of Religious Society* to a very crowded audience in the church in which I was baptised, the Lord's Day following, I set out the next Wednesday to Oxford, where I was received with great joy by my religious friends. My dear and honoured friends the Reverend John and Charles Wesley, being now for some time embarked for Georgia, and one or two more having taken Orders, the interest of Methodism, as it was then and is now termed, had visibly declined, and very few of this reputed mad way were left at the university. This somewhat discouraged me at times, but the Lord Jesus supported my soul and made me easy by giving me a strong conviction that I was where he would have me to be. My degree, I soon found, was of service to me, as it gave me access to those I could not be free with when in an inferior station; and, as opportunity offered, I was enabled to converse with them about the things which belonged to the kingdom of God. The subscriptions for the poor prisoners, which amounted to about £40 per annum, were soon put into my hands. Two or three small charity schools, maintained by the Methodists, were under my more immediate inspection; which, with the time I spent in following my studies, private retirement, and religious converse, sweetly filled up the whole of my day, and kept me from that unaccountable but too common complaint of having any time hang upon my hands. Distributing money and books among the poor prisoners, and employing such as could work, I found was of admirable service. For hereby they were kept from that worst of gaol diseases—idleness; and were not only convinced that we bore a good will towards them, but also led them, as it were, under an obligation to hear the instructions we gave them from time to time. This practice was first taken up by the Wesleys; and would to God all prison chaplains would follow their good example!

Whilst I was an undergraduate, amongst other religious friends, I was very intimate with one Mr Broughton, a professed Methodist, who had lately taken Orders, and was curate at the Tower of London. Being called down for a while into Hampshire, he wrote to me to be of good courage, and bid me hasten to town to officiate in his absence, and be refreshed with the sight and conversation of many who loved me for Christ's sake, and had for a long time desired to see me.

Accordingly, on Wednesday, August 4 (the prisoners being provided for by the coming of Mr Hervey, another young worthy Methodist, who had lately taken deacon's Orders), with fear and trembling I obeyed the summons and went in the stage coach to London. There being no other passenger, I employed myself a good part of the way in earnest supplication to the God of all grace to be my guide and my comforter; at the same time I could not help praising him for changing my heart, and calling me to preach the gospel at a place to which, not many years ago, I would have given much money, if my circumstances had permitted, to have gone up and seen a play. In the evening,

I reached the Tower, and was kindly received by my dear friend. The remainder of the week was spent in visiting Sir John Philips and others who were glad to see me. But God sent me something to ballast it; for as I passed along the streets many came out of their shops to see so young a person in a gown and cassock. One I remember in particular cried out, 'There's a boy parson,' which served to mortify my pride, and put me also upon turning that apostolical exhortation into prayer, 'Don't let anyone look down on you because you are young.'

On Sunday, August 8th, in the afternoon, I preached at Bishopsgate church, the largeness of which, and the congregation together, at first a little dazed me; but by thinking of God and considering in whose name I was about to speak, my mind was calmed, and I was enabled to preach with power. The effect was immediate and visible to all; for as I went up the stairs almost all seemed to sneer at me on account of my youth; but they soon grew serious and exceedingly attentive, and after I came down showed me great tokens of respect, blessed me as I passed along and made great enquiry who I was. No one could answer the question, for I was quite a stranger. I speedily slipped through the crowd and came to the Tower, blessing God for his goodness to me the unworthiest of the sons of men.

Here I continued for two months, reading prayers twice a week, catechising and preaching once, besides visiting the soldiers in the infirmary and barracks daily. I also read prayers every evening at Wapping chapel, and preached at Ludgate prison every Tuesday. God was pleased to give me favour in the eyes of the inhabitants of the Tower. The chapel was crowded on Lord's Days. Religious friends from different parts of the town attended the word, and several young men came on Lord's Day morning, as serious enquirers, to hear me discourse about the new birth and the necessity of renouncing all in affection in order to follow Jesus Christ.

After I had been in town about a month, letters came

from the Wesleys and the Rev. Mr Ingham, their fellow-labourer, a true Israelite, from Georgia. Their accounts fired my soul, and made me even long to go abroad for God too; but having no outward call, and being, as I then thought, too weak in body ever to undertake a sea voyage, I endeavoured to lay aside all thoughts of going abroad. But my endeavours were all in vain; for I felt at times such a strong attraction in my soul towards Georgia that I thought it almost irresistible. I strove against it with all my power, begged again and again with many cries and tears that the Lord would not allow me to be deluded, and at length opened my mind to several dear friends. All agreed that labourers were wanted at home; that I had as yet no visible call abroad; and that it was my duty not to be rash but wait and see what providence might point out to me. To this I consented with my whole heart, and having stayed in London till Mr Broughton came out of the country, I returned to my little charge at Oxford.

What communion did I daily enjoy with God! How sweetly did my hours in private glide away in reading and praying over Mr Henry's *Comment upon the Scriptures*! Nor was I alone happy; for several dear youths were greatly enlivened, and met daily at my room to build each other up in their most holy faith. I was chosen a corresponding member of the Society for Promoting Christian Knowledge, which I rejoiced in, as it gave me an opportunity of procuring books at a cheap and easy rate for the poor people. May the great high priest and apostle of our profession continue to bless that Society, and prosper all their pious undertakings, to the advancement of his own glory, and his people's eternal good!

About the middle of November I was once more called from my beloved, though little, scene of action. The Rev. Mr Kinchin, now with God, had recently been awakened, and accordingly resolved to associate with the despised Methodists, determining to know nothing but Jesus Christ and him crucified. He was then minister of Dummer, in

Hampshire; and being likely to be chosen Dean of Corpus Christi College, he desired me to come and officiate for him, till that affair should be decided. By the advice of friends I went, and he came to supply my place at Oxford. His parish consisting chiefly of poor and illiterate people, my proud heart at first could not well brook it. I would have given all the world for one of my Oxford friends, and mourned for lack of them as a dove that has lost her mate. But upon giving myself to prayer, and reading Mr Law's excellent character sketch of Ouranious in his *Serious Call to a Devout and Holy Life*, my mind was reconciled to such conversation as the place afforded me. Before I came to Dummer, Mr Kinchin had got this people used to having public prayers twice a day, according to the rubric, that is, in the morning (it being the winter season) before it was light, and in the evening after the people returned from their work. He also catechised the lambs of his flock daily, and visited from house to house. He loved his people, and was beloved by them. I prosecuted his plan, and generally divided the day into three parts—eight hours for study and retirement, eight hours for sleep and meals, and eight hours for reading prayers, catechising, and visiting the parish. The profit I reaped by these exercises, and conversing with the poor country people, was unspeakable. I frequently learnt as much by an afternoon's visit as in a week's study. During my stay here, an invitation was sent me to a very profitable curacy in London; but I had no inclination to accept it.

The thoughts of going to Georgia still crowded continually in upon me, and at length providence seemed to point my way there. About the middle of December came a letter from Mr Broughton, informing me that Mr Charles Wesley had arrived at London. Soon after came a letter from Mr Charles himself, wherein he informed me that he had come over to procure labourers; but, added he, 'I dare not prevent God's nomination.' In a few days after this came another letter from Mr John Wesley, wherein were these words—'Only Mr Delamotte is with me, till God shall stir up the hearts of some of his servants, who, putting their lives in his hands, shall come over and help us, where the harvest is so great, and the labourers so few. What if you are the man, Mr Whitefield?' In another letter were these words— 'Do you ask me what you shall have? Food to eat, and clothes to put on; a house to lay your head in, such as your Lord had not; and a crown of glory that does not fade away.' Upon reading this, my heart leaped within me, and, as it were, echoed to the call. Many things concurred to make my way clear. Mr Kinchin was now elected Dean of Corpus Christi College, and being thereby obliged to reside at Oxford he willingly took upon him the charge of the prisoners. Mr Hervey was ready to serve the cure of Dummer. Mr Wesley was my dear friend, and I thought it would be a great advantage to me to be under his tuition. Georgia was an infant, and likely to be an increasing colony; and the government seemed to have its welfare much at heart. I had heard many Indians were near it, and had thought it a matter of great importance that serious clergymen should be sent there. Retirement and privacy were what my soul delighted in. A sea voyage would, in all probability, not do my constitution much hurt; indeed, I had heard the sea was sometimes beneficial to weakly people. And supposing the worst, as I must necessarily return to take priest's Orders, it would then be left to my choice whether I would settle in my native country or go abroad any more. These things being thoroughly weighed, I at length resolved within myself to embark for Georgia; and knowing that I should never put my resolution into practice if I conferred with flesh and blood, wrote to my relations to inform them of my design, and told them, if they would promise not to dissuade me from my intended voyage, I would come and take a personal leave of them; if otherwise, knowing my own weakness, I was determined to embark without visiting them at all.

On New Year's Day, 1737, I went to Gloucester to hear

the bishop's opinion, and to take my leave of my mother and other relations. His lordship received me, as he always did, like a father, approved of my design, wished me much success, and said he did not doubt God would bless me and that I would do much good abroad. My own relations, at first, were not so passive. My aged mother wept sore; and others urged what attractive promotion I might get if I stayed at home. But, at length, they grew more quiet, and finding me so fixed argued no longer.

During my stay here I began to grow rather popular. God gave me honour for a while, even in my own country. I preached twice on the sabbaths. Congregations were very large, and the power of God attended the word; and some I have reason to believe were truly converted, who will be my joy and crown of rejoicing in the day of the Lord Jesus.

In about three weeks I went to Bristol to take leave of some more of my relations who lived there. As it was my constant practice, wherever I went, to attend the daily public services of the church, I went, the Thursday after my coming, to hear a sermon at St John's church. Whilst the psalm was being sung, after prayers, the minister came to my seat, and asked me to give the congregation a sermon. Having my notes about me, I complied. The hearers seemed startled, and after the sermon enquiry was made who I was. The next day there was another sermon at St Stephen's. Many crowded there expecting to hear me again. The preacher asked me to preach, as the other did the day before. I again complied; and the news spread so wide here that on the following Lord's Day many of all denominations were obliged to return from the churches where I preached, for lack of room. Afterwards I was called by the mayor to preach before him and the Corporation. And for some time following I preached all the week-day sermons, and twice on Sundays besides visiting the religious Societies. The word, through the mighty power of God, was sharper than a two-edged sword. The doctrine of the new birth and justification by faith in Jesus Christ (though I was not so clear about it as afterwards) made its way like lightning into the hearers' consciences. The arrows of conviction stuck fast; and my whole time, between one lecture and another, except what was spent in necessary refreshment, was wholly occupied in talking with people concerned about religion. Large offers were made me to stay at Bristol. All wondered why I wanted to go to Georgia, when I might be so well provided for at home; and some urged that if I had a mind to convert Indians I might go amongst the Kingswood colliers, and find Indians enough there. But none of these things moved me. Having put my hand to the plough, I was determined, through divine grace, not to look back. And therefore, at length, I took my leave, but with what mutual affection and concern cannot easily be expressed.

Having stayed about ten days at the university, I took, as I thought, my last farewell of my dear friends, and came up to London at the beginning of March, in order to wait upon James Oglethorpe and the trustees. I was kindly received by both.

I remained in London about three weeks, waiting for Mr Oglethorpe, who expected to sail any day. In this period I preached more frequently than when there before. Many more came to hear me; and the last Sunday I was in town I read prayers twice and preached four times. But, finding Mr Oglethorpe was not likely to go for some time, and having been under particular obligation to the Rev. Sampson Harris, minister of Stonehouse in Gloucestershire, I went down there, at his request, to take his place while he came up to transact some business in town.

I had reason to think God sent me here in answer to prayer, for there was a little sweet Society of seeking souls who had heard me preach at an adjacent town and wrestled with God, if it was his will, to send me to them. They received me with joy, and most of the parishioners were very civil when I came to visit them from house to house. When I examined them I found them more knowledgeable than I expected. Their pastor had catechised the little ones in the summer, and expounded the four lessons every Lord's Day in the church. I followed his good example, and found great freedom and assistance given me both in my public and private administrations. Having the use of the parsonage house, I expounded every night. Many who were not parishioners came to hear, and were edified. On Sundays, besides expounding the lessons, catechising and preaching, I repeated my sermons to the Society. Neither church nor house could hold the people that came. I found uncommon manifestations granted me from above. Early in the morning, at noonday, evening, and midnight, indeed all the day long, did the blessed Jesus visit and refresh my heart. If the trees of a certain wood near Stonehouse could speak, they would tell what sweet communion I and some others enjoyed with the ever blessed God there. Sometimes, as I was walking, my soul would make such sallies as though it would go out of the body. At other times, I would be so overpowered with a sense of God's infinite majesty that I would be constrained to throw myself on the ground and offer my soul as a blank in his hands, to write on it what he pleased. One night was a time never to be forgotten. It happened that there was a lot of lightning. I had been expounding to many people, and some being afraid to go home I thought it my duty to accompany them, and make good use of the occasion to stir them up to prepare for the coming of the Son of Man. As I returned to the parsonage house, whilst others were getting up from bed, frightened almost to death, I and another poor but pious countryman were in the field, exulting in our God and longing for the time when Jesus should be revealed from heaven in a flame of fire! Oh that my soul may be in a similar state when he actually comes to call me! For I think I never had been happier than that night, or, all things considered, more blessed than during my stay at Stonehouse.

The incumbent having returned from London and the

people of Bristol having given me repeated invitations, indeed having insisted on my coming again, since the time of my embarking was deferred, on May 23 I paid them a second visit. Multitudes came on foot, and many in coaches a mile outside the city, to meet me; and almost all greeted and blessed me as I went along the street.

I preached, as usual, about five times a week; but the congregations grew, if possible, larger and larger. It was wonderful to see how the people hung on the rails of the organ loft, climbed on the lead roofs of the church and made the church itself so hot with their breath that the steam would fall from the pillars like drops of rain. Sometimes almost as many would go away, for lack of room, as came in; and it was with great difficulty that I got into the desk, to read prayers or preach. Persons of all denominations flocked to hear. Persons of all ranks not only attended my public ministry but gave me private invitations to their houses. A private Society or two were set up. I preached and collected for the poor prisoners in Newgate two or three times a week; and many offered me large sums not to go abroad.

I went on to Oxford, where we had, as it were, a general meeting of the Methodists; and finding their interests flourishing and being impatient to go abroad I hastened away, after taking a most affectionate leave, and came to London about the end of August.

About this time, through the importunity of friends and aspersions of enemies, I was prevailed upon to print my sermon *On the Nature and Necessity of our Regeneration or New Birth in Christ Jesus*, which under God began the awakening at London, Bristol, Gloucester and Gloucestershire. The Dissenters, I found, were surprised to see a sermon on such a subject from a clergyman of the Church of England, and finding the author came from Oxford were ready to say, 'Can any good thing come out of Nazareth?' This sermon sold well to persons of all denominations and was dispersed very widely both at home and abroad. A second impression was called for; and finding another of my sermons was printed without my leave, and in a very incorrect manner, at Bristol, I was obliged to publish in my own defence; and afterwards, thought I had a clear call to print any other discourses, though in themselves insignificant, if I found them blessed to the good of souls.

I was invited to preach at Cripplegate, St Anne's and Forster Lane churches, at six on the Lord's Day morning, and to assist in administering the holy sacrament. I embraced the invitations, and so many came that sometimes we were obliged to consecrate fresh elements two or three times; and stewards found it somewhat difficult to carry the offerings to the communion table. I also preached at Wapping chapel, the Tower, Ludgate, Newgate and many of the churches where weekday sermons were kept up. The congregations continually increased, and generally, on a Lord's Day, I used to preach four times to very large and very moved audiences, besides reading prayers two or three times and walking perhaps twelve miles in going backwards and forwards from one church to the other. But God made my feet like hind's feet, and filled me with joy unspeakable at the end of my day's work. This made me look upon my friends' kind advice which they gave me, to spare myself, as a temptation. For I found by daily experience, the more I did the more I might do for God.

About the latter end of August, finding there were many young men belonging to the Societies that attended my administrations, I entered into one of their singing societies, hoping to have greater opportunities of doing them good. It answered my design. Our Lord gave me to spiritualise their singing. And after they had taught me the notes, they would gladly hear me teach them some of the mysteries of the new birth, and the necessity of living to God. Many sweet nights we spent together in this way; and many of these youths afterwards, to all appearance, walked with God, and will, I trust, join the heavenly choir in singing praises to the Lamb, and him who sits on the throne for ever.

About the middle of September, my name first appeared in the newspapers. The Sunday before, I was prevailed upon to preach a charity sermon at Wapping chapel. The congregation was very large, and more was collected than had been for many years on a similar occasion. My friends entreated me to preach another charity sermon, at Sir George Wheeler's chapel, and through the importunity of Mr Habersham (more recently my faithful assistant in the orphan house) I agreed to do it. I spoke on the widow's giving of her two mites. God bowed the hearts of the hearers as the heart of one man. Almost all, as I was told by the collectors, offered most willingly. This still drew on fresh requests. The Sunday following, I preached in the evening at St Swithin's, where £8 was collected instead of ten shillings. The next morning, as I was at breakfast with a friend at the Tower, I read in one of the newspapers that there was a young gentleman going as a volunteer to Georgia; that he had preached at St Swithin's, and collected £8 instead of ten shillings, £3 of which were in half-pence; and that he was to preach next Wednesday before the Societies, at their general quarterly meeting. This advertisement chagrined me. I immediately sent to the printer, desiring he would put me in his paper no more. His answer was that he was paid for doing it, and that he would not lose two shillings for anybody. By this means, people's curiosity was stirred up more and more. On the Wednesday evening, Bow church in Cheapside was crowded exceedingly. I preached my sermon on early piety, and at the request of the Societies printed it.

I now preached generally nine times a week. The early sacraments were exceedingly awe-inspiring. At Cripplegate, St Anne's and Forster Lane, how often have we seen Jesus Christ crucified, and clearly presented before us! On Sunday mornings, long before day, you might see streets filled with people going to church with their lanterns in their hands, and hear them conversing about the things of God. Other Lecture Churches near at hand would be filled with persons who could not come where I was preaching; and those who did come were so deeply moved that they were like persons struck with pointed arrows, or mourning for a firstborn child. People gave so liberally to the charity schools that this season nearly £1000 was collected at the several churches, besides many private contributions and subscriptions sent in afterwards. I always preached free of charge, and gave myself.

The Blue Coat boys and girls looked upon me as their great benefactor; and I believe frequently sent up their infant cries on my behalf. Worthy Mr Seward, afterwards my dear fellow-traveller, was their hearty friend and advocate. He was concerned in over twenty charity schools, and, as I found some months afterward, inserted the paragraph that so chagrined me.

The tide of popularity now began to run very high. In a short time I could no longer walk on foot as usual, but was constrained to go from place to place in a coach to avoid the hosannas of the multitude. They grew quite extravagant in their applauses, and had it not been for my compassionate high priest, popularity would have destroyed me. I used to plead with him to take me by the hand and lead me unhurt through this fiery furnace. He heard my request and let me see the vanity of all commendations but his own.

Not that all spoke well of me. No; as my popularity increased, opposition increased also. At first, many of the clergy were my hearers and admirers; but some soon grew angry, and complaints were made that the churches were so crowded that there was no room for the parishioners, and that the pews were spoiled. Some called me a spiritual pick-pocket, and others thought I made use of a kind of charm to get the people's money. A report was spread abroad that the Bishop of London, upon the complaint of the clergy, intended to *silence* me. I immediately went to see his lordship, and enquired whether any complaint of this nature had been lodged against me. He answered, 'No.' I asked his lordship whether any objection could be made against my doctrine. He said, 'No,' for he knew a clergyman who had heard me preach a plain spiritual sermon. I asked his lordship whether he would grant me a licence. He said I needed none, since I was going to Georgia. I replied, 'Then your lordship would not forbid me?' He gave me a satisfactory answer, and I took my leave. Soon after this, two clergymen sent for me and told me they would not let me preach in their pulpits any more unless I renounced that part of my sermon on regeneration where I wished that my brethren would entertain their audiences more often with sermons on the new birth. This I had no freedom to do, and so they continued to oppose me.

What I believe irritated some of my enemies the more was my free conversation with many of the serious Dissenters, who invited me to their houses and repeatedly told me that if the doctrine of the new birth and justification by faith was preached powerfully in the church there would be but few Dissenters in England. One minister called me a *pragmatical rascal*, and vehemently inveighed against the whole body of Dissenters. This stirred up people's corruptions, and having an overweening fondness for me, whenever they came to church and found that I was not preaching, some of them would go out again. This spirit I always endeavoured to quell, and made a sermon on purpose from those words, 'Consider carefully how you listen.' One time, on hearing that a churchwarden intended to take £8 a year from his parish minister because he refused to let me preach his sermon, I composed a sermon on 'Love your enemies,' and delivered it where I knew the churchwarden would be. It had its desired effect. He came after the sermon and told me he was convinced by my talk that he should not resent the injury the minister had done me, and then thanked me for my care.

I had a sweet knot of religious friends, with whom I at first attempted to pray extempore. Some time, I think in October, we began to set apart an hour every evening to intercede with the great head of the church to carry on the work begun, and for the people we knew, according to what we knew they needed. I was their spokesman before God, and he only knows what enlargement I felt in that divine service. Once we spent a whole night in prayer and praise; and many a time at midnight and one in the morning, after I have been wearied almost to death in preaching, writing, and conversation, and going from place to place, God imparted new life to my soul and enabled me to intercede with him for an hour and a half and two hours together.

At length, on December 28, I left London and went on board the *Whitaker*, after having preached in a good part of the London churches, collected about £1,000 for the charity schools, and got upwards of £300 for the poor of Georgia among my friends, for which I have since publicly accounted. At the same time God raised me a sufficiency to supply my own temporal necessities and gave me repeated proofs that if we *seek first the kingdom of God and his righteousness, all other things* (I mean food and clothing, which is all a Christian should desire) *shall be added unto us*. For which, and all his other unmerited mercies, I desire to praise him in time, and magnify his holy name through the boundless ages of eternity.

First Journal

A Journal of a Voyage
from London to Savannah in Georgia
(December 1737—May 1738)

The sole motive (if my heart does not deceive me) which induced me to leave my native country was a full conviction that it was the divine will. What reasons I can urge for this persuasion it is needless to mention, because few in this case would judge impartially; and what seems a reason to me may not be deemed so by another. Let it suffice to inform you that, after earnest prayer for a year and a half that if the design was not of God it would come to naught, though strongly solicited to act in a contrary manner I found myself eagerly bent on going abroad as ever.

Accordingly, on Wednesday, December 28, 1737, after having continued instant in prayer with my friends at Mr James Hutton's, and afterwards receiving the holy sacrament at St Dunstan's, being recommended to the grace of God by a great number of weeping Christian brethren at the Rev. Mr John Hutton's, I set out at night for Deptford in a coach, accompanied by four friends, and got there safe at ten. Here a widow gladly received us into her house, and many of my friends came from London on foot intending to accompany me to the ship. With them I took a little bodily refreshment, spent two or three hours praying particularly for our friends and enemies and all mankind, sang psalms and hymns and spiritual songs, and then took ourselves off to rest; and the Lord made us dwell in safety. Oh who can express the unspeakable joy of religious friends!

Thursday, December 29. Rose early in the morning, and continued in urgent intercessions, chanting and singing of psalms with my friends until nine, at which our hearts were much rejoiced. After this we went in quest of our ship, but finding she had slipped down to Purfleet, and was not to move to Gravesend for some time, we returned to Deptford praising God, and praying for a blessing on our intended voyage. The Lord perform our petitions!

Having returned to Deptford with my friends, we dined comfortably together, joined in a psalm, read the lessons for the day, and concluded with prayer. Some were then obliged to depart for London. After they had gone, I continued with the rest in special intercession for nearly two hours, and then God was pleased to comfort my heart. If parting from a few earthly friends for a time is so grievous, how will the wicked bear to be parted from God and good men for all eternity!

Friday, December 30. Went with our baggage and nine or ten friends in a Gravesend boat to Purfleet, where the *Whitaker* had got to. Spent the time we were on the water in singing psalms and special intercession, and came on board about ten in the morning.

Saturday, December 31. Began this morning to have public prayers on open deck, at which the officer and soldiers attended with decency and reverence. After prayer, I enlarged a little on those words of St Paul, 'I resolved to know nothing while I was with you except Jesus Christ and him crucified.'

Today, also, I began to visit the sick, and took that opportunity of talking to those around me about the uncertainty of life and the certainty of a future judgement; and God was pleased not to let my words fall on stony ground.

Sunday, January 1, 1738. Blessed be God for the happy beginning of a new year; for it has been a day of fat things. We rose in the morning, and retired to an adjacent hill with my friends, to prayer; and afterwards were most agreeably surprised with the coming of several more London friends who came all night on the water to see me.

About ten, we went to church, where I preached; and the curate was so kind, at our request, as to give us the sacrament. In the afternoon I preached again to a more numerous congregation than in the morning; and as we were to stay there only one Lord's Day, I was pressed to preach and read prayers a third time at six in the evening. It was a thing I found entirely new, but upon the curate's readily complying to lend the pulpit, and my friends' and the people's urging, I looked upon it as a call of providence, and accordingly read prayers and preached to a very crowded audience; and this I did without notes, having brought only two sermons with me. Oh, who can express the loving kindness of the Lord, or show all his praise?

Monday, January 2. Sat up till twelve at night, to take leave of some of my friends, whose business obliged them to be at London the next morning; and then, after three or four hours' rest, rose and walked to Greenhithe with the remainder of my friends, intending to take a boat there, and so return to my charge at Purfleet. But just as we were entering the boat, providentially came a boy telling us the *Whitaker* had slipped down to Gravesend, and was ready to sail, if not actually under sail. We immediately hastened back to where we had come from, and went on our way rejoicing.

About eleven, we reached Gravesend, and found the ship was not to sail till the morrow. This put gladness in my heart, as it gave me an opportunity of settling some affairs of consequence and conversing a little longer with my dear friends.

About twelve o'clock I went on board, leaving my

friends to dine on shore, and as I went along God was pleased to show me he had given a blessing on my talks.

Tuesday, January 3. Went on board, read prayers and preached, visited the sick; and then took a final leave, as I thought, of my friends. Spent the afternoon in writing letters and putting things in order.

This evening began to read prayers between decks, judging it would be too cold above.

Wednesday, January 4. I could not have public prayers, because the soldiers were engaged with their officer. But I visited the sick, and perceived the soldiers were attentive to hear me when I applied myself to those around the sick persons.

Thursday, January 5. Read prayers and preached; visited the sick, and had God with me all the day long. Began to catechise six or seven of the young soldiers on open deck. I was surprised they would submit to it, but God has the hearts of all men in his hands.

Great civility was shown me on board by the officers; and Captain Whiting sent his boat to fetch me to Gravesend.

My health of body, I could perceive, increased, and my soul was much refreshed. I now began once more to feel the comforts of a retired life, and blessed God from my heart that he had called me to the place I was going to.

Friday, January 6. About nine, I came on board, read prayers, and preached between decks; and Mr H. sang a psalm, as he generally does. Meanwhile the ship loosed from Gravesend and sailed by twelve o'clock to the Nore. We had a very brisk gale of wind. God gave me great comfort, and I went below decks and sat down on the floor and read Arndt's *True Christianity*. Part of the time I stood on deck, and admired the wonders of God in the deep.

Three or four were added today to my catechumens, of some of whom I have great hopes. I read prayers, preached upon deck and catechised my own companions; interceded upon deck near the forecastle; wrote my journal;

and climbed up into my cabin to bed, where my friend Habersham and I lay as comfortably as on a bed of state. Some of the passengers, amongst whom was Mr Habersham, began now to be sick, but I felt very little of it; on the contrary, God enabled me to rejoice with exceeding great joy. My heart was warm by talking to the sailors, and I was lifted even above myself. I found that over a hundred, excluding the ship's company, were on board. God grant that not one of them may perish through my neglect!

Saturday, January 7. Breakfasted with some of the gentlemen in the great cabin, who were very civil, and let me put in a word for God.

Read public prayers, and began to expound the Lord's prayer to the soldiers by way of sermon; and God enabled me to do it with power. After that, I instructed my catechumens, who now amounted to twelve or thirteen. God make them soldiers of Christ as well as of the king.

Had an hour's conversation with a gentleman on board on our fall in Adam, and the necessity of new birth in Christ Jesus; and hope it was not unpleasant to him.

Today I obtained what I prayed for, namely a place to retire to; for Captain Whiting, on my bare mentioning my want of such a thing, offered me the free use of his own cabin, a place very commodious for that purpose.

Catechised those who went with me on open deck, as an example to others; and found that they improved. Captain Whiting, the two cadets and sergeants, sat very serious and attentive. But when the Captain of the soldiers came, my heart sank a little, though without reason; however, I did not leave off. O corruption, you are my sister!

Sunday, January 8. My friend Habersham and I have great reason to be thankful to God; for we slept as well as we could desire, though the wind blew very hard, and the sailors were very busy in taking care of the ship, which by the morning had dragged her anchor two miles.

I went early and visited the seasick soldiers and their families between decks, gave them some sage tea and sugar, etc., and excited them all to thankfulness and repentance, out of gratitude for their preservation from the last night's storm, and returned public thanks at morning prayers.

Monday, January 9. Mr Habersham began to learn Latin. I had nearly twenty catechumens with my own companions, who I believe made some advances.

Weighed from the Nore, and sailed before the wind in company with several others, which carried us on so briskly that we anchored before Margate about one. Here I enjoyed a wished-for opportunity of writing to some of my London friends, and found my heart greatly enlarged towards them.

After dinner, having some necessaries to buy, Mr H. and I went on shore to Margate. The wind blew very fresh, and the sea raged horribly, but he who dwells on high was mightier, and kept us from the least fright, and filled me with great joy, and brought us safe ashore.

We had the most abandoned man with us I ever saw, who came out of an East India ship. He had so much of the devil in him that the very boatmen, profane as they were, abhorred him; from which I infer that were the devil himself to appear as he is, the wickedest sinners could not but detest him.

Tuesday, January 10. About seven, we took boat and praised and blessed God to see the floods clap their hands. About eight we came on board, and found we had great reason to be thankful that we were on shore last night. The sailors told us that the lightning shone on the sea all night, that the storm was very great and the ship's long boat was lost.

I read public prayers, returned thanks for our deliverance, and expounded by way of sermon the second article of the creed, which I began yesterday, and did the same after evening prayers. Spent the remainder of the day in writing letters; and have not enjoyed a more calm delightful frame of mind a long time.

The sick increased on my hands, but were very thankful for furnishing them with sage tea, sugar, broth, etc. At the sight of so many objects of pity, I felt touched with a fellow-feeling of their miseries. I could not but change round the prodigal's complaint, *How many of my father's children are ready to perish with hunger, whilst I have enough and to spare?*

Wednesday, January 11. Had no public prayers this morning, being much hurried in writing letters to go by post; and when I went to read, the soldiers were engaged in their military affairs upon deck, so that I did nothing but visit the sick. I fear I did foolishly.

Went on in explaining the creed after evening prayers, and was enabled to talk of the crucifixion of our Lord. I believe it pricked them to the heart. O that I could hear them cry out, 'What shall we do to be saved?'

After evening prayers and visiting the sick, went ashore with Mr Habersham to Deal, and were so delighted with a prospect of the Downs that we expressed our thankfulness by singing psalms all the way. The boatmen, I believe, wondered at it at first, but they were not ashamed to blaspheme, and I thought I had no reason to be ashamed to praise God. I had the satisfaction before we got to Deal, to hear one of them join seriously with us; and perceived a surprising alteration in their behaviour always after. Blessed be God!

Thursday, January 12. Read prayers and went on explaining the creed to the soldiers; visited and prayed with the sick, and began this afternoon to explain the catechism to the women by themselves. I find there are about sixteen of them. Blessed be God! they were much moved. Prosper this work of my hands, Lord!

Had some religious talk with the surgeon of the soldiers, who seems very well disposed. I seldom, if ever, see him idle, and find he has many good qualities. God grant Christianity may be grafted in him!

Friday, January 13. Remained on shore all day, the weather being too rough to go on board. Was concerned about leaving my flock so long; but hope this short absence will make our meeting more agreeable tomorrow. Had the pleasure of joining in public worship at Deal, in a pretty chapel, which was more pleasant on account of our being confined for some time within the narrow limits of a ship.

Saturday, January 14. Spent the morning in writing letters, and was much pleased with the pious conversation of a poor woman who was one of my listeners last night, and who I believe has passed through the pangs of the new birth.

Hastened on board about eleven, the wind promising fair to take us out of the channel, and was affectionately received by the people.

Monday, January 16. Was rather moved by seeing a poor soldier tied neck and heels, for several mutinous words he had spoken. The captain related the case to me, and said if I could make him realise his crime, I might beg him off. I endeavoured to do it, but alas in vain; he continued obstinate, and thereby hindered my design taking effect. After this, the captain ordered him to be tied down between decks; so I took the opportunity of this in my morning sermon to exhort the soldiers to obey those who had authority over them, and to avoid those sins that would provoke God to command them to be tied hand and foot and to be cast into outer darkness, where would be weeping and gnashing of teeth.

About twelve, a Deal boat coming alongside, I was minded to go on shore to answer my letters. The sea was very boisterous, but God brought us to shore rejoicing. O why did I fear in the least? What am I, when left to myself!

Tuesday, January 17. Was awakened with a call that the ship was about to sail, but found it soon contradicted. Spent an hour in special intercession, and the rest of the morning in writing letters and teaching Mr H. Latin. Oh that I may be made an instrument of breeding him up for God!

Came on board about two in the afternoon, and found

all things quiet in the ship; I was most kindly received, and the women were very attentive when I proceeded to explain the catechism to them. May God open their hearts as he did that of Lydia, that these may give diligent heed to the things that are spoken.

Wednesday, January 18. Spent all the morning in retirement, reading the scriptures, public prayer, and preaching, the weather being extremely pleasant. Began to live by rule more than ever, for nothing I find is to be done without it. All who had been sick and recovered came to prayers, for whom I gave thanks; at the end of my sermon exhorting them with the utmost earnestness to sin no more, lest a worse evil should befall them, and to show their thankfulness not only with their lips but in their lives. O that there may be always in them such a mind!

Finished my exposition on the creed. Read public prayers, and preached as usual in the afternoon. Catechised both my own companions and the soldiers, and was pleased to see many others were attentive to hear. Had great comfort in reading the scriptures. Was afterwards a little inclined to heaviness, but drove it off by a long intercession. Prayer is an antidote against every evil.

Thursday, January 19. Was much comforted by hearing from my friends. Began, after prayers this morning, to explain the catechism to the soldiers, and drew proper inferences by way of sermon. I find it is much approved of, and for them by far the fittest way of instruction.

Friday, January 20. Spent all the morning in composing a sermon. Happily settled a difference between a soldier and his wife, who were one of the four couples I married when first I came on board. The man had resolved to leave her, but upon my reminding him of his marriage vow, and entreating him with love, he immediately took to her again. What may not a minister do through Christ, when his flock love him? Almost finished the sermon I began yesterday.

Went on in expounding the catechism after evening prayer, and now began to read the first lesson, which I purposely omitted before, not knowing whether they would bear it.

Proposed to the captain to read a few prayers in the great cabin every night, which he readily consented to, and indeed said he would be glad to hear me preach whenever I thought proper.

Was surprised in the midst of my evening's talk by the chief mate, who came and told me that the minister of Upper Deal had sent a boat for me, desiring me immediately to come on shore. Accordingly, after I had concluded, Mr H. and I went and found the minister who was left to officiate, who desired me, at the request of the inhabitants, to preach the Sunday following. After this, we retired to our lodging in Deal, and after a sermon and long intercession was comforted by the reception of several letters from persons who I believe sincerely fear God.

Sunday, January 22. About nine, went on board with Captain Whiting, who is always extremely civil. Visited the sick, and read prayers in the great cabin. Read prayers and preached my sermon on early piety on open deck to the soldiers; the officers and other gentlemen listening seriously. The weather was very cold, but preaching warmed my heart.

About noon went on shore with Captain Whiting and Mr Habersham. Dined at the postmaster's, who received us hospitably. In the afternoon, preached at Upper Deal on Acts 28:26. Many seemed pricked to the heart, and some given such life that they expressed a desire to follow me wherever I should go. O free grace in Christ Jesus! I have scarce known a time I have preached anywhere without seeing some effect of my doctrine. From the hearts of the mighty the word of the Lord has not turned back, the sword of the Spirit has not returned empty. A proof of this, I hope, that the words are not my own and that God is truly with me. May I never by pride and vainglory provoke him to depart from me.

Stayed all night on shore to expound the Lord's prayer

and had a large company to hear me; and should have had seven hundred, my hostess told me, if the house had been able to hold them—so swiftly did the word of God run and prevail.

Monday, January 23. Was much comforted by receiving five more letters; answered some of them, and about eleven in the morning went on board the *Amy* to pay my respects to Colonel C., and to visit the soldiers, whom I looked upon as part of my charge. I was received very civilly by the officers and went among the soldiers and enquired into the state of their souls; gave them a word or two of exhortation, promised to bring them some books (I saw their wants), and at the officers' request to come and preach to them, if opportunity should offer before we left the Downs.

After this, I visited the *Lightfoot*, our other transport ship, in which were about twelve soldiers and a sergeant; they received me kindly. I sat down and conversed with them, promised to send them some books, and to come and preach to them also, if providence should permit. The Downs being exceedingly calm, and the weather clear, going from ship to ship was very pleasant. Mine are but little flocks. O that it may be my heavenly Father's good pleasure to give them the kingdom.

Wednesday, January 25. Went on board in the morning with my friends intending to read prayers and preach to the soldiers; but they were engaged about their own affairs, and I could not stay long. Had great civilities shown us by the officers, etc., who treated my friends respectfully; and the captain, at my request, pardoned a woman who otherwise was to have been sent on shore.

After breakfast, returned on shore with my friends; and read prayers, and preached at Upper Deal to a large congregation. I was surprised to see such a number of people, but all Deal seems to be in a holy flame, and if I was prepared for it I should see still greater things than these.

Thursday, January 26. I had a visit paid me by an

anabaptist teacher, who came to talk with me about things to do with the kingdom of God. From what I could find out he was a spiritual man. I asked him several questions about assuming the ministerial function without being called, as was Aaron; but he did not answer to my satisfaction. However, we both agreed in this, that unless a man is born again, he cannot enter the kingdom of God.

Friday, January 27. About two, a clergyman came on board from a neighbouring village to pay me a visit, with whom I spent an hour or two agreeably; had prayers on open deck, and emphasised the duty of keeping holy the sabbath day, which then came in course to be explained, but was afraid to sing a psalm, Mr H. being at Deal with friends. Where was my courage then? Lord what am I when left to myself!

At five, returned ashore with the clergyman, to whom I promised some books for his parishioners. Glad tidings of great joy sent me by four or five correspondents; sat up till one in the morning answering them, and then went to bed and felt in possession of my God. And will God really dwell in this heart of mine? O free grace of Christ! Praise the Lord, O my soul, and all that is within me praise his holy name!

Sunday, January 29. Went on board early in the morning, read prayers, preached to the soldiers, and visited the sick; then returned on shore, and, accompanied by a troop of pious friends, hastened to Shroulden church, about a mile and a half from Deal, where I preached to a weeping and crowded congregation at the request of the minister, who at my request gave me and my friends the blessed sacrament. Others stayed also, sixteen of them, and—something which I have never come across before—the clerk pronounced a loud Amen to every person who received either bread or wine. An excellent custom, and in my opinion worth following in all churches. After this I and my friends went on our way rejoicing; dined at Mr R.'s, and in the afternoon preached at Upper Deal. The church was quite crowded, and many went away for lack of room; some stood on the lead roofs of the church outside, and looked in at the top windows, and all seemed eager to hear the word of God. I preached against worldly-mindedness, and had great reason to think God gave it his blessing.

In the evening, such numbers came to hear me that I was obliged to divide them into four groups, and God enabled me to expound to them from six till ten. Some would have persuaded me to send the last group away without expounding, but I could not bear to let so many go away empty. I find the more we do for God the more we may. My strength held out surprisingly, and I was little if at all fatigued. Afterward, I gave thanks with my friends for the blessings of the day, and we went to our respective beds about twelve at night. Oh who can express the loving kindness of the Lord, or show all his praise?

Monday, January 30. At the request of the inhabitants, and by permission of Mr R. (who sent a most obliging message from Canterbury), I preached again at Upper Deal, to as crowded and attentive an audience as I had yesterday; and afterwards, with Mr H., I visited the Rev. Mr W., who read prayers and most courteously invited me to come and see him. Our conversation ran chiefly on the expediency of baptising infants at church. I continued with him about an hour, and then at his request visited a poor woman of the parish, who was grievously troubled in mind; and God was pleased to bless my ministry to her comfort. To him be all the glory!

Soon after this we went to Mr R.'s, where our friends were waiting for us. But we had not been long there before the wind shifted about suddenly, and a cry came, 'the wind is fair, prepare yourselves for sailing'. We immediately retired, intending to intercede for all mankind before we parted; but the people were in such a hurry, for fear the sea should grow too tempestuous to go off, that we were obliged to be very brief. Having therefore recommended ourselves to God, I took my leave.

Thursday, February 2. About ten o'clock there sprang up a fair pleasant gale, which carried us from the Downs nearly forty miles that day, during which time I read prayers, preached to and catechised my soldiers, wrote some letters, and had an opportunity of sending them as we sailed by Dover.

Anyone would think I would have been glad to have heard from Mr Wesley, as he went by Deal, but I considered God ordered all things for the best, and therefore I now joyfully went, but not knowing where I was going to, and did not doubt that he who strengthened David when he went out against Goliath would also strengthen me against all my spiritual adversaries, and send his Holy Ghost to guide, assist and comfort me in all emergencies. The good Lord keep me always in this frame of mind!

Friday, February 3. Let this day be noted in my book, for God worked a wonderful deliverance for us! About seven in the morning, the men on deck not keeping a good look-out, one of the East India ships in shifting to the wind ran near us so very briskly that had Captain Whiting not providentially been on deck and beseeched them for God's sake to tack about, both the ships must inevitably have split against one another. They were within four yards of each other. The captain said he never was in so great danger in his life. Mr Habersham and I knew nothing of it till it was over; but when I was told about it, I endeavoured to excite everyone to thankfulness, and returned public thanks at prayers. Too many seemed to be oblivious of the mercy received.

Read public prayers and preached to the soldiers as usual; explained the catechism to the women, and exhorted them particularly to be obedient to their own husbands, which they have lately been failing to do; and was pleased to hear the captain, as I came on deck, remind me of the suggestion I made to him some time ago about having prayers daily in the great cabin, and indeed desired that from now on I would read prayers morning and evening to them. This I most readily consented to, it being what I had long desired and prayed for, and what I was just then about to propose to him again. Accordingly I went immediately and acquainted the lieutenant, etc., of the captain's desire, and we began this night to have full public prayers; and at Captain Whiting's request, expounded the second lesson, and a glorious lesson it was. Blessed be God! I hope we shall now begin to live like Christians, and call upon the name of the Lord daily. The very thought of God's answering this prayer filled me with joy.

Saturday, February 4. Began to have prayers in the great cabin in the morning, read prayers and preached twice to the soldiers as usual, and expounded the second lesson in the evening to the gentlemen after prayers in the great cabin, which from now on I intend, God willing, to continue. The benefit of it will be unspeakable, for it gives me an opportunity of saying many salutary truths, and affords us matter for serious table-talk afterwards.

I was much pleased to see our ship sail directly before the wind; furnished three soldiers with books, who began today to learn to read. God enable them not only to read, but to do their duty! Mr Habersham's scholars increase. The Lord increase his strength!

Sunday, February 5. Joined in spirit with absent friends in holy ordinances; spent some time most delightfully in reading the word of God; read prayers, and made some observations on both the lessons to the soldiers. Oh that the Lord would open our understandings, for they are but a dead letter without the illumination of his Holy Spirit.

Read prayers and preached my sermon on justification in the afternoon to the officers, etc., in the great cabin.

Wednesday, February 8. Had public worship and expounded as usual to both my congregations. Was pleased to hear a gentleman talk for some time of the utter inability of anything to make us happy but God.

In the afternoon I preached and read prayers on open deck, at the captain's desire, who ordered chairs to be brought and boards put across them for the soldiers to sit on. My subject was the eternity of hell torments, and I was earnest in delivering it, being desirous that none of my dear hearers should experience them. Praying and singing psalms on open deck enlarged my heart.

Was enabled to make good part of a sermon this evening, and lay down to sleep. God grant that I may die daily!

Sunday, February 12. Did as usual, and preached my sermon on glorification to the gentlemen in the great cabin. Oh that God may make us partakers of it!

Honest Joseph, my servant, returned thanks after morning prayer for his recovery from a late severe fit of sickness. I hope now Christ has touched him by the right hand of his healing power, he will get up and serve him. He tells me he can say with David, 'It is good for me that I have been afflicted.' God be praised! for sanctified afflictions are signs of special love.

Tuesday, February 14. May I never forget this day's mercies, since the Lord was pleased to deal so lovingly with me! About twelve at night a fresh gale arose, which increased so much by four in the morning that the waves broke in like a great river on many of the poor soldiers who lay near the main hatchway. Friend Habersham and I knew nothing of it, but perceived ourselves restless, and could not sleep at all. He complained of a grievous headache. I got up and called upon God for myself and those who sailed with me, absent friends, and all mankind. After this I went on deck; but surely a more noble, awful sight my eyes never yet beheld! For the waves rose mountain high, and sometimes came on the quarter-deck. I endeavoured all the while to magnify God, for thus making his power to be known. Then, creeping on my knees (for I did not know how else to go), I followed my friend H. between decks, and sang psalms and comforted the poor wet people. After this, I read prayers in the great cabin, but we were obliged to sit all the time. Though things were tumbling, the ship rocking, and persons falling down unable to stand, and sick about me, I never was more cheerful in my life, and was enabled, though in the midst of company, to finish a sermon before I went to bed, which I had begun a few days before. Praise the Lord, O my soul, and all that is within me praise his holy name!

Friday, February 17. Found honest Mr D. particularly useful to me, I being a little sick by the recent shaking of the ship, and the heat and smell of the people between decks, who as yet have scarce had time to recover since the storm. O how soon are these frail tents of ours put out of order! Happy the man who serves God in his health, and has nothing to do when sickness seizes him but quietly to lie down and die.

Saturday, February 18. Performed the usual duty, and finished the Lord's prayer. Perceived my bodily disorders to go off, and was enabled to preach to the soldiers. The captain noticed I was a little out of sorts, and gave Mr H. a cordial for me.

After dinner, I grew better, and was exceedingly delighted by sitting on deck, praising God for the pleasantness of the weather, and reading Archbishop Cranmer's *Life*. Surely he was a righteous man. But why should you be cast down, O my soul? Still trust in God. He who has begun will carry on and finish the good work. Even so, Lord Jesus.

Though the weather was exceedingly pleasant all the day, yet it grew more and more so in the evening, and our ship sailed at the rate of nine miles an hour, and as steady as though we were sitting on shore. The night was unusually clear, and the moon and stars appeared in their greatest lustre, so not having patience to stay below I went up on deck with friend Habersham and praised God for his wonderful loving kindness, singing psalms, and gave thanks for the blessings and asked pardon for the offences of the last week; and then had a long intercession. God grant I may learn a lesson from this good providence of God; and the nearer I come to my journey's end, the quicker may my pace be.

Sunday, February 19. For these two days our ship has sailed at the rate of a hundred and sixty miles in twenty-four hours, and rode in triumph directly before the wind, and cast anchor about two in the morning, until which time I sat up on purpose to give thanks in Gibraltar Haven. Oh that my friends would therefore praise the Lord for his goodness, and extol him for the wonderful works he does for me, the least of the sons of men.

Monday, February 20. Spent the morning on board, writing letters to my dear friends in England, to acquaint them of my safe arrival. Went in the afternoon on shore to Gibraltar, and was delighted with the appearance of the place. My friend Habersham and I dined at an inn, and went afterwards with Captain Whiting and some other company to view one side of the fort, which to us seemed impregnable, and at the sight of it I could scarce avoid crying out, 'Who is so great a God as our God?'

Seeing persons of all nations and languages gave me great pleasure; and the difference of the value of their money and ours gave me occasion to reflect on the stupidity of those who place their happiness in that which has no intrinsic worth in itself, but only so much as we arbitrarily put upon it.

Went into a Romish chapel, wherein were the relics of a vast deal of pageantry, and several images of the Virgin Mary, dressed up, not like a poor Galilean, but in her silks and damasks. Oh, thought I, who has bewitched this people, that they should depart like this from the simplicity of Christ and go a-whoring after their own inventions? Surely were the great St Paul to rise from the dead and come and view the Romish church his spirit would be stirred up within him, as it was in Athens, to see them, thus wholly given over to idolatry.

Tuesday, February 21. After having read prayers, and written some more letters to my friends in England, I went again to Gibraltar to pay my respects to Governor Sabine, being told by Captain M. that he expected to see me. The worthy old gentleman, like Sergius Paulus, received me with the utmost openness, and gave me a general invitation to come and dine with him every day, during my stay at Gibraltar. I thanked him for his kindness, had a quarter of an hour's conversation with him, and took my leave for that time.

Wednesday, February 22. This day I went again on shore, and paid both the ministers of Gibraltar a visit, who received me very affectionately, and offered me the use of the pulpit. Oh what a blessed thing it is for the clergy to dwell together in unity!

At eleven, went to public prayers, and was much pleased to see many officers and soldiers attend the General to church. I think religion looks doubly attractive in a soldier.

Went in the afternoon to visit a deserter, who had sent me a letter asking me to intercede for him with the Governor. He being apprehensive he should die for desertion, I intended to answer his request; but the Governor was so merciful that he ordered him to be whipped only, which I thought punishment little enough. O sin, what mischief you make in the world!

Friday, February 24. Blessed be God, who this day has shown me that he has heard my prayer, and not taken his loving kindness from me. Long before I reached Gibraltar, I prayed that God would open an effectual door at the place where we were going to, and direct me where I should lodge, and lo! this day he has answered me. About ten in the morning Captain Mackay came on board, telling me that one Major S. (a person I had never seen) had provided me with a convenient lodging at one merchant B.'s, and desired that I should come on shore. I looked on this as a call from providence, received it with all thankfulness and went ashore with friend Habersham, first praying that God would direct us how to behave.

About the middle of the town, Major S. conducted us to our new lodgings, which were very commodious, and engaged us to dine with him and Captain Mackay. 'When I sent you without purse or bag or shoes, did you lack anything?' And they said, 'Nothing, Lord!'

About eleven I was introduced by Doctor C. to General Columbine, who was desirous of meeting me. He received me exceeding kindly; and after a little religious conversation we went to Governor Sabine's, and from there to public prayers. I was highly pleased to see so many officers attending on the Generals to church. Doctor C. told me he had not known Governor Sabine absent himself from prayers once in several years, except when he was hindered by sickness. Oh that all others would let their light so shine before men!

Saturday, February 25. About six this morning went with friend Habersham to the church to pray with some devout soldiers, who I heard used to meet there at that time, and with whom my soul was joined immediately. After we had finished our devotion, I made an enquiry into their state, and found that their Society had been subsisting about twelve years, and that one Sergeant B. (a devout soldier indeed), now amongst them, was the first beginner of it. At first, they told me they used to meet in dens and mountains, and caves in the rocks; but afterwards, when they applied for leave to build a little place to retire in, Doctor C. and Governor Sabine gave them the free use of the church, where they constantly meet three times a day to pray, read, and sing psalms, and at any other season when they please. They have met with contempt, and are now in derision called *The New Lights*. A glorious light they are indeed; for I conversed closely with several of them, and they made me quite ashamed of how little proficient I am in the School of Christ. Many have joined with them for a time, but a servile fear of man—that bane of Christianity—made them draw back. However, some continue steadfast and immoveable, though despised by the world. Governor Sabine countenances them much, and has spoken of them often to me with respect. Blessed be God, the Father of our Lord Jesus Christ, who has not left himself without witness in any place, but has some everywhere who serve him and do what is right!

There is also another Society of the Scottish church, who in contempt are called *Dark Lanterns*. It has subsisted about a year, and is made up of many serious Christians, I was informed. I did not think it a good idea to visit them; but I sent them, as well as the other Society, some suitable books. I had religious talk with several of them, and endeavoured to unite both Societies together. Oh, when will that time come, when all differences about externals shall be taken away, and we all with one heart and one mouth shall glorify our Lord Jesus Christ!

I spent nearly two hours with the devout soldiers in the church. Many of them conversed most spiritually, and seemed well acquainted with the pangs of the new birth. May God perfect the good work begun in their hearts!

Sunday, February 26. Between five and six in the morning went with Mr Habersham (which I did all the while I was at Gibraltar) and sang psalms, prayed and expounded the lessons to the devout soldiers in the church, and was much enlarged. Thanks be to you, O God!

Intended to go and preach to my people, but was prevented by the violence of the wind. I was pleased to hear from some Gibraltar officers who dined that day on board the *Whitaker* that some of my flock had the courage to read prayers and sing psalms themselves, and (as I found afterwards) continued so to do during my absence from them. Blessed be God! I hope I shall have some who dare be singularly good, and will not be kept out by the throng.

Preached in the morning at Gibraltar, before such a congregation of officers and soldiers as I never before saw. The church, though very large, was quite crowded; and God was pleased to show me that he had given extraordinary success to my sermon. O how is the divine strength magnified in my weakness! O grant I may, like a pure crystal, transmit all the light you pour over me, and never claim as my own what is your sole property!

Monday, February 27. Went to the church, and did as yesterday; and was visited afterwards by two of the Nonconforming Society, who seemed to be true Israelites. I exhorted them to love and unity, and not to let a little difference about a few externals occasion any narrow-spiritedness to arise in their hearts. I advised them to come and hear me expound in the church, which they did; and providentially the lesson was the fourth chapter of Ephesians, from which I took occasion to urge on them the necessity of loving one another with a catholic disinterested love, to be of one heart and one mind, and to join without respect of persons in hastening the kingdom of our Lord Jesus Christ. I hope God gave a blessing to what was said, for I observed they came constantly afterwards, and was told there was a perfect harmony between them. What infinite mischief have needless divisions occasioned in the Christian world! Divide and rule is the devil's motto.

Tuesday, February 28. Was asked by Dr C. in the name of the Governor and Colonel C. to preach every Prayer Day whilst I stayed at Gibraltar, which I promised to do. Many of the inhabitants pressed me to stay with them, and were exceeding kind to those who were with me. Blessed be God for thus giving me favour in his people's sight! Lord, what am I, that you should so highly honour me like this? Grant, O Lord, the more you exalt me, the more I may abase myself, and look to the rock from which I was hewn!

Conversed with one of the devout soldiers, who was under strong spiritual trials; and God was pleased to give him comfort. I find it necessary more and more every day that ministers should be tempted in all things, that they may be able to succour by their own experience those that are tempted.

Wednesday, March 1. Expounded in the morning, and was pleased at my entrance into the church to see several soldiers kneeling in several parts of the house of God at their private devotions. O happy Gibraltar, that you have seen such a set of praying men! Some, I hear, often come in by two o'clock in the morning to pour out their hearts before God. The Lord grant all their petitions!

Preached, according to my promise, to a numerous and much moved audience of officers, soldiers, etc. Dined, at his invitation, at Governor Sabine's; and expounded at night to nearly 200 people, amongst whom were many of the officers, and not a few of the honourable women. Oh that they may with meekness receive the engrafted word, and that it may be a means of saving their souls!

Thursday, March 2. Spent part of the day in writing letters. Dined and supped at Mr Argat's, chief civil magistrate in Gibraltar. Expounded twice in the church, as usual, and at night had over 300 hearers, amongst whom were many officers, ladies, and Dr C., the minister of the church himself, who would have had me go up into the reading desk so that I might have had greater command of the people, but I declined it that night. God be praised for sending me abroad, and prospering the work of his hands upon me!

Friday, March 3. Still God lets me see greater things than before. Oh that my thanks may increase proportionately! This morning, besides a great number of the soldiers, nearly if not more than a dozen of the townspeople came to church to hear me expound. Afterwards we breakfasted with a gentlewoman, who sent by Major S. to invite us, and most gladly received us into her house. About ten I preached my sermons against *Swearing*, and made a farewell application to the soldiers who were going over to Georgia out of that garrison. The Governor had that morning reviewed them; and as I could not be in the same ship with them, I desired they might be ordered to come to church, that I might have an opportunity of telling them how to behave in the land which they were going over the sea to protect. The Colonel and Governor most readily consented; there was a most crowded audience, and God was pleased to set his seal on my sermon. Many officers and soldiers wept sorely, and a visible alteration was observed in the garrison for some days after. Oh that their convictions may end in their conversion, and that they may bring forth the fruits of the Spirit!

Bought some wine out of the money which I had collected for the use of the sick poor in Georgia. The parsonage house ought to be the poor's storehouse.

Saturday, March 4. Went in the afternoon to the Jewish synagogue, and was surprised to see one of the heads of them come from the farthest end and put me in one of their chiefest seats. But afterwards he told me he had heard my sermon yesterday against swearing, and thanked me for it. I remained with them for the whole of their service, and spent most of my time there in secret prayer to God that the veil might be taken from their hearts, and that blessed time might come when his chosen people should again be engrafted into their own olive tree, and all Israel be saved.

Visited an unhappy man in prison, who last night, in a drunken fit, murdered a fellow-soldier. I providentially met him just as he was apprehended, and laid before him the terrors of the Lord. At first he seemed unconcerned, but in a short time he was pricked to the heart, desired me to come and see him, and today trembled, and wept bitterly. Oh Drunkenness, what mischief you have done! Your name is legion, for behold a troop of sins come along with you.

In the evening, I had nearly, if not more than, a thousand hearers; and I took occasion, from the poor man's example just mentioned, to warn the soldiery not to be drunk with wine, wherein is excess—a sin that most easily besets the men of Gibraltar. I had a great hoarseness upon me, but even so God enabled me to speak with power. When we are weak, then are we strong. What mercies has God shown me this last week! Oh that my friends, when they hear of it, may praise him, for surely God has heard their prayer!

Sunday, March 5. After morning exposition in the church, went and saw the Roman Catholics at their High Mass; and shall only make this remark: that there needs no other argument against Popery than to see the pageantry, superstition and idolatry of their worship.

Monday, March 6. About twelve, went to the church, as arranged, and made a farewell exhortation, as God gave me utterance, to a great number of weeping soldiers, women, etc. After which we kneeled down, and having commended each other to the care of God I left them and went and took my leave of the two Generals, visited the confined prisoner, dined at a gentlewoman's house of the town, left nearly fifty letters to be sent to England, and about four went on board, accompanied to the seaside by nearly two hundred soldiers, women, officers, etc., who sorrowed at my departure, and wished me good luck in the name of the Lord. Surely I may now expect greater success abroad, having such an addition of intercessors on my behalf. O Lord put their tears into your bottle, and let their cry come to you!

Tuesday, March 7. Went and conversed with, and distributed some books amongst, the soldiers whom we took from Gibraltar. Three of them belonged to one of the Societies, and desired with some others to come with me in our ship. God sanctify my ministry to them. Most of the rest are of the Scots church, but seem very willing to conform. What a pity it is that Christ's seamless coat should be rent in pieces on account of things in themselves purely indifferent!

At dinner we were likely to be struck against by the man-of-war, but God had mercy on us, commanded the wind to shift about, and delivered us out of so great a danger. Oh that we may show our thankfulness not only with our lips but in our lives! How ought creatures to live who are every moment liable to be hurried away by death to judgement!

This day we set sail from Gibraltar.

Wednesday, March 8. Gave myself, as much as my indisposition of body would give me leave, to the word of God and prayer; and was much moved by what is said of Hezekiah in 2 Chronicles 32:25, that because he did not respond, was not thankful enough for the great things God had done for him, he was permitted to fall through the pride of his heart. Alas, what danger am I in of sharing the same fate! O my friends, cry mightily to God, that no such evil come upon me.

Thursday, March 9. Married a couple on deck. I endeavoured to give them a suitable exhortation after the solemnity was over, and hope this couple did call Christ to their marriage. It is through a neglect of this that we have so few happy matches.

The contrary wind still continuing, my sea-sickness increased, so that I was obliged to omit reading prayers to the soldiers, and go to bed sooner than usual. I find this sickness will purge my body.

Friday, March 10. My bodily indisposition still increased; there was a great storm without, but, blessed be God, a calm within. Sometimes, indeed, my will would inwardly rebel; but I hope through inward and outward sufferings I shall at length be able to say in all things, 'Father, not my will, but yours be done.'

Did my usual duty in the great cabin, and began expounding the ten commandments; interceded for friends on deck, and went to bed full of a sense of my own unworthiness. Oh that I could always see myself in my proper colours! I believe I should have little reason to fall down and worship myself. God be merciful to me a sinner!

Saturday, March 11. Blessed be God, this morning the storm began to blow over, and light broke in upon my soul. Was enabled to read prayers and expound both in the cabin and to the soldiers, with more vigour than I have done since we left Gibraltar. Had reason to think my late indisposition has been sanctified to me. Suffering times are a Christian's best improving times, for they break the will, wean us from the creature, test the heart, and by them God teaches his children as Gideon by thorns and briars taught the men of Succoth.

Sunday, March 12. Expounded with more enlargement than usual, and gave my people notice that I intended speaking to them one by one; to see what account they could give of their faith. 'I have not ceased warning every one of you,' says the apostle. May I follow his steps!

Monday, March 13. Blessed be God, this is the most comfortable day I have had since I last came aboard; slept better than usual; was enabled to compose freely; perceived my appetite to return; was enlarged much in intercession, and found I had reason to give thanks for my late indisposition. O how gently does my gracious master deal with me! Though sorrow may endure for a night, yet joy comes in the morning. Lord, grant that I may spend that health which you have now restored to me to your honour and service! It is good for me that I have been a little chastised; for who knows but I might otherwise have perished by being lifted up above measure with my last success? Lord give me humility, even though it be through sufferings! So shall your blessings never prove my ruin.

Tuesday, March 14. Began to put in execution what I promised on Sunday, i.e. enquired into the faith of those committed to my charge; and though all of them were not so greatly proficient as I could wish, yet I find they know enough to save them, if they put what they know into practice, so that they cannot blame God if they miscarry. Oh that the Lord may give them his blessing!

Wednesday, March 15. Was much pleased with my present situation, and had reason to bless God for some further visible effects of my ministry. Was highly delighted in seeing friend Habersham active in teaching the lambs of my flock. He has now got a regular school, and the children began today to come at regular set hours. Several also of the soldiers learn to write and read, so that my friend is likely to make a useful man.

Thursday, March 16. Preached this afternoon my sermon against *Swearing*, at which several of the soldiers wept. Blessed be God, that sin is much debated amongst us; and I think visible alteration may be perceived through the whole ship.

Saturday, March 18. The weather being exceeding fair, and the sea calm, I went with Captain Whiting on board the *Lightfoot*; dined with the gentlemen belonging to the ship and Colonel C., who came on board to pay them a visit; married a couple; distributed Bibles, Testaments, Soldiers' Monitors amongst the men; exchanged some books for some cards, which I threw overboard; preached a sermon against drunkenness, which God enabled me to finish yesterday; and returned in the evening, delighted with seeing the porpoises roll about the great deep. O Lord, the sea is full of your riches!

Sunday, March 19. Went with Captain Whiting on board the *Amy*; read prayers and preached to more than two hundred and twenty hearers, and married a couple, who did not behave so well as I could wish. The bridegroom laughed several times in the middle of the solemnity, at which I shut up my prayer book. He began to weep; I then proceeded, and gave him and the bride a Bible, as the best present I could make them, and exhorted all to holiness of life. God give them a hearing ear, and an obedient heart!

Dined with Colonel Cochrane, who treated me with the utmost civility and took care to dispose of some books I brought with me to suitable persons. About three, we returned to the *Whitaker*, read prayers and preached my sermon against drunkenness; after which, Captain Mackay made a useful speech to the men, and exhorted them to give heed to the things that had been spoken. Religion is likely to go on well when both civil and ecclesiastical powers are engaged in keeping up the purity of it. But, Lord, unless you help us, all our endeavours are but in vain.

Promise, then, we beseech you, to give us your blessing!

Monday, March 20. Today Colonel Cochrane came to dine with us, and in the midst of our meal we were entertained with a most agreeable sight. It was a shark about the length of a man, which followed our ship, attended with five little fishes called the pilot fish, much like a mackerel, but larger. These, I am told, always keep the shark company, and what is most surprising, though the shark is so ravenous a creature, yet however hungry it is it never touches one of them. Nor are they less faithful to him, for if at any time the shark is hooked, these little creatures will not forsake him but cleave close to his fins and are often taken up with him. Go to the pilot fish, you that forsake a friend in adversity, consider his ways and be abashed. This simple sight one would think sufficient to confute any atheist (if there be such a fool as a speculative atheist) in the world.

Tuesday, March 21. The weather growing warmer, friend Habersham had some cloths hung over to cover his school. His children come very regularly both to learn and say their prayers at night. Captain Whiting takes great delight in them, and Captain Mackay much encourages the soldiers to learn to read and write, so we begin to live as regularly now as we could wish to do on shore.

Friday, March 24. Today the sick still increased, and friend Habersham was very ready to assist and carry things to them. Nothing more useful than visiting sick beds! How are those to be pitied, who purposely shun such improving sights!

Sailed a hundred and forty-four miles the last twenty-four hours, and was much delighted in seeing many porpoises playing about the ship, one of which Captain Whiting caught, and part of its liver we had dressed for dinner. It had a head much like a pig, and was about six feet long. The works of the Lord are exceeding great, and to be admired of all those who have a delight in them.

Churched a woman who lately gave birth to a dead child,

and afterwards gave her an exhortation applicable to her circumstances. God grant she may apply it to her heart!

Sunday, March 26. This day, God, I trust, magnified his power in the conversion of a young gentleman on board, whom he has been pleased to visit with a fever. His convictions were strong, and as far as I could determine, a thorough renovation began in his heart. The Lord perfect it till the day of his dissolution. Now God begins to show me why he has sent me. O that I was humble, so that I might be fit for the high and lofty one who inhabits eternity to work through me!

Preached a sermon in the afternoon on Luke 3:14, *Then some soldiers asked him, 'And what should we do?' He replied, 'Don't extort money and don't accuse people falsely—be content with your pay.'* I made it at the request of Captain Mackay who seems in earnest about the great work of his salvation. He has read Arndt's *True Christianity*, and is now reading Law's *Christian Perfection*—books worth their weight in gold, and which God has blessed to the conversion of many. But what are books without your Spirit, O Lord? If you bless them to man's use, they will be blessed.

Exchanged some bad books that were on board (which I threw immediately into the sea) for some good ones. All that I have found with them, as yet, have been ready to surrender them up, and I find by daily experience more and more, that people who are truly awakened to a sense of the divine life cannot bear to read anything trifling, but throw away their useless books, as we read in Acts chapter 19 that books of divination and the occult were surrendered by those who were converted.

Monday, March 27. Last night God was pleased to take away a black boy of Captain Whiting's, after he had been ill of a violent fever for some days. He was never baptised, but I had a commission from his master, who seemed very moved at his death, to instruct and baptise him, if it had pleased the most high that he should recover; but God saw fit to order it otherwise. His holy will be done. About ten in the morning he was wrapped up in a hammock and thrown into the sea. I could not read the funeral service over him as he was unbaptised, but Captain Mackay ordered the drum to be beaten, and I exhorted all the soldiers, sailors, etc., as God gave me utterance, to remember their creator in the days of their youth, and to prepare for that time when the sea should give up its dead, and all nations be called together to appear before the Son of God. Oh that they may be made wise by it, that they may lay to heart what has been said, and practically consider their latter end!

Had our blessed Lord been here, I believe he would have wept to see what havoc sin had made amongst us. Lord, teach us so to count our days that we may apply our hearts to wisdom.

Tuesday, March 28. Today Captain Mackay began to come at six in the morning and join in prayers on deck, instead of having prayers in the great cabin. Surely our soldiers will be without excuse since the captain sets so good an example. I have no reason to complain of them, for they come very regularly twice a day to prayer, and an oath seems to be a strange thing amongst most of them. Many marks of a sound conversion appear in several on board, and we live in perfect harmony and peace, loving and beloved by one another.

Thursday, March 30. Had still more proofs of a thorough conversion being worked in some in the ship. I hope many of us shall have reason to bless God for coming on board the *Whitaker*. God grant, while I preach to others, I myself may not be a castaway! But God is love, and he will not, if I remain single-minded, let his blessings destroy me. O let your power be exerted in preserving me, even me always, O my saviour.

Friday, March 31. This being the crucifixion of our blessed redeemer Lord, I preached a sermon on the penitent thief; and I hope God gave it his blessing. We began prayers later than usual, so that before I had done, darkness came upon us, which reminded me of that darkness which overwhelmed the world when the God of nature suffered. Oh that our hearts may rend like the rocks, and our souls arise from the death of sin, as the bodies of those people rose from their graves and appeared to many in the holy city, after our Lord's resurrection.

Had a good instance of the benefit of breaking children's wills early on. Last night going between decks (as I do every night) to visit the sick and to examine my people, I asked one of the women to bid her little boy, who stood by her, say his prayers; she answered that his elder sister would, but she could not make him. At this, I bid the child kneel down before me, but he would not till I took hold of his two feet and forced him down. I then bid him say the Lord's Prayer (being informed by his mother he could say it if he wanted to); but he obstinately refused, till at last, after I had given him several blows, he said his prayer as well as could be expected, and I gave him some figs for a reward. And this same child, though not more than four years old, came on deck tonight and when the other children came to say their prayers to my friend Habersham, he burst into tears, and would not go away till he had said his too. I mention this as a proof of the necessity of early correction. Children understand it sooner than parents imagine. And if they would have resolution to break their wills thoroughly when they are young, the work of conversion would be much easier, and they would not be so troubled with perverse chldren when they are old.

Saturday, April 1. Wonderfully pleasant sailing still, and what was infinitely better, had reason to think several went forward in the great work of their salvation. Oh that we may be buried with Christ in baptism, and rise with him to newness of life.

Sunday, April 2. Rose early this morning, and joined in spirit with my dear absent friends, who were receiving the holy eucharist, and celebrating our blessed Lord's resurrection. I find my not being in priest's Orders is a great hindrance to my ministry, which will oblige me to return to

England as soon as possible. The good Lord prepare me for that second imposition of hands.

Preached a sermon in the afternoon on Philippians 3:19, *I want to know Christ and the power of his resurrection.* Oh that we may all experience it in our hearts! For without it, Christ as to us is dead in vain.

Monday, April 3. Had some further conversation with the young gentleman whose conversion I mentioned before, and who I hope is really given life from above. He told me he used to wonder to hear me talk that all our thoughts, words, and actions ought to be dedicated to God; but now he perceived what I said to be true. How does the new nature give us new notions! It seems a difficult task to the natural man to turn his whole life into one continued sacrifice, but the spiritual man does it with ease. He feels a divine attraction in his soul, which he feels drawing his heart towards God just as the lodestone attracts the needle. Draw us then, O God, and our affections will rise up to you.

Friday, April 7. If it were not for the corruptions of my own heart, which are continually stirring, what have I to disturb my peace? But as long as those Amalekites remain in my soul, I shall never be perfectly at ease. Lord, just keep me struggling, and at last I shall be more than conqueror through Jesus Christ who loved me.

Saturday, April 8. We live more comfortably in the great cabin than can easily be imagined. We talk of little else but God and Christ. God has greatly blessed the *Country Parson's Advice to his Parishioners*, that excellent book, and scarce a word is to be heard among us when together but what has reference to our fall in the first, and our new birth in the second Adam, the Lord from heaven; so that we all, I trust, are resolved to put my afternoon's text into practice, and are determined not to know anything save Jesus Christ, and him crucified. Grant this, O Father, for your dear Son's sake. Oh that I knew how to be thankful! Oh that heaven and earth would join with me in praising God!

April 12 or 13. Today Captain Whiting caught a dolphin which was most beautiful when drawn out of the water, but its colour soon changed. Just so is man; he flourishes for a little while, but once death comes how quickly is his beauty gone! A Christian may learn a lesson of instruction from everything he meets with.

Friday, April 14. Today I could have wished for some young prodigals aboard the *Whitaker*, to see one of our soldiers dying. Alas, how did his breast heave, his heart pant, and great drops of sweat trickle down his face! His eyes looked ghastly, and the whole man was in a bitter agony. Captain Whiting went down between decks with me once or twice to see him. I used the last prayer several times. About nine at night he expired, I fear without hope, for he killed himself by drinking. Oh that all drunkards would learn from him to be wise in time, and practically consider their latter end!

Today I was called in a hurry to pray by one of the devout soldiers who came from Gibraltar, and who was supposed to be expiring. I came, I saw, and rejoiced in spirit, for his soul seemed full of God. Instead of being frightened at the approach of the king of terrors, he welcomed it, and said he was going to his dear redeemer; then he fell as it were into a trance, and poured out his heart in repeating some very appropriate verses out of the Psalms. At this point we thought he was going to die, but God brought him from the nethermost hell. From that instant the fever left him, and he recovered. Oh what a difference there is between the person who fears God, and the one who does not fear him, in their last hours! Lord, let me die the death of the righteous, and let my future state be like his.

Exercised a little discipline this evening on a boy whom Captain Mackay noticed more than a week ago for behaving badly at church, and said he would send him to me. I therefore, by the advice of his master, ordered him to be tied till he could say the 51st Psalm, which he repeated tonight very solemnly in the midst of the congregation. May it be a warning to him for the future!

Sunday, April 16. This evening I was sent for by a sailor who has been the most remarkable swearer on board, and whom I specially warned about two days ago, telling him I believed God would deal with him in a remarkable way. He laughed, and said he hoped not. But tonight he sent for me trembling and burning with a fever; he told me what grievous sins he had been guilty of, and prayed most fervently for repentance. Two or three of the same stamp have been taken in the same manner. God grant that they may flee from the wrath to come! Sinners must either bend or break.

Tuesday, April 18. Was greatly delighted to see two waterspouts, which ran along for several miles, and by the special providence of God missed us. We saw one of them coming, and were surprised to observe a sudden calm for about six minutes round the *Whitaker*, when the other parts of the sea boiled like a pot. Surely the everlasting I AM said to the sea at that instant, *Let there be a calm in that place*; for our ship was immediately stopped in her course, and so the waterspout passed by before we came up to it; otherwise, it would have torn our sails in pieces. God's hand was so visible in this that several people said they had never seen anything like it before. Oh how providence watches over us, when we think nothing of it! How well we do to live under the immediate protection of such an overruling power! After this, several squalls came upon us which gave me glorious matter for adoring that great and good God who is obeyed by winds and storms. The sailors were in a great hurry and confusion, but to my relief not a single oath was heard all the time—a proof, this, that sailors can pull their ropes without swearing, and the words spoken to them have not altogether fallen on stony ground! Blessed be God!

Monday, May 1. This morning went out on deck, after being confined to my bed for a week by a violent fever, which all except three or four in the ship have had. I was blooded three times, and blistered and vomited once, and, blessed be God, can say, *It is good for me that I have been afflicted*; for as afflictions abounded, consolations much more abounded, and God enabled me to rejoice with joy unspeakable. Satan desired to have me to sift me as wheat; but Jesus Christ prayed for me, and my faith did not fail. I had all the conveniences I could have on shore: Captain Whiting gave up his own bed for me; J.D. and friend H. sat up with me every night, and nothing was lacking to make my sickness comfortable and easy. Blessed be God for these abundant mercies in Christ Jesus!

I hope I shall now sympathise with those who are sick, from my own experience, and learn to be more tender-hearted to my fellow Christians. I am now better. May I sin no more, and be more fervent in spirit, serving the Lord lest a worse thing happen to me!

Friday, May 5. About ten o'clock this morning I buried the cook of the ship, who expired last night. I could have wished for a hundred tongues to have sounded a loud alarm to the people; but the sight of the corpse, and the weakness of my body, would only just let me read out the service. Lord, what is man?

In the afternoon I privately baptised a new-born infant. Thus it is, some coming into the world, others going out of it continually. Good God! Who can desire to live here always?

This afternoon, after having lain about a week on this coast, we saw Savannah River, and sent off for a pilot. Oh what joy appeared in everyone's face! How infinitely more joyful will the children of God be, when having passed through the waves of this troublesome world they arrive at the haven of everlasting rest? Hasten, O Lord, that blessed time, and let your kingdom come!

Second Journal

A Continuation
of the Reverend Mr Whitefield's Journal
from his arrival at Savannah
to his return to London
(May 1738—December 1738)

Sunday, May 7. Arrived at Savannah Town about seven this evening, and joined in prayer, and a psalm of thanksgiving with Mr Delamotte and some pious souls who rejoiced at my arrival.

Monday, May 8. Began to read public prayers and expound the second lesson at five in the morning, to seventeen adults and twenty-five children. May God open their hearts that they may attend to the things that were spoken. In the afternoon, Mr Causton sent word that he and the magistrates would come to see me; but I chose rather to go to see them. I was received with great civility, and our chief conversation was about where I should live; at last it was resolved that I should have a house and place of worship built at Frederica, and serve at Savannah when, and as long as, I pleased. I find there are many divisions amongst the inhabitants; but God, I hope, will make me an instrument of healing them. Grant this, O Lord, for your dear Son's sake!

Sunday, May 14. After another week's confinement by

the return of my fever, under which God showed me great mercies, and which went off with a fit of the ague, I attempted to read prayers; but was so exceedingly faint and weak that I had to stop before I began the second service.

Tuesday, May 16. Having by the blessing of God got a little strength, I went to see Tomo Chachi, who, I heard, was almost dying at a neighbour's house. He lay on a blanket, thin and meagre, and little else but skin and bones. Senauki, his wife, sat by, fanning him with some Indian feathers. There was nobody who could talk English, so I could only shake hands and leave him.

Friday, May 19. God still strengthened me more and more, so I went this morning to two little villages, Hampstead and Highgate, about five miles off Savannah: the former consists of three families, making in all eleven souls, one man a Jew, two men, one woman and seven children Swiss. I was much delighted with seeing the improvements a few pairs of hands had made in their respective plantations, and was surprised to see what hard work can do. Surely they do not speak the truth, who say that the Georgia people have been idle; for I never saw more hardworking people than are in these villages. They live exceedingly hard, but with a little assistance may do very well. I was at a loss because I could not speak French, but I resolved under God to follow my worthy predecessor's example and to visit them once a week, and read prayers to as many as could understand me. I also enquired into the state of their children, and found there were many who might prove useful members of the colony if there was a proper place provided for their maintenance and education. Nothing can effect this but an orphanage, which might easily be erected at Savannah if some of those who are rich in this world's goods would contribute towards it.

Saturday, May 20. Went once more to see Tomo Chachi, hearing his nephew Tooanoowee was there, who could talk English. I desired him to enquire of his uncle whether he thought he was going to die. He answered that he did not know. I then asked where he thought he would go after death. He replied, 'to heaven'. But alas, how can a drunkard enter there? I then exhorted Tooanoowee (who is a tall, good-looking youth) not to get drunk, telling him he understood English, and therefore would be punished the more if he did not live better. I then asked him whether he believed in heaven. He answered, 'Yes.' I then asked whether he believed in a hell, and described it by pointing to the fire; he replied, 'No,' from which we may easily gather how natural it is to all mankind to believe there is a place of happiness, because they wish it to be true, and on the contrary how averse they are to believe in a place of torment, because they wish it may not be so. But God is true and just, and as surely as the good will go into everlasting happiness, so the wicked will go into everlasting punishment.

Friday, June 2. This evening, parted with kind Captain Whiting and my dear friend Delamotte, who embarked for England about seven at night. The poor people lamented the loss of him, and went to the waterside to take a last farewell. And good reason they had to do so, for he has been indefatigable in feeding Christ's lambs with the sincere milk of the word, and many of them (blessed be God) have grown thereby. Surely, I must labour most heartily, since I come after such worthy predecessors. The good which Mr John Wesley has done in America, under God, is inexpressible. His name is very precious among the people; and he has laid such a foundation that I hope neither men nor devils will ever be able to shake. Oh that I may follow him, as he has Christ!

Monday, June 5. Had a conference with a certain person of the parish who, I heard last night, had been broaching many heretical doctrines to one of my friends, particularly in denying the eternity of hell torments. I therefore visited him this morning for breakfast, and after imploring God's assistance, in the spirit of meekness, I asked him whether he believed in the eternity of hell torments. He answered frankly, 'No.' I replied, 'What do you mean, sir, when you repeat the twelfth article of our creed? He said he believed wicked men were to be annihilated. I then read Pearson's exposition of the last article, but he denied it all, said he thought himself in the right, and believed it his duty to inform mankind that they were right to be annihilated. At this I repeated to him that passage out of the Revelation, 'If anyone takes words away from this book of prophecy, God will take away from him his share in the tree of life and in the holy city, which are described in this book.' This, he said, he believed. Afterwards we talked afresh, but finding him resolute to propagate his principles I then told him with the utmost calmness that I was sorry I gave him the cup yesterday at the sacrament; but for the future, he must pardon me if I refused ever to give it him again. This staggered him a little, but he bore it pretty patiently, yet thought me uncharitable.

Saturday, June 10. Placed one who came with me, at Highgate, to teach the children English that belong to that village and Hampstead. There are about twenty in all, of French extraction, but a few of them are able to speak a little in our common language. I thought placing a master there would be of great consequence. First, because I cannot think children will ever be naturalised to the colony till they can talk our language. Secondly, because the present generation will soon wear off, and these children being well instructed in ours, will make them forget their own tongue, and should they marry and have children, they would naturally teach their children the same; so that at length we shall all be of one speech. Thirdly, as they are but few in number, and no likelihood of any French minister coming amongst them, I or my successors will be unable to catechise or bring them to hear the word of God at our church unless they are acquainted with the English language.

Monday, June 12. Opened a school today for the girls of

Savannah, a friend, whose heart God was pleased to touch on board the ship, having at my request undertaken to teach them. The work is for my master, and therefore I do not doubt we shall be supplied some way or another with a sufficient fund for the support of it. May God enable him who is set over them to feed them with the sincere milk of the word, and give them grace to grow thereby!

Thursday, June 22. Was taken (as all about me thought for death) with a violent purging and vomiting, which in a period of five hours quite exhausted my spirits, and brought me in appearance almost to the point of death. But God supported me by his inward comforts, caused me to rejoice in it, and cast me into a deep sleep, out of which I awoke perfectly well, to the surprise of all about me. O who can express the loving kindness of the Lord, or show all his praise!

Friday, June 23. To the great surprise of myself and people, was enabled to read prayers and preach with power before the Freemasons, with whom I afterwards dined, and was treated with the utmost civility. May God make them servants of Christ, and then and not till then will they be free indeed.

Tuesday, July 11. Returned this evening from Ebenezer (where I went yesterday), the place where the people from Salzburg are settled; and was wonderfully pleased with their order and hard work. Their lands are improved surprisingly for the time they have been there, and I believe they have far the best crop of any in the colony. They are blessed with two such pious ministers as I have not often seen. They have no law courts, but all little differences are immediately and implicitly decided by their ministers, whom they regard and love as their fathers. They also have an orphanage in which are seventeen children and one widow, and I was much delighted to see the regularity with which it is managed. Oh that God may stir up the hearts of his servants to contribute towards that and another which we hope to have erected at Savannah. Mr

Boltzius, one of the ministers, being with me on Saturday, I gave him some of my poor's store for his orphans, and when I came to Ebenezer, he called them all before him, catechised and exhorted them to give God thanks for his good providence towards them; then sang a psalm, and afterwards the little lambs came and shook me by the hand, one by one, and so we parted, and I scarcely ever was better pleased in my life. Surely, whoever contributes to the relief of the Salzburg people will perform an acceptable sacrifice to our blessed master. They are very poor, but with a little assistance might live comfortably and well. They lack a place for public worship, and money to buy cattle, and other necessaries for the orphanage and people. May the great God raise up instruments to assist and relieve them, for surely they are worthy.

Tuesday, July 25. I am now waiting for the scout-boat which Mr Horton has sent to take me to Frederica, to preach the gospel there also. For that is what I am sent for.

On Sunday morning at five o'clock I publicly expound the second lesson for the morning or evening service as I see most suited to the people's edification; at ten I preach and read prayers; at three in the afternoon I do the same; at seven expound part of the church catechism, at which great numbers are usually present. I visit from house to house, read public prayers, and expound twice, and catechise (unless something extraordinary happens), visit the sick every day, and read to as many of my parishioners as will come three times a week. And blessed be God, my labours have not been altogether vain in the Lord. For he has been pleased to set his seal on my ministry in a manner I could not, I dared not in America, expect. Not unto me, O Lord, not unto me, but unto you be the glory!

At Frederica

Tuesday, August 8. After a pleasant passage of five or six days, I arrived at Frederica, a town situated more than a hundred miles to the south from Savannah, and consisting of about a hundred and twenty inhabitants. The people received me most gladly, having had a famine of the word for a long time.

Wednesday, August 9. Began today visiting from house to house and found the people in appearance desirous of being fed with the sincere milk of the word, and keen to have me stay among them.

This evening, had prayers in a house which Mr Horton hired for us during my stay, and most of the inhabitants, I believe, were present. Blessed be God, timber is sawing for the erecting of a more commodious place for public worship, till a church can be built. God grant we may always worship him in spirit and in truth, and then we may be assured that at all times and in all places he will hear us.

Saturday, August 12. This afternoon was alarmed with the news of a family disaster. My dear friend H.'s brother went to find a horse that was lost in the woods, got lost himself, and many guns shot after him for several days, but in vain. I endeavoured to give thanks to God for this and everything that happens to me, because it is his will, and resolved to set out for Savannah immediately, knowing what concern my dear friend H. must be in at so sudden a loss.

In the evening, because I was to go about midnight, I gave notice I would preach as well as expound, at which almost all the inhabitants were present.

Sunday, August 13. A report reached Frederica that the Spaniards had taken possession of Fort St George, and fired at one of our boats; but this was quickly found to be entirely groundless.

At Savannah

Wednesday, August 16. Arrived today at Savannah, and had the pleasure of meeting my friend who had been lost; he was roving about in the woods from Tuesday till Friday, during which time the great guns were fired according to custom, and the people showed what a great respect they had for me and my friends, many of them going out all day and night after him. As soon as I had refreshed myself, I went and visited my parishioners from house to house to thank them for their kindness to my friends. An unusual joy appeared in their faces at my unexpected return, and they were ready to say, 'How beautiful are the feet of the messenger bringing good news of salvation.' At evening prayers (and a very large congregation was present) I returned my dear hearers' hearty thanks for the recent example of their sincere affection; I publicly exhorted my friend who was lost to show his thankfulness not only with his lips but with his life, and desired their prayers to God for me that I might now devote myself more to my blessed master's service, and study daily to purify my corrupt nature, that I might be made an instrument under him of winning their souls to God.

Wednesday, August 23. Today I had to express my resentment against unbelief, by refusing to read the burial service over the most professed unbeliever I ever yet met with. God was pleased to visit him with a lingering illness, in which time I went to see him frequently. Particularly about five weeks ago, I asked what religion he was of; he answered that religion was divided into so many sects that he knew not which to choose. Another time, I offered to pray with him but he would not accept it, at which I resolved to go and see him no more; but being told two days before he died, that he had an inclination to see me, I went to him again, and after a little conversation I put to him the following questions. 'Do you believe Jesus Christ to be God, the one mediator between God and man?' He said, 'I believe Christ was a good man.' 'Do you believe the holy scriptures?' 'I believe', he replied, 'something of the Old Testament, the New I do not believe at all.' 'Do you believe, sir, in a judgement to come?' He turned himself about, and replied, 'I know not what to say to that.' 'Alas,' said I, 'Sir, if all these things should be true'—which words, I believe, gave him concern, for he seemed after that to be very uneasy, grew delirious, and departed in a day or two. Unhappy man, how quickly was he convinced that all I said was true! Now he and I are of one mind. The day after his decease, he was carried to the ground, and I refused to read the service over him, but went to the grave and told the people what had passed between him and me, warned them against unbelief, and asked them whether I could safely say, 'as our hope is this our brother doth'. At this I believe they were thoroughly satisfied that I had done right. God grant this may be a warning to surviving unbelievers.

Thursday, August 24. Today I went to Highgate with a friend or two and read prayers, preached and baptised a child, and catechised in a house recently erected by the inhabitants. When I sent a master to teach their children, one offered to give me a part of his land, and the rest to give their labour. So I accepted it, found materials, and today it was fit to preach in and be made into a school house. The children, though foreigners, answered admirably well, which gave me great hopes that the other foreign children of the colony may also learn our English language when a proper master is provided. After the service, we refreshed ourselves together, thanked our good God, and ate our bread with gladness of heart.

Sunday, August 27. God having now shown both me and my friends that it was his will I should return for a while to England, this afternoon I preached my farewell sermon.

Monday, August 28. This being the day of my departure, it was mostly spent in taking leave of my flock, who expressed their affection now more than ever. They came to me from the morning to the time I left them with tears in their eyes, wishing me a prosperous voyage and safe return, and gave me other tokens of their love, for they brought me wine, ale, cake, coffee, tea, and other things for my passage, and their love seemed genuine.

Charleston

Arrived here last night, and preached twice today, I hope

with some good effect. The Bishop of London's commissary, the Rev. Mr Garden, a good soldier of Jesus Christ, received me in a most Christian manner. He and several others offered me a lodging, and were more than civil to me. How God raises me up friends wherever I go! Who is so good a God as our God?

Was much pleased with the neatness of the buildings, and the largeness of the place. The church is very beautiful, and the inhabitants seem to be excellently well settled. God's judgements have recently been among them with the spread of smallpox. I hope they will learn righteousness.

On board the Mary, *Captain Coc, commander, bound from Charleston to England*

Saturday, September 9. About noon, came on board with great composure of mind, and thought of my absent friends; settled my things, wrote my journal, and finished some other matters. The wind being fair, weighed anchor, and set sail about five in the evening. The Lord send us a prosperous voyage, and bring us in his appointed time to the haven where we want to be.

Saturday, September 16. Had contrary winds all the week, and got only a few leagues from Charleston, yet God showed me great mercies, for he enabled me to write several things, and correct others. I have only been a little seasick, and though I have not had my clothes off, and lay on deck or on a chest every night, yet the goodness of God keeps me healthy and strong, and makes me feel his Holy Spirit within me. My sphere of action is now contracted into a very narrow compass. There are only a few souls on board, and all that I can do is to read public prayers, and add a word of exhortation twice every day, and catechise those I brought with me. The captain and all are very civil.

Saturday, September 23. God is pleased to send us contrary winds, except one night about the middle of the week. However, he enables me to give thanks, and great reason have I to do so, for the Holy Spirit has truly been with me.

I have observed that before God calls me to a public work he always sends me into some retirement, but never to so great a one as now. A sign this, I hope, that a greater work is yet to come. Lord, fit and prepare me for it.

Sunday 24. Monday, September 25. Was oppressed much in spirit these two days. The wind was contrary, and the sea churned and was tempestuous; but blessed be God, he enabled me to be resigned to his will, this outward and inward trial being only what was to be expected after how he has recently helped me. We cannot always be on the mountain in this life.

Friday, October 6. Before I left Savannah, the lesson appointed for the morning was St Paul's shipwreck, out of Acts, and before I left Charleston the lesson was the first chapter of Jonah, both of which made such a deep impression on me that I wrote to my friend Habersham to tell him I was worried we might have a dangerous voyage. Since I have been on board, what St Paul said to his companions, that he perceived their voyage would be with much damage, has frequently been pressed on my heart; and God has now shown me why he gave the forewarnings. For last Tuesday night, after we had sailed 150 miles, the last twenty hours, about eleven o'clock, there arose a sudden violent east wind, which continued till about four in the morning, and put all the sailors to their wits' end. Most of them declared they had never seen the like before. The mainsail was slit in several pieces, and several of the other sails, and much of the tackling all tattered. Not a dry place was to be found in all the ship. The captain's hammock, in the great cabin, was half filled with water, and though I lay in the most dry part of the ship, yet the waves broke in upon me two or three times. In short, all was terror and confusion, men's hearts failing them for fear, and the wind and the sea raging horribly. But God (for ever be to me. I felt a sweet complacency in my will, in submission to his. Many particular promises that God has made me from his word, that I should return in peace, flowed in upon my heart; and he enabled me to rejoice greatly. Most of our fresh provisions have been washed overboard, and our tackling is much out of order, so we have the prospect only of an indifferent voyage; but, blessed be God, the prospect pleases me, for now I shall learn, I trust, how to go without as well as how to abound, and how to endure hardship like a good soldier of Jesus Christ. O Lord, let your strength be magnified in my weakness, say to my soul, 'It is I; don't be afraid,' and then let storms and tempests do their worst.

Saturday, October 7. Today, adored be the divine goodness, the weather has cleared up more and more, and our ship has sailed directly before the wind, at the rate of four or five miles an hour. A desire to see my friends in England, to see to my business, and to return to my poor flock, prompts me secretly to wish for a continuance of this prosperous gale. But Lord, I know not what to pray for as I ought. Do with me as seems good in your sight. Only I beseech you to sanctify my present retirement, that the longer I am upon the sea, the more zealous I may be in your service when I come upon dry land.

Saw a Jamaica ship, Captain Phillips, who has been out nine weeks. What reason we have to be thankful!

Having had no opportunity before, since the storm, of getting the people together, gave a word or two of exhortation to my shipmates, to bless God for our recent deliverance, and to sin no more lest a worse storm should befall us.

Saturday, October 14. Sailed this week about 600 miles; but yesterday God was pleased to send us a contrary wind, which still continues. A few days ago I flattered myself we should soon be at our desired port, but God is pleased to defer the accomplishment of my hopes. However, blessed be his name! He enables me to give thanks. Most of this week has been spent in searching the scriptures, and in retirements for direction and assistance in the work before me. My fresh provisions are gone, and the people are allowed a quart of water each man for a day. I hope now the spiritual man will grow, having so little for the natural man to feed on. Amen, Lord Jesus! Blessed be God! I can by his grace say that I rejoice in going without, and in everything give thanks. Had this sentence out of Matthew Henry much pressed on my heart to comfort me in my retirement: 'The mower loses no time whilst he is whetting his scythe.'

Saturday, October 21. Made but slow advances in our voyage, having had only one or two days of fair wind. But even so, I believe we shall now soon reach shore; for God has been pleased to visit me all the week with a variety of inward trials, which is a sign to me that I shall experience yet more and more of his mercies. How good is God thus to prepare me by sufferings, so that his blessings may not be my ruin. These things are not joyful to the natural man, but grievous; but God enables me to take comfort in him, to thank him sincerely for his loving correction, and therefore when I am sufficiently exercised by it I hope it will bring out in me the peaceable fruits of righteousness.

Sunday, October 22. At the desire of the captain, preached my sermon on rash anger, having only expounded until now. In the lesson were these remarkable words, 'Return to your own house, and show what great things God has done to you.' And again, 'It happened that when Jesus had returned, the people received him gladly, for they were all waiting for him.' These last words were remarkably impressed on me at Savannah, when I was asking God in prayer whether it was his will that I should go to England. Thus God's word is in particular cases as well as in general ways a light to our feet, and a lantern to our paths.

Thursday, October 26. Was much comforted this evening in reading the 33rd and 34th chapters of Ezekiel, where I could not but notice many circumstances of God's dealing with him similar to what I have experienced in myself.

Saturday, October 28. Sailed about 300 miles in the first four days of this week. Had a little storm on Wednesday night, and a great calm ever since. We are now within 150 leagues of land, and our provisions and water very scanty, and our ship very weak; but the time of our arrival has not yet come. Lord, teach me to be resigned and thankful.

Monday, October 30. Still God is pleased that the wind, what there is of it, should be contrary, and our ship's company are now brought into great straits. Their allowance of water is a quart a day, and our constant food for some time has been salt beef and water dumplings, which do not agree with the stomachs of some among us. But God enables me to rejoice in that and all our other needs. When we are destitute of outward comforts, then God comforts our souls more. Great blessings await me on shore, and great trials must come first.

Was comforted tonight in my present circumstances by these verses out of this evening's lesson—'I have learned to be content whatever the circumstances. I know what it is to be in need, and I know what it is to have plenty. I can do everything through him who gives me strength.' 'Even so come, Lord Jesus.' Amen, and Amen.

Reading afterwards in the Book of Maccabees, and thinking of my present situation, this verse was pressed with unspeakable comfort upon my soul: 'After this they went home, and sang a song of thanksgiving and praised the Lord in heaven, because it is good, because his mercy endures for ever.' I hope my friends will take care to fulfil this when we meet together on shore.

Wednesday, November 1. As soon as we found the wind fair, we joined in thanksgiving and in singing the first part of the 34th Psalm (new version), which was very appropriate to our circumstances. For they tell me they have not more than three days' water on board, allowing a quart to each man a day. But he who at one time at the request of his disciples thought of the crowd and worked a miracle for their relief, and at another time at the intercession of Moses gave water to the wandering Israelites, I trust now has heard our prayers, and sent this wind with a commission to bring us where he will meet all our needs. If not, O blessed Jesus, your will be done.

Thursday, November 2. For these two days past, God has been pleased greatly to humble my soul, and bring me low by spiritual depression. And today he has thought fit once more to send us a contrary wind. Our allowance of water is now just a pint a day, so we dare not eat much beef. Our sails are exceedingly thin, some more of them were split again last night, and no one knows where we are; but God does, and that is sufficient.

Last night he lifted up the light of his blessed face upon me, and today fills me with joy unspeakable and full of glory, so that, though I have little to eat, yet I inwardly possess all things. I am sometimes afraid lest continued abstinence may cause a bodily sickness. But why am I afraid? If it does, that and everything else I know will work for my good.

This is now the eighth week I have been on board. If my friends ask me why I arrived no sooner, I may truly answer, Satan hindered us. For I believe it is he who is permitted to do this; but this still gives me greater hope that a more effective door than ever will be opened in England for preaching the everlasting gospel. O Satan, you may toss me up and down, and bring me into jeopardy on every side, but Jesus Christ is praying for me on the mountain.

Sunday, November 5. I used part of the commination service (as well as solemn prayer and psalms three times) and spoke about these words of St James: 'Consider it pure joy, my brothers, when you face trials of many kinds, because you know that the testing of your faith develops perseverance. Perseverance must finish its work.' I hope this had a good effect on my hearers' hearts, and calmed their spirits; for indeed we are brought very low. But I can say with the penitent thief that I suffer justly, and do not receive the ten thousandth part of the reward due to my crimes. Lord, remember me now you are in your kingdom.

Wednesday, November 8. When my spirits are gone, then I find my faith less lively; but I trust that is only because of my bodily state. At all other times I have great confidence in God, and if he were now to let me choose whether this trial should continue, or we should have a fair wind, I should humbly refer it back to him, for I do not know what is best for me.

Most people in the great cabin are now beginning to be weak, and look hollow-eyed; just a little longer, and we shall come to extremities, and then God's arm will bring us salvation. May we patiently wait for the Lord's pleasure. Amen, amen.

Many now, I believe, bless God that I am with them. For, they say, 'How we should have been blaming and cursing one another if Mr Whitefield had not been among us!' Blessed be God, if my ministry or presence can be instrumental to prevent sin against you, O Lord, toss me on the ocean as long as it pleases you.

Friday, November 10. Was much strengthened in our present distress by the second lesson for the day. It was our saviour's turning the water to wine at the wedding at Cana. We have asked him, as the holy virgin did, and told him in prayer, that we have very little water. At present he seems to turn away his face and say, 'What have I to do with you?' But this is only because the hour of extremity has not yet come. When it has, I do not doubt that he will richly supply our wants now as he did theirs then. May we in patience possess our souls.

Saturday, November 11. Still we are floating about, not knowing where we are, but our people seem yet to have hopes of seeing Ireland.

Our ship is much out of repair, and our food by no means enough to support nature in an ordinary way, being of the most indifferent kind, too—an ounce or two of salt beef, a pint of muddy water, and a cake made of flour and skimmings of the pot. I think often of him who preserved Moses in the ark of the bulrushes. So long as I look upwards my faith will not fail.

Sunday, November 12. This morning, the doctor of our ships took up the prayer book and noticed that he opened at these words, 'Blessed be the Lord God of Israel, for he hath visited and redeemed his people'. And so, indeed, he has, for about eight o'clock this morning news was brought that our men saw land, and I went and was a joyful spectator of it myself.

As soon as I had seen the land, we joined together in a prayer and psalm of thanksgiving, and already began to reflect with pleasure on our recent difficulties. Thus it will be later on, the storms and tempests of this troublesome world will serve to render our haven of eternal rest doubly pleasing. I fear now nothing so much as the treachery of my heart, lest like the ungrateful lepers I should not turn to God and give thanks by leading a holy life. But all things are possible with God, on whose rich mercies and free grace in Jesus Christ I alone depend for wisdom, righteousness, sanctification and redemption.

Spent a good part of this afternoon in walking on deck, and blessing God for the sight I saw all round. His good providence has been pleased to bring us into a fine large bay, surrounded on each side with high lands and hummocks, much like those near Gibraltar, and a large lighthouse on the foreland, from which in the evening was shown a light. It lies on the north-west of Ireland, and most suppose we are near Limerick, but are not certain, only one of our men having been here before.

Tuesday, November 14. I spoke to the captain, and he to the mate, who in the morning went with a boat, and about noon today returned loaded with provisions and water, and not only so, but told us he was kindly treated by the people he met with, especially by a great country gentleman, who came from his seat at midnight on purpose to relieve him and his companions; furnished them with a fresh boat and other necessaries, most kindly invited me, though unknown, to his house, to stay as long as I please, and has ordered horses to wait ready to take me thither.

Who is so great, so good a God as our God? Our hour of extremity had indeed come, for we had just half a pint of water left, and my stomach was exceedingly weak through my long abstinence, but now his almighty arm has brought us salvation.

As soon as the provisions came, we kneeled down and returned hearty thanks to our good God, who has heard our prayers and sent his angel before us to prepare our way.

Why God deals with me like this I do not know now, but I shall find out later. However, this I know, that this voyage has been greatly for my good; for I have had a glorious opportunity of searching the scriptures, composing talks, writing letters and communing with my own heart. We have been on board just nine weeks and three days—a long and perilous, but profitable voyage to my soul; for I hope it has taught me in some measure to endure hardships as a minister of Christ should. My clothes have not been off (except to change) all the passage. Part of the time I lay on deck; part on a chest; and the remainder on a bedstead covered with my buffalo skin. Many inner trials also God has been pleased to send me, which I believe he has sanctified to my great good. I am now going on shore to the house of a wealthy gentleman, whom God has commanded to receive me. I may yet be exposed to many perils by land before I see my dear friends; but his grace who has preserved me from so many perils by water will also be sufficient for me on dry land. While I continue on this side of eternity, I never expect to be free from trials, only to change them. For it is necessary to heal the pride of my heart, that such should come.

As for the success of my ministry whilst on board, I shall

only say much sin has been prevented, and one I hope effectually converted, who is to be my fellow-traveller to England.

About seven at night I dressed myself and went on shore, and was received in a strong castle belonging to Mr MacMahon, the gentleman who sent me an invitation. He himself was not at home, having gone some miles to meet me, but his maidservant kindly received us. I asked for water, and she gave me milk, and brought out butter in a lordly dish, and never did I eat a more strengthening meal. About ten, the gentleman (having missed me at the place appointed) came through the rain, and entertained us most hospitably, and about one we went to bed—I hope with hearts full of a sense of the divine love.

Kilrush in Ireland

This morning about 11 o'clock, after being most hospitably entertained by Mr MacMahon, and furnished with three horses, I and my servant and my new convert set out for Dublin and reached Kilrush, a little town, eight Irish miles from Carrigaholt, about two in the afternoon, where we were refreshed and stayed the rest of the day with Captain Coc, who last night with his whole crew was almost shipwrecked, but this morning by the good providence of God was brought on shore here. Surely my shipmates will of all men be most miserable if they continue impenitent, having such loud and repeated calls from God.

As I rode along, and noticed the meanness of the poor people's living in these parts, I said if my parishioners at Georgia complain to me of hardships I must tell them how the Irish live, for their habitations are far more despicable, and their living as hard, I believe, as to food; and yet no doubt contentment dwells in many of these low huts.

When I first came into our inn, we kneeled down and prayed, and again at night sang psalms and prayed with the captain and several of my shipmates—the first time, I believe, the room was ever put to such a use by a ship's crew and their chaplain.

Fourthfargus

Friday, November 17. Had a very pleasant ride, over a fine fruitful open country to Fourthfargus, a village that was reckoned ten, but at a moderate computation thirty English miles from Kilrush. But this is not the first piece of Irish I have met with—their innocent blunders often extort smiles from one.

As I stopped to have my horses shoed I went in to one of the poor people's cabins, as they call them; but it may as well be called a sty, a barn, or a poultry-coop. It was about twenty feet long, and twelve broad, the walls built with turf and mud. In it was a man threshing corn, two swine feeding, two dogs, several geese; a man, his wife, three children, and a great fire. Georgia huts are a palace to it. Indeed, the people live very poorly in this part, some walk barefoot with their shoes in their hands to save them from wearing out, others out of necessity. I observed many of their feet to be much swollen, and ready to gush out with blood, through extremity of cold.

Whilst I was in the cabin, as they call their little Irish huts, I talked with the woman in the house, and found she was a Roman Catholic; and indeed the whole community almost are of the Romish profession, and seem to be so very ignorant that they may well be termed the wild Irish. No wonder, when the key of knowledge is taken from them. Woe to their blind guides. I can think of no likelier means to convert them from their erroneous principles than to get the Bible translated into their own native language, to have it put in their houses, and charity schools erected for their children, as Mr Jones has done in Wales.

Limerick

Saturday, November 18. Presuming the people where I stayed last night were Roman Catholics, I neglected to call them in to join in prayer; but to my great grief found afterwards that some were Protestants, and expected prayers from me. Oh base ingratitude! Is this my zeal for recent deliverance? Oh treacherous heart! Fie upon thee, fie upon thee. God be merciful to me a sinner.

About two this afternoon we reached Limerick, a large garrison town with a cathedral in it, about twenty-one English miles from Fourthfargus. The roads, as we came along, grew better, but the people much more subtle and designing. Here are also many beggars, which I put down to the lack of parish provision for them. At evening prayer we went to the cathedral, and returned public thanks for our safe arrival.

Sunday, November 20. Having sent last night to inform Dr Burscough, Bishop of Limerick, that I had recently arrived, at his lordship's appointment I went to see him this morning and was received with the utmost candour and civility. At his lordship's request, I preached this morning at the cathedral to a very numerous congregation, who all seemed moved, and fully expecting me to preach in the afternoon; but providence did not seem to open a door. But why should not a visiting minister always offer his service? I think it is a wrong piece of modesty not to do it, for a sermon from a stranger may do more good than many from those the people are constantly used to.

Parkgate, in England

Thursday, November 30. After nearly twelve months' absence from London, three months from Georgia, and a pleasant passage from Dublin, to my inexpressible comfort God brought me to Parkgate, and so fulfilled a promise which was pressed upon my heart last Innocents' Day, in Hampshire, when I was under a great concern what my mother would say to the resolution I had then made to go to Georgia.

Third Journal

A Continuation
of the Reverend Mr Whitefield's Journal
from his arrival at London
to his departure from thence on his way to Georgia
(December 1738—June 1739)

Friday, December 8, 1738. About noon, I reached London; was received with much joy by my Christian friends, and joined with them in psalms and thanksgiving for my safe arrival. My heart was greatly enlarged by this. In the evening went to a truly Christian Society in Fetter Lane, and perceived God had greatly watered the seed won by my ministry when last in London. The Lord increase it more and more.

Sunday, December 10. When I was on board the *Mary*, those particular parts of the book of Jeremiah which relate to the opposition he met with from the false prophets deeply impressed me. Now I began to see the wisdom of God in it, for five churches have already been denied me, and some of the clergy, if possible, would oblige me to depart from these coasts. But I rejoice in this opposition, it being a certain sign that a more effectual door will be opened, since there are so many adversaries.

However, I had an opportunity of preaching in the morning at St Helen's, and at Islington in the afternoon, to large congregations indeed, with great evidence of the

Spirit, and with power. Here seems to be a great outpouring of the Spirit, and many who were awakened by my preaching a year ago have now grown strong men in Christ, by the ministrations of my dear friends and fellow-labourers, John and Charles Wesley. Blessed be God, I rejoice in the coming of the kingdom of his dear Son.

The old doctrine about justification by faith alone I found much revived, and many letters had been sent concerning it to me, all which I providentially missed, for now I come unprejudiced, and can the more easily see who is right. And who dare assert that we are not justified in the sight of God merely by an act of faith in Jesus Christ, without any regard to works past, present or to come?

In the evening, I went to Fetter Lane Society, where we had what might not improperly be called a love feast—eating a little bread and water, and spending about two hours in singing and prayers. I found my heart greatly united with the brethren. Surely a primitive spirit is reviving among us. May God join my heart to theirs more and more.

Sunday, December 24. Preached twice, and in the evening went to Crooked Lane Society, where God enabled me to withstand several persons who cavilled against the doctrine of the new birth. But the passion with which they oppose it shows that they themselves have not experienced it. Lord make them partakers of it, for your dear Son's sake.

After I left Crooked Lane, I went and expounded to a company at Mr B.'s in Little Britain; then I went to another love-feast at Fetter Lane, and, as it was Christmas Eve, carried on till nearly four in the morning in prayer, psalms and thanksgiving, with many truly Christian brethren, and my heart was much enlarged and full of love. God gave me a great spirit of supplication. May his free grace in Christ Jesus be adored. Amen and Amen.

Monday, December 25. About four this morning, went and prayed, and expounded to another Society in Redcross Street, consisting of something like two or three hundred people—the first time I ever prayed extempore before such a number in public. The room was exceedingly hot. I had been watching in prayer all night, yet God so filled me with his Holy Spirit that I spoke with as great a power as ever I did in my life. My body was weak, but I found a supernatural strength and the truth of that saying, 'When I am weak, then I am strong.'

At six I went to Crutched Friars' Society, and expounded as well as I could, but perceived myself a little oppressed with drowsiness. How the corruptible body weighs down the soul! When shall I be delivered from the burden of this flesh?

Preached three times, and assisted in administering the sacrament the same day. This day 24 years ago I was baptised. Lord! to what little purpose I have lived! However, I sealed my baptismal covenant with my dear saviour's most blessed body and blood, and trust in his strength I shall keep and perform it. Amen, Amen.

Saturday, December 30. Preached nine times this week, and expounded something like eighteen times, with great power and enlargement. There is no end of people coming and sending to me, and they seem more and more desirous, like new-born babes, to be fed with the sincere milk of the word. What a great work has been wrought in the hearts of many within this year! Now I know that thousands might come at first out of curiosity, yet God has gone before them and given them life by his free grace.

Before my arrival, I thought I might envy my brethren's success in the ministry, but blessed be God, I rejoice in it, and am glad to see Christ's kingdom come, whatever instruments God uses to bring it about. Sometimes I seem to be deserted for a little while, and much oppressed, especially before preaching, but comfort soon flows in. The kingdom of God is within me. Oh, free grace in Christ!

Sunday, December 31. Preached twice to large congregations, especially in the afternoon, at Spitalfields. I was very hoarse, and was deserted before I went up into the pulpit; but God strengthened me to speak, so as to be heard by all.

After I left Spitalfields, my cold was so bad that I despaired of speaking much more that night; but God enabled me to expound to two groups in Southwark, and I was never more enlarged in prayer in my life.

Monday, January 1, 1739. Received the holy sacrament, preached twice, and expounded twice, and found this to be the happiest New Year's Day that I ever yet saw. Oh what mercies has the Lord shown me since this time last year! And yet I shall see greater things than these. Oh that my heart may be prepared to see them! Oh that my old things may pass away, and all things become new!

Tuesday, January 2. From seven in the morning till three in the afternoon, people came, some telling me what God had done for their souls, and others crying out, 'What shall we do to be saved?' I had to go out after this, so I put several off until Thursday. God enabled me to give them answers of peace.

Friday, January 5. Held a conference at Islington, concerning several things of very great importance, with seven true ministers of Jesus Christ, despised Methodists, whom God has brought together from the east and the west, the north and the south. What we were in doubt about, after prayer, we determined by lot, and everything was carried on with great love, meekness, and devotion. We continued in fasting and prayer till three o'clock, and then parted with a full conviction that God was going to do great things among us.

Perceived something a little bordering on envy towards my brother H. I find more and more that true humility consists in being submissive to those who are a little above or a little below us. Oh when shall I come to rejoice in others' gifts and graces as much as in my own. I am resolved to wrestle with Jesus Christ by faith and prayer till he thus blesses me.

Sunday, January 7. Preached twice today, and

expounded to three Societies, one of which I never visited before. God grant I may pursue the method of expounding and praying extempore. I find God blesses it more and more.

Monday, January 8. Though I sat up all night, yet God carried me through the work of the day with about an hour's sleep. Expounded in the evening, and confuted a virulent opposer of the doctrine of the new birth and justification by faith alone. Spent the remainder of the evening with our bands, which are little groups of six or seven Christians meeting together to compare their experiences.

Tuesday, January 9. Stayed at home again today to talk with those who came to consult me, and found that God has awakened several, and excited in them a hunger and thirst after righteousness by my sermon on the power of Christ's resurrection, and 'Have you received the Holy Spirit?' Every day I hear of someone or other who has been awakened to a new sense of the divine life. Oh what abundant reason I have to be thankful!

Oxford

Sunday, January 14. Got up in the morning and prayed and sang psalms lustily, and with a good courage, and afterwards was ordained priest at Christ Church. *Before*, I was a little dissipated, but *at* imposition of hands, my mind was in a humble frame and I received grace in the holy sacrament.

London

Wednesday, January 17. Dined with and convinced several who were prejudiced against extempore prayer. Went to see the Trustees, and was most kindly received.

Thursday, January 18. Perceived myself much disordered, so that I was obliged to lie down to sleep; but afterwards God greatly enlarged my heart, and enabled me to expound to two Societies. I took a collection for two poor housekeepers. I find action is the best way to take all oppression off the spirits. God will meet and bless us when doing his work.

Sunday, January 21. Went this morning and received the sacrament at the hands of the minister who wrote against me. Blessed be God, I do not feel the least remonstrance against, but a love for him; for I believe he has a zeal for God, though in my opinion not according to knowledge. Oh that I could do him any good.

Preached twice with great power and clearness in my voice to two crowded congregations, especially in the afternoon, when I believe nearly a thousand people were in the churchyard, and hundreds more returned home that could not get in. This first set me thinking of preaching outdoors. I mentioned it to some friends, who looked upon it as a *mad* idea. However we kneeled down and prayed that nothing may be done rashly. Thus God magnifies his power most when opposed.

Expounded twice afterwards, where the people pressed most vehemently to hear the word. God enabled me to speak with the demonstration of the Spirit, and with power; and the remainder of the evening he filled me with a humble sense of his infinite mercies. I think I am never more humble than when exalted.

Tuesday, January 23. Stayed at home today as usual, to receive people, and still had the comfort of having many come to me, who have been awakened to a sense of the new birth. What reason I have to bless God for sending me to England! How he daily sets his seal on my ministry!

Friday, January 26. Went to see an opposing clergyman, and had a conference with him of nearly two hours. His grand objection was against our private Societies, and using extempore prayer, which he grounded on the authority of the Canons, and the Act of Charles II. In answer, I showed that that Act was entirely levelled against seditious schismatical meetings, contrary to the Church of England, which confines us to a form in public worship only. He replied that ours was public worship, but this I deny. For ours were

Societies never intended to be set up in opposition to the public worship, by law established, but only in imitation of the early Christians, who continued daily with one accord in the Temple, and yet in fellowship building one another up, and exhorting one another from house to house.

Monday, January 29. Expounded twice, and sat up till about one in the morning with my honoured brother and fellow-labourer John Wesley, in conference with two clergymen of the Church of England, and some other strong opposers of the doctrine of the new birth. God enabled me with great simplicity to declare what he had done for my soul, which made them look upon me as a madman. We speak what we know, and testify about what we have seen, and they do not receive our witness. Now, therefore, I am fully convinced there is a fundamental difference between us and them. They believe only an outward Christ, we further believe that he must be inwardly formed in our hearts also. But the natural man does not accept the things of the Spirit of God, for they are foolishness to him: nor can he know them, because they are spiritually discerned.

Friday, February 2. Had a great number of communicants. This is the first time I have preached without notes (for when I preached at Deptford and Gravesend, I only repeated a written sermon); but I find myself now, as it were, constrained to do it.

Saturday, February 3. About nine times God has enabled me to preach this week, and to expound 12 or 14 times; about £40, I believe, has been collected for the orphanage. I find I gain greater light and knowledge by preaching extempore, so that I fear I should quench the Spirit if I did not go on to speak as he gives me utterance.

Tuesday, February 6. Went to St Helen's, where Satan withstood me greatly—for suddenly I was deserted, and my strength went from me. But I thought it was the devil's doing, and therefore was resolved to resist him steadfast in the faith. Accordingly, though I was exceedingly sick in reading the prayers, and almost unable to speak when I entered the pulpit, yet God gave me courage to begin, and before I had done, I waxed warm and strong in the Spirit, and offered Jesus Christ freely to all who would lay hold on him by faith.

Windsor

Thursday, February 8. I find much service might be done to religion on journeys, if we only had courage to show ourselves Christians in all places. Others sing songs in public houses, why should we not sing psalms? And when we give the servants money, why may we not with that give them a little book, and some good advice? I know by experience it is very beneficial. God grant this may be always my practice.

Basingstoke

Left Windsor about ten in the morning, dined at Bagshot, and reached Basingstoke at five in the evening. Not meeting with our friends, who were coming from Dummer, I wrote to some Christian brethren I had left behind me, and afterwards was agreeably surprised by several people who came uninvited to see me. After a little conversation, I perceived they wanted to hear the word of God, and being in a large dining room in the public house, I gave notice I would expound to as many as would come. In a short time, I had over a hundred very attentive hearers, to whom I expounded for more than an hour, for which they were very thankful. Blessed be God for this opportunity! I hope I shall learn more and more every day that no place is amiss for preaching the gospel. God forbid that the word of God should be bound because some out of a misguided zeal deny the use of their churches. Though they bid me no more speak to the people in this way, yet I cannot but speak the things that I have seen and felt in my own soul. The more I am bidden to hold my peace, the more earnestly will I lift up my voice like a trumpet and tell the people what must be done in them before they can be finally saved by Jesus Christ.

Friday, February 9. In the evening I went to a large room prepared for the purpose, and expounded for an hour. The place was very crowded, many were very noisy, and others did us the honour of throwing stones up at the windows. But I spoke so much the louder, being convinced some good must come from a place where there is opposition. I should doubt whether I was a true minister of Christ, if I were not opposed. And I find it does me much good, for it drives me nearer to my Lord and master, Jesus Christ, with whom I long to dwell.

Bristol

Thursday, February 15. Sat up till past one in the morning answering my friends' letters, having no time otherwise. Received a letter from a dear Christian brother, in which were these words: 'I was told that Mr B. said to Mr C., "I believe the devil in hell is in you all. Whitefield has set the town on fire, and now he is gone to kindle a flame in the country." Shocking language for one who calls himself a minister of the gospel. But my dear friend, I trust this will not move you unless it is to pity him, and pray the more earnestly that he may experience the power of those truths he is now opposing, and have the same fire kindled in his breast, against which he is so much engaged. For I trust I am persuaded it is not a fire of the devil's kindling, but a holy fire that has proceeded from the Holy and Blessed Spirit. Oh, that such a fire may not only be kindled, but blow up into a flame all England, and all the world over!'

After breakfasting and praying with some religious friends, I went with Mr Seward to public worship; from there to the Rev. Mr Gibbs, minister of St Mary Redcliffe, who, I was informed, had promised to lend me his church to preach in for the orphanage. But he in effect gave me a refusal, telling me that he could not lend his church without a special order from the Chancellor. At this I immediately went to see the Chancellor, to whom I had sent a message the night before. But he told me frankly that he would not give any positive leave, neither would he prohibit anyone who would lend me a church; but he would advise me to withdraw to some other place till he had heard from the bishop, and not preach on that or any other occasion. I asked him his reasons. He answered, 'Why do you want to press me so hard? The thing has given a general dislike.' I replied, 'Not the plan for the orphanage: even those who disagree with me in other particulars approve of that. And as for the gospel, when was it preached without dislike?' Soon after this I took my leave, and went to see the Dean, who received me with great civility. When I had shown him my Georgia accounts, and answered him a question or two about the colony, I asked him whether there could be any just objection against my preaching in churches for the orphanage. After a pause for a considerable time, he answered that he could not tell. But, somebody knocking at the door, he replied, 'Mr Whitefield, I will give you an answer some other time; now I am expecting company.' 'Will you be pleased to fix a time, sir?' 'I will send a message to you,' said the Dean. O Christian simplicity, where have you gone? Why don't the clergy speak the truth—that it is not against the orphanage but against me and my doctrine that their enmity is levelled.

About three in the afternoon, God having given me great favour in the jailor's eyes, I preached a sermon on the penitent thief to the poor prisoners in Newgate, and collected fifteen shillings for them. Many seemed much affected, and I hope the power of the Lord was present to awaken them.

Friday, February 16. Began this morning to settle a daily exposition, and reading prayers to the prisoners in Newgate. I opened it by enlarging on the conversion of the jailor, and I trust the same good work will be experienced in this prison before I leave it.

Saturday, February 17. Read prayers and expounded

the parable of the Prodigal Son at Newgate to a great number of people; and afterwards was much refreshed by the coming of a dear London friend, and the receipt of several letters. One thing moved me much in these letters, namely the news of a great opposer's being given up by the physicians. Alas poor man! We all prayed most heartily for him, knowing how shortly he must give an account of what he had most unjustly said and written against me and many true servants of Jesus Christ.

About one in the afternoon, I went with my brother Seward and another friend to Kingswood, and was most delightfully entertained by an old disciple of the Lord. My heart has long since yearned toward the poor colliers, who are very numerous, and like sheep without a shepherd. After dinner, therefore, I went up on a hill and spoke to as many people as came to me. There were more than two hundred. Blessed be God that I have now broken the ice! I believe I never was more acceptable to my master than when I was standing to teach those hearers in the open fields. Some may censure me, but if I were to please men in the matter I should not be the servant of Christ.

Sunday, February 18. Got up this morning at about six, being called up by about fifty young persons, whom I appointed to meet me at my sister's house, and with whom I spent over an hour in prayer, psalm-singing and a warm exhortation. Soon after this, I read prayers, and preached at St Werburgh's to a large audience. I thought yesterday I would not have the use of any pulpit, but God who has the hearts of all men in his hands disposed the Rev. Mr Penrose to lend me his, and he thanked me for my sermon; and the Rev. Mr Gibbs sent a message to offer me the use both of St Thomas's and St Mary Redcliffe. The latter of these I accepted, and preached to such a congregation as I had never seen before, with great liberty and demonstration of the Spirit. Many people went away for lack of room, and Mr Gibbs and his lady were exceedingly civil both to me and Mr Seward.

After the sermon, and taking a little refreshment, I hastened to a Society in Baldwin Street, where many hundreds were assembled to hear me, so that the stairs and court below, besides the room itself, were crowded. Here I continued to expound for about two hours, and then for as long at another Society in Nicholas Street, equally thronged. Surely, that same Jesus who came to his disciples while the doors were shut when they assembled together, was truly with us; for great numbers were quite melted, and God so caused me to renew my strength that I was better when I returned home than when I began to exhort my young fellow-soldiers at six in the morning. I could not do this if Jesus Christ did not strengthen me. By his free grace alone, I am what I am. Not to me but to your name alone, O Lord, be all the glory.

Tuesday, February 20. Today my master honoured me more than ever before. About ten in the morning, in response to a summons received from the Apparitor yesterday, I went to see the Rev. Mr R., the Chancellor of Bristol, who now plainly told me he intended to stop my proceedings. 'I have sent for the Registrar here, sir,' said he, 'to take down your answer.' At which, he asked me by what authority I preached in the diocese of Bristol without a licence. I answered that I thought that custom had grown obsolete. 'And why, pray, sir,' I asked him, 'did you not ask the Irish clergyman this question, who preached for you last Thursday?' He said that was nothing to him. He then read over part of the ordination service, and those Canons that forbid any minister preaching in a private house, etc., and then asked me what I said to them. I answered that I understood those Canons did not apply to professed ministers of the Church of England. 'But', he said, 'they do.' 'There is also a Canon', said I, 'forbidding all clergymen to frequent taverns and play cards. Why is that not put into practice?' 'Why doesn't somebody complain of them?' said he, 'and then it would.' When I asked him why I was being singled out in this way (referring to my printed

talks for my principles), he said, 'You preach false doctrine.'
I did not answer this, but told him that despite those Canons
I could not but speak of the things that I knew, and was
resolved to proceed as usual. 'Note his answer, Mr Registrar,' he said, and turning to me added, 'I am resolved, sir, if
you preach or expound anywhere in this diocese till you
have a licence, I will first suspend, and then excommunicate
you.' I then took my leave—he waited upon me very civilly
to the door, and told me that what he did was in the name of
the clergy and laity of the city of Bristol; and so we parted.

Being taken ill, just before I went to the Chancellor, on
my return home I found I had not so much joy as peace.
But I did not perceive the least feeling of resentment in my
heart, and to show how little I regarded such threats, after
I had joined in prayer for the Chancellor, I immediately
went and expounded at Newgate as usual, where God gave
me great joy, and wondrously pricked many to the heart,
as though to say, 'This is the way, walk in it.' After this we
dined with several Christian friends with the kind keeper
of the prison, and rejoiced exceedingly at the thought that
we should one day or other sing together in such a place as
Paul and Silas did. God prepare us for that hour, for I
believe it will come. I shall be exalted, I must be humbled.

Wednesday, February 21. At three in the afternoon, as
arranged, I went to Kingswood amongst the colliers. God
highly favoured us in sending a fine day, and nearly two
thousand people were assembled on that occasion. I
preached on John 3:3, and enlarged for about an hour—I
hope to the comfort and edification of those who heard
me. God grant the seed sown may not fall on stony or
thorny, but on good ground.

Bristol

Friday, February 23. After dinner, I was taken very ill, so
I had to lie on the bed; but looking on it as a thorn in the
flesh, at three I went, as arranged, and preached to about
four or five thousand people from a hill in Kingswood.

The sun shone very bright, and the people standing in such an awe-inspiring manner round the hill, in the profoundest silence, filled me with a holy admiration. Blessed be God for such a plentiful harvest. Lord, send out more workers into your harvest.

This done, God strengthened me to expound to a Society outside Lawford's Gate, and afterwards to another in the city, and afterwards to a third. I spoke with more freedom the last time than at the first. When I am weak, then am I strong.

Saturday, February 24. About ten in the morning I went to see the Chancellor, and showed him a letter I had received from the Lord Bishop of Bristol. My master gave me great boldness of speech, and I asked the Chancellor why he did not write to the Bishop as he had promised? I think he answered he was to blame. I then insisted on his proving I had preached false doctrine, and reminded him of his threat to excommunicate me in the name of the clergy and laity of the City of Bristol. But he tried to make me believe he had said no such thing; and confessed, this time, that he had neither heard me preach, nor read any of my writings. I asked him his reasons for prohibiting my collecting for the orphanage. He answered, 'It would hinder the people's benefactions to the Bristol clergy.' I replied, 'It would by no means hinder their contributions, and the clergy ought first to subscribe themselves for example's sake.' After much conversation on this subject I with meekness told him I was resolved to go on preaching, and that if collections were not made here for the poor Georgians I would lay it entirely upon him, adding that I would not be one who would hinder such a plan for the universe.

This evening I declined going to any Society, that I might have a little time to write letters; amongst which I wrote the following one to the Bishop of Bristol.

Bristol, Feb. 24, 1739

My Lord,—I humbly thank your Lordship for the

favour of your Lordship's letter. It gave abundant satisfaction to me, and many others, who have not failed to pray in a particular manner for your Lordship's temporal and eternal welfare. Today, I showed your Lordship's letter to the Chancellor, who (notwithstanding he promised not to prohibit my preaching for the Orphan House, if your Lordship was only neutral in the affair) has influenced most of the clergy to deny me their pulpits, either on that or any other occasion. Last week, he was pleased to charge me with false doctrine. Today, he has forgotten that he said so. He also threatened to excommunicate me for preaching in your Lordship's diocese. I offered to take a licence, but was denied.

If your Lordship should ask what evil I have done, I answer none save that I visit the religious Societies, preach to the prisoners in Newgate and to the poor colliers in Kingswood who, they tell me, are little better than heathens. I am charged with being a Dissenter, though many are brought to the church by my preaching, not one taken from it. The Chancellor is pleased to tell me my conduct is contrary to the Canons, but I told him those Canons which he produced were not intended against such meetings as mine are, where His Majesty is constantly prayed for and everyone is free to see what is done.

I am sorry to give your Lordship this trouble, but I thought it proper to mention these particulars, that I might know of your Lordship wherein my conduct is exceptionable.

I heartily thank your Lordship for your intended benefaction. I think the design is truly good, and will meet with success, because so much opposed.

God knows my heart, I desire only to promote his glory. If I am spoken evil of for his sake, I rejoice in it. My master was long since spoken evil of before me. But I intrude on your Lordship's patience.

Sunday, February 25. What mercies has my good God

shown me today! When I got up in the morning I thought I would be able to do nothing, but the divine strength was greatly magnified in my weakness. About six in the morning I prayed, sang with and exhorted my young morning visitors, as I did last Lord's Day. At eight I read prayers, and preached to a very crowded congregation at Newgate, and from there I rode to Brislington, a village about two miles from Bristol, where there was such a vast congregation that after I had read prayers in the church I thought it right to go and preach in the churchyard, so that no one might be sent away empty. The people were exceedingly attentive, and God gave me utterance and, what was best of all, by permission of the minister who invited me there we had a sacrament and I hope it was a communion of the gospel; why then should I fear what man can do to me?

At four I hastened to Kingswood. At a moderate computation, there were about ten thousand people to hear me. The trees and hedges were full. All was hush when I began; the sun shone bright, and God enabled me to preach for an hour with great power, and so loudly that everyone, I was told, could hear me. Mr B. was right. The fire is kindled in the country, and I know all the devils in hell shall not be able to quench it.

Finding myself strengthened from above, I went and expounded at Baldwin Street Society, when more than £5 was collected for the orphanage. Afterwards, I went to another, and about nine at night came home rejoicing at the great things God had done for my soul. Today I have been exalted; I must expect now to be humbled. Anything is welcome to me that God sends.

Thursday, March 1. Amongst my other letters by today's post, I received the following one from the Rev. Mr John Wesley:

Feb. 20, 1739

My dear Brother,—Our Lord's hand is not shortened among us. Yesterday I preached at St Katherine's, and at Islington, where the church was almost as hot as some of the Society rooms used to be. I think I never was so much strengthened before. The fields, after the service, were white with people praising God. About three hundred were present at Mr S.'s; from there I went to Mr B.'s, then to Fetter Lane, and at nine to Mr B.'s, where too we simply lacked room. Today, I expound in the Minories at four, at Mrs W.'s at six, and to a large group of poor sinners in Gravel Lane (Bishopsgate) at eight. The Society at Mr Crouch's does not meet till eight, so I expound before I go to him near St James's Square, where one young woman has recently been filled with the Holy Spirit, and overflows with joy and love.

On Wednesday at six, we have a noble company of women, not adorned with gold or costly apparel, but with a meek and quiet spirit, and good works. At the Savoy, on Thursday evening we have usually two or three hundred, most of them at least thoroughly awakened. Mr A.'s parlour is more than filled on Friday, as is Mr P.'s room twice over, where I think I have commonly had more power given to me than at any other place. A week or two ago a note was given me there, as near as I can remember in these words: 'Your prayers are desired for a sick child that is lunatic, and sore vexed day and night, that our Lord should heal him, as he did those in the days of his flesh; and that he should give his parents faith and patience till his time is come.'

On Saturday week, a middle-aged, well-dressed woman at Beech Lane (where I expound usually to five or six hundred before I go to Mr E.'s Society) was seized, as it appeared to several about her, with little less than the agonies of death. We prayed that God who had brought her to the birth would give her strength to bring forth, and that he would work speedily, that all might see it and fear, and put their trust in the Lord. Five days she travailed and groaned, being in bondage. On Thursday evening our Lord got himself the victory, and from that moment she has been full of love and joy, which she openly declared at the same on Saturday last; so that thanks also were given to God by many on her account. It is to be observed, her friends have accounted her mad for these three years, and accordingly bled, blistered her, and what not. Come and let us praise the Lord, and magnify his name together.

The weather being fair, after I had preached and collected thirty-seven shillings at Newgate I went on the hill at Kingswood, where about fifteen hundred colliers and country people were gathered together, and were very attentive to hear me. I have reason to believe, by what I have heard, that my words have not altogether fallen to the ground. Some of the colliers, I find, have been much moved.

Sunday, March 4. Got up much refreshed in spirit, and gave my early attendants a warm exhortation as usual. Went to Newgate, and preached with power to an exceedingly crowded congregation. Then hurried to Hannam Mount, three miles from the city, where the colliers live all together. God favoured us in the weather. More than four thousand were ready to hear me, and God enabled me to preach with the demonstration of the Spirit. The ground not being high enough, I stood on a table, and the sight of the people covering the green fields, and their deep attention, pleased me much.

At four in the afternoon, I went to the hill on Rose Green and preached to more than fourteen thousand souls, and so good was my God that everyone could hear.

In the evening I expounded at Baldwin Society, but could only get up to the room with the utmost difficulty, the entrance and court being so crowded. Blessed be God, the number of hearers much increases, and as my day is, so is my strength! Tonight I returned home much more refreshed in my spirits than in the morning when I set out. I was full of joy, and longed to depart and to be with Jesus Christ. This has been a sabbath indeed to my soul!

Monday, March 5. Had the pleasure of having many whom God has touched by my ministry come to me enquiring about the new birth. At eleven, I preached at Newgate and collected thirty-nine shillings for the poor prisoners; and being invited by many colliers, at three in the afternoon I went to a place called the Fishponds, on another side of Kingswood, where about two thousand were gathered together. The sight pleased me much, and having no better place to stand upon, the wall was my pulpit; and I think I never spoke with greater power. My preaching in the fields may displease some timorous, bigoted men, but I am thoroughly persuaded it pleases God, and why should I fear anything else?

At my return home, I was much refreshed with the sight of two pious friends. After some conversation, they went with me to a Society where I prayed and expounded for over an hour, and then spent the remainder of the evening with them and many other Christian brethren, in warming one another's hearts by mutual exhortation, and singing of psalms.

New Passage

Tuesday, March 6. At the inn where we put up there was an unhappy clergyman who would not go over in the passage boat because I was going in it. Alas, thought I, this very temper would make heaven itself unpleasant to that man, if he saw me there. I was likewise told that in the public kitchen he charged me with being a Dissenter. A little after, as I passed by, I saw him playing dice at a gaming table. I heartily wish those who charge me causelessly with schism, and being too righteous, would consider that the Canon of our church forbids our clergy to frequent taverns, to play cards or dice, or any other unlawful games. Their indulging themselves in these things is a stumbling-block to thousands.

After supper, in the evening, I called the family of the inn together, and was pleased to see about twenty come to hear the word. God enabled me to speak and pray, and having dispersed my friends went to bed early, being told that we were to be woken up in good time. Blessed be God for any opportunity of doing good.

Cardiff

Wednesday, March 7. Got up about twelve at night, sang psalms and prayed, and the wind being fair we had a speedy passage over to the Welsh shore. Our business requiring haste, God having of his good providence sent someone to guide us, we rode all night, stopped at Newport to refresh us, where we met two friends, and reached Cardiff about eleven in the morning.

I was much refreshed with the sight of my dear brother Howell Harris, whom, though I did not know him personally, I have long since loved with the affection of Jesus Christ, and have often felt my soul drawn out in prayer for him. A burning and shining light has he been in those parts, a barrier against profaneness and immorality, and an indefatigable promoter of the true gospel of Jesus Christ. For about three or four years God has inclined him to go about doing good. He is now about twenty-five years of age. Twice he has applied (being every way qualified) for Holy Orders, but was refused, under a false pretence that he was not of age, though he was then twenty-two years and six months. About a month ago he offered himself again, but was put off. At this, he was and is still resolved to go on in his work; and indefatigable zeal he has shown in his master's service. For these three years (as he told me from his own mouth) he has talked almost twice every day for three or four hours at a stretch, not authoritatively, as a minister, but as a private person, exhorting his Christian brethren. He has been, I think, in seven counties, and has made it his business to go to wakes, etc., to turn people from such lying vanities. Many alehouse people, fiddlers, harpers, etc. (Demetrius-like) sadly cry out against him for spoiling their business. He has been made the subject of numbers of sermons, has been threatened with public prosecutions, and had constables sent to apprehend him. But God has blessed him with inflexible courage—instantaneous strength has been communicated to him from above, and he still continues to go on from conquering to conquer. He is of a most catholic spirit, loves all who love our Lord Jesus Christ, and therefore he is styled by bigots a Dissenter. He is condemned by all who are lovers of pleasure more than lovers of God; but God has greatly blessed his pious endeavours. Many call and own him as their spiritual father, and I believe would lay down their lives for his sake. He generally speaks in a field, but at other times in a house, from a wall, a table, or anything else. He has established nearly thirty Societies in South Wales, and still his sphere of action is enlarged daily. He is full of faith and the Holy Spirit.

When I first saw him my heart was united to him. I wanted to catch some of his fire, and gave him the right hand of fellowship with my whole heart. After I had greeted him, and given a warm exhortation to a great number of people who followed me to the inn, we spent the remainder of the evening in taking sweet counsel together, and telling one another what God had done for our souls. My heart was still drawn out towards him more and more. A divine and strong sympathy seemed to be between us, and I was resolved to promote his interest with all my might. Accordingly, we took an account of the several Societies, and agreed on such measures as seemed most conducive to promote the common interest of our Lord. Blessed be God, there seems to be a noble spirit gone out into Wales, and I believe ere long there will be more visible fruits of it. What inclines me strongly to think so is that the partition wall of bigotry and party-zeal is broken down, and ministers and teachers of different communions join with one heart and mind to carry on the kingdom of Jesus Christ. The Lord make all the Christian world thus minded! For till this is done, I fear, we must despair of any great reformation in the church of God. After much comfortable and encouraging talk with each other, we knelt down and prayed, and God was pleased to give me great enlargement of heart in that duty.

Thursday, March 8. About ten, as agreed, I went to the Town Hall, and preached for about an hour and a half to a large assembly of people. My dear brother Howell Harris sat close by me. I did not notice any scoffers inside, but some outside were pleased to honour me so far as to trail a dead fox, and hunt it about the Hall—but, blessed be God, my voice prevailed.

Newport in Wales

Friday, March 9. I preached to about a thousand people, and then, with my brother Howell Harris, Seward, etc., we went rejoicing and blessing God for opening an effectual door on the way. I think Wales is excellently prepared for the gospel of Christ. They have many burning and shining lights among both the Dissenting and church ministers, amongst whom Mr Griffith Jones shines in particular. No less than fifty charity schools have been erected by his means, without any settled visible fund, and fresh ones are being set up every day. People think nothing of coming twenty miles to hear a sermon, and great numbers there are who have not only been hearers, but doers also of the word; so that there is a strong prospect of the spreading of the gospel in Wales.

Bath

Monday, March 12. Finding many in Bath wanted to hear me, I gave a short notice and about five in the evening preached out on the town common, to a much larger audience than could reasonably have been expected. It snowed a good part of the time, but the people stayed very contentedly.

Bristol

Sunday, March 18. Had the pleasure of seeing my morning

audience so much increased, that more than a hundred people had to stand outside in the street. Was taken ill for about two hours, but even so was enabled to go and preach at Hannam to many more than were there last Sunday; and in the afternoon I really believe no less than twenty thousand were present at Rose Green. Blessed are the eyes which see the things which we see. Surely God is truly with us. To see such crowds stand about us in such an awe-inspiring silence, and to hear the echo of their singing run from one end of them to the other, is very solemn and surprising. My talk continued for about an hour and a half, and at both places more than £14 was collected for the Orphan House; and it pleased me to see with what cheerfulness the colliers and poor people threw in their mites.

Bath

Monday, March 19. After dinner, through great weakness of body and sickness in my stomach I had to lie down on the bed; but when the time came for my preaching I went, weak and languid as I was, relying on the divine strength, and I think scarcely ever preached with greater power. There were about four or five thousand of high and low, rich and poor, to hear. As I went along I noticed many scoffers, and when I got up on the table to preach, many of them laughed; but before I had finished my prayer everything was hushed and silent, and before I had concluded my talk God by his word seemed to impress a great awe upon their minds, for everyone was deeply attentive and seemed much moved by what had been spoken.

Keynsham

Thursday, March 22. Received unspeakable pleasure from a letter of today's post which brought me word of the flourishing of the gospel at Oxford. Had many come to consult me in spiritual cases, and could not but rejoice to see how secretly and irresistibly the kingdom of Jesus Christ is carried on, in spite of all opposition. In the afternoon, I preached again at Baptist Mills, where somebody was so kind as to put some turf together for me to stand on. I had a great freedom of speech, and insisted much on original sin, because there are many in this city who, I fear, have imbibed the principles of that polite preacher Mr F.

Friday, March 23. Dined with many Quakers at Frenchay, who entertained me and my friends with much Christian love; but we could by no means agree about the disuse of the two outward signs in the sacrament, nor of their absolute refusing to pay tithes. But I think their ideas about walking and being led by the Spirit are right and good. I should rejoice to find all Quakers thus minded. Much sincerity and simplicity seems to be amongst them, but I think, at the same time, they insist so much upon the inward life that they place too much religion in their not using externals.

Sunday, March 25. God put it into the hearts of some gentlemen to lend me a large bowling-green, where I preached to about five thousand people, and took a collection for my poor orphans, till my hands were quite weary. Blessed be God, that the bowling-green is turned into a preaching place! This, I hope, is a sign that assembly rooms and playhouses will soon be put to the same use. O may the word of God be mighty to the pulling down of these strongholds of the devil!

Preached at Hannam to a larger congregation than ever, and again in the afternoon to upwards (as was computed) of 23,000 people. I was aferwards told that those who stood farthest off could hear me very plainly. Oh may God speak to them by his Spirit, at the same time that he enables me to lift up my voice like a trumpet!

Tuesday, March 27. At four this afternoon, being invited several times, I preached in a yard belonging to the glasshouses, where many dwell who I was informed neither feared God nor regarded man. The congregation consisted of thousands, and God enabled me to lay before them his threats and promises, so that none might either despair or presume. Oh that I may be taught by God rightly to explain the word of truth!

Whilst I was preaching, I heard many people behind me, hallooing and making a noise, and supposed somebody must have set them to disturb me deliberately. I was not in the least bothered, but rather increased all the more in strength, but when I had finished and enquired the cause of that noise I was informed that a gentleman (being drunk) had taken the liberty of calling me *dog*, and saying that I ought to be whipped at the cart's tail, and had offered money to anyone who would pelt me. Instead of that, the boys and people nearby began to throw stones and dirt at him. I knew nothing of it till afterwards, when I expressed my dislike of their behaviour, but could not help noticing what sorry wages the devil gives his servants.

Thursday, March 29. Blessed be God, I hope a good work is begun today. Having had several notices that the colliers of Kingswood were willing to subscribe, I went to dinner with them near a place called Two Mile Hill, and collected over twenty pounds in money, and got over forty pounds in subscriptions towards building them a charity school. It was surprising to see with what cheerfulness they parted with their money on this occasion. If I were to stay here, I would try to settle schools all over the wood, as also in other places, as Mr Griffith Jones has done in Wales; but I have only just time to set it on foot. I hope God will bless the ministry of my honoured friend Mr John Wesley, and enable him to bring it to good effect. It is a pity that so many little ones as there are in Kingswood should perish for lack of knowledge.

After dinner I preached a farewell sermon, and recommended the charity school to their consideration; and they all seemed willing to assist, either by money or their labour, and to offer such things as they had. I do not doubt that the Lord will prosper this work of my hands.

Friday, March 30. Preached this afternoon near Coal-Pit Heath, seven miles from Bristol, a place to which I was earnestly invited, and where great numbers of colliers live.

I believe there were over two thousand people assembled on this occasion. The weather was exceedingly fair, the hearers behaved very well, and the place where I preached being near the maypole I took the opportunity of warning them about misspending their time in revelling and dancing. Oh, that all such entertainments were put a stop to. I see no other way to effect it, but by going boldly and calling people from such lying vanities in the name of Jesus Christ. That reformation which is brought about by a coercive power will be only outward and superficial; but that which is done by the force of God's word will be inward and lasting. Lord, make me fit by your grace for such a work, and then send me.

Saturday, March 31. Went this morning and visited the poor man who was misused at the glasshouse. He seemed much concerned for what he had done, and confessed he did not know what he had done; at which, I took the opportunity of dissuading him from the sin of drunkenness, and parted from him very friendly.

Monday, April 2. Several thousands of little books have been distributed among the people, about £200 collected for the Orphan House, and many poor families relieved by the bounty of my friend Mr Seward. What gives me greater comfort is the consideration that my dear and honoured friend, Mr Wesley, is left behind to confirm those who are awakened, so when I return from Georgia I hope to see many bold soldiers of Jesus Christ.

Kingswood

I came about two to Kingswood, where the colliers, unknown to me, had prepared a hospitable entertainment, and were keen for me to lay the first stone of their school. At length I complied, and a man giving me a piece of ground (in case Mr C. should refuse to grant them any), I laid a stone, and then kneeled down and prayed God that the gates of hell might not prevail against our design. The colliers said a hearty Amen, and after I had given them a word of exhortation, I took my leave, promising that I would come amongst them again if ever God should bring me back to England. I hope a reformation will be carried on amongst them. For my own part, I would rather preach the gospel to the unprejudiced, ignorant colliers, than to the bigoted, self-righteous, formal Christians. The colliers will enter into the kingdom of God before them.

Abergavenny and Comihoy

Thursday, April 5. Here I expected much opposition, having been informed that many intended to disturb me.

But God impressed a divine awe upon everyone, so that though there were many opposers present when I preached, yet none dared utter a word. God caused me to speak with extraordinary authority, and I did not spare the polite scoffers in the least.

If God were not calling me elsewhere, I could spend some months in Wales very profitably. The longer I am in it, the more I like it. To me they seem a people sweetly disposed to receive the gospel. They are simple and artless. They have left bigotry more than the generality of our Englishmen, and through the exhortations of Howell Harris and the ministry of others they are hungering and thirsting after the righteousness of Jesus Christ.

Gloucester

Wednesday, April 11. Was treated today as I expected, and as I told my friends I would be, when I first entered the city. The minister of St Michael's was pleased to lend me his church yesterday and today, but some wealthy Demetriuses were offended at the size of the congregations and alleged that it kept people from their business, so he was influenced by some of them to deny the use of his pulpit any more on a weekday. Alas, what enmity there is in the natural man against the success of the gospel!

Thursday, April 12. I am, and profess myself, a member of the Church of England. I have received no prohibition from any of the bishops; and having had no fault found by them with my life or doctrine, have the same general licence to preach which the rectors are willing to think sufficient for their curates; nor can any of them produce one instance of their having refused the assistance of a stranger clergyman because he did not have a written licence. And have their lordships the bishops insisted that no one shall ever preach occasionally without such special licence? I have never been charged by his lordship with teaching or living otherwise than as a true minister of the Church of England. I keep close to the Articles and Homilies, which if my opposers did we should not have so many dissenters from her. But it is most notorious that for the iniquity of the priests the land mourns. We have *preached* and *lived* many sincere people out of our communion. I have now conversed with several of the best of all denominations; many of them solemnly protest that they left the church because they could not find food for their souls. They stayed among us till they were starved out.

Evesham

Stayed at Cheltenham, for the sake of a little peace and some private business, till after dinner, and got safe to Evesham (where Mr Seward's relations live) about seven at night. Several persons came to see me, amongst whom was Mr Benjamin Seward, whom God has been pleased to call by his free grace very recently. His circumstances both before and in conversion much resemble those of St Paul. For he was brought up at the feet of Gamaliel, being at Cambridge for some years. As regards the law, so far as outward morality went, he was blameless; as concerning zeal, opposing the church. My proceedings he could by no means approve, and he once had a mind, he said, to write against Mr Law's spiritually live ideas in his *Christian Perfection*. But recently it has pleased God to reveal his dear Son, by eight days' sickness in which he hardly ever ate or drank or slept, and underwent great inward agonies and tortures.

After this, the scales fell more and more from the eyes of his mind. God sent a poor travelling woman, that came to sell straw toys, to instruct him in the nature of the second birth, and now he is resolved to prepare for Holy Orders and to preach Christ and those truths straightaway in every synagogue which he had once endeavoured to destroy. He is a gentleman of a very large fortune, which he has now devoted to God. I write this to show how far a man may go and yet know nothing of Jesus Christ. Behold, here was one who constantly attended on the means of grace, who was exact in his morals, humane and courteous in his conversation, who gave much to charity, was frequent in private duties; and yet, till about six weeks ago, as destitute of any saving knowledge of Jesus Christ in his own experience as those on whom his name was never called and who still sit in darkness and the shadow of death. Blessed be God that although not many rich, not many mighty, not many noble are called, yet some are. Who would just be called a fool for Christ's sake? How often has my companion and honoured friend, Mr William Seward, been deemed a madman even by this very brother, for going to Georgia; but now God has made him an instrument of converting his brother.

Oxford

Saturday, April 21. I had been much pressed in spirit to hasten here, and now I found the reason for it; for alas, the enemy had got great advantage over three of our Christian brethren, and driven them to deny Christ's visible church on earth. They had so far influenced and deluded Mr Kinchin, a sincere and humble minister of Jesus Christ, that I found through their persuasion he had actually left his fellowship and intended to resign his living. This, I must confess, gave me a great shock. For I knew what dreadful consequences would attend a needless separation from the established church. For my own part, I can see no reason for my leaving the church, however I am treated by the corrupt members and ministers of it. I judge the state of a church not by the practice of its members but its original and public constitutions; and so long as I think the Articles of the Church of England are consistent with scripture, I am resolved to preach them up without either bigotry or party zeal. For I love all who love the Lord Jesus.

Sunday, April 22. Being much concerned about Mr Kinchin's conduct, this morning I wrote him the following letter:

Oxon, April 22, 1739

Dearest Mr Kinchin,—Just now I have received the blessed sacrament and have been praying for you. Let me exhort you, by the mercies of God in Christ Jesus, not to resign your parsonage till you have consulted your friends at London. It is undoubtedly true that all is not right when we are afraid to be open to our dear brethren.

Satan has desired to sift you as wheat. He is dealing with you as he did with me some years ago, when he kept me in my room for about six weeks, because I could not do anything wholeheartedly. So he would have you not preach till you have received the Holy Spirit in the full assurance of it; and that is the way never to have it at all. God will be found in the use of means; and our Lord sent out his disciples to preach *before* they had received the Holy Spirit in that most plentiful manner at the day of Pentecost.

Besides, consider, my dear brother, what confusion your separation from the church will occasion. The prison doors are already shut, our Society is stopped; and most are afraid almost to converse with us. I can assure you that my being a minister of the Church of England, and preaching its Articles, is a means under God of drawing so many after me.

As for objecting about the habits, robes, etc., good God! I thought we long since knew that the kingdom of God did not consist in any externals, but in righteousness and peace and joy in the Holy Spirit.

Oh my dear brother, I labour in pain for you. Never was I more shocked at anything than at your proceedings. I do not doubt that you will pray to God to be kept from delusion at reading this. I am not ignorant of Satan's devices, and I know he never more successfully tempts us than when he turns himself into an angel of light. Oh my dearest Mr Kinchin, do nothing rashly. Consult your friends and do not break the heart of your most affectionate, though unworthy, brother in Christ,

George Whitefield

Tuesday, April 24. Perceived myself much strengthened yesterday and this morning, and told my friends how these words were impressed upon me, *And more than meet the gathering storm.* About nine o'clock, after I had exhorted the brethren, the Vice-Chancellor came in person to the house where we were assembled, having threatened to do so some time ago if they continued to build up one another in that manner. He sent for me downstairs, being informed that I was in the house. When I first saw him I perceived he was in a passion, which he soon expressed in such language as this: 'What do you mean by going about, alienating the people's affections from their proper pastors? Your works are full of vanity and nonsense. You pretend to inspiration. If you ever come again in this manner among these people, I will lay you first by the heels, and these shall follow.' Upon this he turned his back, and went away. I soon found by the comforts God gave me, how glorious it was to suffer anything for the sake of Jesus Christ. However, I must not forget to mention that I exhorted all the brethren not to forsake the assembling themselves together, though no pastor should be permitted to come amongst them; for so long as they continued steadfast in the communion of the established church, I told them no power on earth could justify hindering them from continuing in fellowship, as the early Christians did,

in order to build each other up in the knowledge and fear
of God.

London

Sunday, April 29. Preached in the morning at Moorfields,
to an exceeding great multitude. At ten, went to Christ
Church, and heard Dr Trapp preach most virulently
against me and my friends, upon these words, 'Do not be
over-righteous ... why destroy yourself?' God gave me
great serenity of mind, but alas the preacher was not so
calm as I wished him. His sermon was founded upon
wrong suppositions (the necessary consequence of his
hearing with other men's ears), not to say that there were
many direct untruths in it. And he argued so strenuously
against all *inward feelings* that he plainly proved that with
all his learning he knew nothing yet as he ought to know.
I pray God rebuke his spirit, and grant that that sermon
may never rise up in judgement against him.

Being weakened by my morning's preaching, in the
afternoon I refreshed myself with a little sleep, and at five
went and preached at Kennington Common, about two
miles from London, where no less than thirty thousand
people were supposed to be present. The wind being for
me, carried the voice to the extremest part of the audience.
All stood attentive and joined in the psalm and Lord's
Prayer most regularly. I scarcely ever preached more
quietly in any church. The word came with power. The
people were much affected, and expressed their love to me
many ways. All agreed it was never seen like this before.
Oh what need have all God's people to rejoice and give
thanks! I hope a good inroad has been made into the
devil's kingdom this day.

Monday, April 30. Declined preaching today, so that I
might have leisure to write to some of my correspondents
and make preparations for my poor orphans in Georgia.
Received letters this evening from there, telling me of the
affairs of that colony. At present they look melancholy; but

our extremity is God's opportunity. Lord, you called me; lo, I come to do your will. Heard also that Mr Kinchin had got over his scruples, and of the wonderful success of my honoured friend Mr John Wesley's ministry in Bristol, and of much opposition at Oxford. Certainly God is about to bring mighty things to pass.

Tuesday, May 1. Preached after public service in Islington churchyard to a greater congregation than ever. In the evening went to expound on Dowgate Hill, at the house of Mr C.; but when I came to the door, no less than two or three thousand people were gathered round it, so that to avoid a noise I had to stand up in the Fore Street window and preach to them in the street. I think they behaved well; and they would have behaved much better had they not been disturbed. Now I know more and more that the Lord calls me into the fields, for no house or street is able to contain half the people who come to hear the word. This is a time for doing; yet a little while, and a suffering time will come. I cannot follow him now, but I shall follow him afterwards.

Wednesday, May 2. Preached this evening again to more than ten thousand, at Kennington Common, and spent the remainder of the evening in conference with our brethren in Fetter Lane Society. I hope we build up one another in our most holy faith. Our brethren who have fallen into errors have left us voluntarily. Now the old leaven is purged out, we walk in the comforts of the Holy Spirit, and are edified.

Thursday, May 3. Was fully employed all day in making preparations for my voyage, and preached at six in the evening (a time I choose that people may not be drawn away from their business) at Kennington, and great power was amongst us. The audience was more numerous and silent than yesterday, the evening calm, and many went away moved. Glory be to God, I begin to find an alteration in the people's behaviour already. God grant it may increase more and more.

Saturday, May 5. Preached yesterday and today as usual at Kennington Common, to about twenty thousand hearers, who were very much moved. The remainder of my time I spent in preparing things for Georgia. I am not usually so much engaged in secular work; but I as readily do this as preach, when it is the will of God. It is a great mistake that some run into, to suppose religion consists only in saying our prayers. I think a man is no further holy, than he is relatively holy, and he only will adorn the gospel of Jesus Christ in all things if he is careful to perform all the civil offices of life, whether servant, master or mistress, with a single eye to God's glory, and from a principle of a living faith in Jesus Christ our saviour. This is the morality which I preach, and which shall stand as long as the rock on which it is founded, for ever and ever.

Sunday, May 6. Preached this morning in Moorfields to about twenty thousand people, who were very quiet and attentive, and much moved. Went to public worship morning and evening; and at six preached at Kennington. Such a sight I never saw before. Some supposed there were above 30 or 40,000 people, and about eighty coaches, besides great numbers of horses. There was an awesome silence amongst them. God gave me great enlargement of heart. I continued my talk for an hour and a half, and when I returned home I was filled with such love, peace, and joy, that I cannot express it. I believe this was partly owing to some opposition I met with yesterday. It is hard for men to kick against the pricks. The more they oppose, the more Jesus Christ will be exalted. Our adversaries seem to have come to an extremity, while for lack of arguments to convince, they are obliged to call out to the civil magistrates to compel me to be silent; but I believe it will be difficult to prove our assemblies in the fields to be either disorderly or illegal.

Tuesday, May 8. Preached in the evening, as usual, on Kennington Common. Some considerable time before I set out from town, it rained very hard, so that once I thought of not going; but several pious friends joined in the hearty prayer to God to withhold the rain, which was done immediately. To my great surprise, when I came to the Common I saw more than twenty thousand people. All the while, except for a few moments, the sun shone out upon us; and I trust the sun of righteousness arose on some with healing in his wings. The people were melted down very much at the preaching of the word, and put up hearty prayers for my temporal and eternal welfare.

Wednesday, May 9. At noon went to see the Honourable Trustees for Georgia. They received me with the utmost civility, agreed to everything I asked, and gave a grant of five hundred acres of land, to me and my successors for ever, for the use of the Orphan House. My friend Habersham also writes me word today from Georgia, that the General and officers are very kind to him upon my account, so that there is a comfortable prospect of all things going on as I could wish.

After God had enabled me to preach to about twenty thousand for more than an hour on Kennington Common, he inclined the hearers' hearts to contribute most cheerfully and liberally towards the Orphan House. I was one of the collectors, and it would have delighted anyone to have seen with what eagerness and cheerfulness the people came up both sides of the eminence on which I stood, and afterwards to the coach doors, to throw in their mites. Surely God must have touched their hearts. When we came home, we found we had collected more than £46, amongst which were £16 in halfpence; for which we endeavoured to give thanks. God was pleased to pour into my soul a great spirit of supplication, and a sense of his free distinguishing mercies so filled me with love, humility, and joy, and holy confusion, that I could at last only pour out my heart before him in an awed silence. It was so full that I could not well speak. Oh the happiness of communion with God!

Thursday, May 10. Preached at Kennington, but it

rained most of the day. There were not more than ten thousand people, and thirty coaches. However, God was pleased so visibly to interpose in causing the weather to clear up, and the sun to shine out just as I began, that I could not avoid pointing it out to the people in my talk. Our petty philosophers, indeed and our Christians falsely so called, laugh at the idea of a particular providence. But to suppose a general providence without holding a particular providence is as absurd as to imagine there can be a chain without being composed of links. Search the scriptures, and we shall find that not a sparrow can fall to the ground without our heavenly Father, and that even the very hairs of our head are all numbered.

Friday, May 11. Preached at Kennington to a larger audience than last night, and collected £26 15s. 6d. for the Orphan House. The people offered willingly. They could not have taken more pains, or expressed more earnestness, had they all come to receive charity from me.

Saturday, May 12. Arranged today for myself and eleven more to go on board the *Elizabeth*, Captain Allen, to Pennsylvania, where I design, God willing, to preach the gospel on my way to Georgia, and buy provisions for the Orphan House. Many came to me this morning telling me what God had done for their souls by my preaching in the fields. In the evening, I preached to about twenty thousand people at Kennington as usual, the weather continuing remarkably fair whilst I was delivering my master's message. I offered Jesus Christ to all who could apply him to their hearts by faith. Oh that all would embrace him! The Lord make them willing in the day of his power.

Sunday, May 13. Preached this morning to a prodigious number of people in Moorfields, and collected for the orphans £52 19s. 6d., more than £20 of which was in halfpence. Indeed, they almost wearied me in receiving their mites, and they were more than one man could carry home. Went to public worship twice, and preached in the evening to about sixty thousand people. Many went away because they could not hear; but God enabled me to speak so that the best part of them could understand me well, and it is very remarkable what a deep silence is preserved whilst I am speaking. After the sermon, I made another collection of £29 17s. 8d., and came home deeply humbled with a sense of what God has done for my soul. I do not doubt that many self-righteous bigots, when they see me spreading out my hands to offer Jesus Christ freely to all, are ready to cry out, 'How glorious did the Rev. Mr Whitefield look today when, neglecting the dignity of a clergyman, he stood venting his enthusiastic ravings in gown and cassock upon a common, and collecting mites from the poor people.' But if this is to be vile, Lord grant that I may be more vile. I know this foolishness of preaching is made instrumental to the conversion and edification of numbers. Pharisees mock on, I rejoice, yes, and will rejoice.

Monday, May 14. Spent most of this day in visiting some friends, and settling my Georgia affairs. Spent the evening very agreeably with several Quakers at the house of Mr H. How much comfort do people lose when they only converse with people of their own communion!

Thursday, May 17. Preached, after several invitations there, at Hampstead Heath, about five miles from London. The audience was of the more genteel sort, and I preached very near the horse course, which gave me occasion to speak home to their souls concerning our spiritual race. Most were attentive, but some mocked. Thus the word of God is either a savour of life unto life, or of death unto death. God's Spirit blows when and where it chooses.

Friday, May 18. Dined with several of the Moravian church, and could not avoid admiring their great simplicity, and deep experience in the inward life. At six, I preached in a very large open place in Shadwell, being much pressed by many to go there. I believe there were upwards of twenty thousand people. At first, through the size of the throng, there was a little commotion; but afterwards all was hushed and silent. Very close to £20 was collected for the Orphan House. Blessed be God, we now begin to surround this great city. As the walls of Jericho once fell down at the sound of a few rams' horns, so I hope even this foolishness of preaching, under God, will be a means of pulling down the devil's strongholds, which are in and about the City of London.

Received several excellent letters, amongst which was one from Mr Ralph Erskine, a field preacher of the Scots church, a noble soldier of the Lord Jesus Christ. Oh that all who were truly zealous knew one another! It must greatly strengthen each other's hands.

Saturday, May 19. Had the pleasure of being an instrument under God with Mr Seward of bringing a young man out of Bethlehem, who was recently put into that place for being, as they term it, *Methodically mad*. The way I came to be acquainted with him was by his sending me the following letter:

To the Rev. Mr Whitefield.

Bethlehem Hospital, No. 50.
Dear Sir,—I have read your sermon upon the new birth, and hope I shall always have a due sense of my dear redeemer's goodness to me. He has so infinitely extended his mercy to me, which sense be pleased to confirm in me by your prayers, and may almighty God bless and preserve you, and prosper your ministerial function. I wish, sir, I could have some explanatory notes upon the New Testament, to enlighten the darkness of my understanding, to make me capable of becoming a good soldier of Jesus Christ; but above all, should be glad to see you.

I am, dear sir, yours affectionately with my whole heart,

Joseph Periam

At his request I paid him a visit, and found him in perfect health both in body and mind. A day or two after, I and

Mr Seward went and talked with his sister, who gave me the three following symptoms of his being mad. 1. That he fasted for about a fortnight. 2. That he prayed so as to be heard four storeys high. 3. That he had sold his clothes, and given them to the poor. This the young man himself had explained to me before, and ingenuously confessed that when his soul was first awakened he was one day reading the story of the young man whom our Lord commanded to sell all and to give to the poor, and thinking it must be taken in the literal sense, out of love to Jesus Christ he sold his clothes, and gave the money to the poor. This is nothing but what is common to persons at their first setting out in the spiritual life. Satan will, if possible, drive them to extremes. If such converts were left to God, or had some experienced person to consult with, they would soon come into the liberties of the gospel. But how should those who have not been tempted like their brethren be able to succour those that are tempted?

On May 5 I received a second letter from him.

Bethlehem, No. 50. May 5, 1739.

Worthy Sir,

Query 1. If repentance does not include a cessation from sin and turning to virtue, and though despite the fact that I lack that deep contrition mentioned by some divines, yet I do not live wilfully in any known sin, and firmly believe the gospel of our Lord Jesus Christ, may I not thereby be entitled to the benefits of Christ's death and resurrection, in the perseverance of knowledge, and practice of my duty?

Query 2. If I am in prison, whether I may not without offence to God make use of endeavours to be discharged, by which I may be enabled to get into a pious family, and consequently be grounded and firmly settled in the love of God, which is my desire; for I am surrounded with nothing but profaneness and wickedness.

Query 3. If my objections to being imprisoned are inconsistent or wicked, which are that I am obliged to submit to the rules of the house, in going to my cell at seven or eight o'clock at night, and not let out till six or seven in the morning, by which I am debarred the use of candle, and consequently books, so that all the time, except what is spent in prayer and meditation, is lost: which exercises, though good, are by so constant repetition, and for lack of change, deadened.

Query 4. If I should, by the goodness of God, be discharged, whether I may without offence to the gospel of Jesus Christ follow the business of an attorney-at-law, to which I was put as a clerk, and by a conscientious discharge of that duty be thereby entitled to a heavenly inheritance? My fear in this point arises from our Lord's advice about going to law. Matthew 5:40.

Query 5. If I cannot be discharged by proper application (which application pray be pleased to let me have), how can I best spend my time to the glory of God, myself and brethren's welfare? And please to give me rules for the same.

These questions, whether important or not, I leave to your judgement. If you think they deserve an answer, should be glad to have them solved, for as I am aware of the power of my adversary the devil, surely I cannot but act with the utmost circumspection, which gives me occasion to trouble you herewith. I hope, sir, the circumstance of the place I am in may excuse the manner in which I have written to you, and count it not an affront, for God is witness how I love and esteem the ministers of Jesus Christ, for whose dear sake may the God of infinite love and goodness stablish and confirm you in the daily success of your ministerial labours, which are the daily prayer of your most unworthy but faithful humble servant,

Joseph Periam

To this I sent the following answer:

May 7, 1739

Dear Sir,—The way to salvation is by Jesus Christ, who is the way, the truth, and the life. The way to Christ is by faith. 'He who believes in me will live,' says our Lord, 'even though he dies.' This faith, if it is a saving faith, will *work* by love. Come, then, to Jesus Christ as a poor sinner, and he will make you a rich saint. This, I think, serves as an answer to your first query.

It is, no doubt, your duty whilst you are in the house to submit to the rules of it; but then you may use all lawful means to get yourself out. I have just now been with your sister, and will see what can be done further. *Watch and pray.*

As for the business of an attorney, I think it unlawful for a Christian—at least exceedingly dangerous. Avoid it, therefore, and glorify God in some other station.

I am, dear Sir, your affectionate friend and servant,
George Whitefield

A day or two after I received a third letter, which is as follows:

Wednesday, May 9, 1739
Worthy Sir,—I received your letter, which was a full answer to my queries, and give you my hearty thanks for the trouble you have taken (the only gratitude I can at present repay); but he whom I have perfectly at heart will supply the deficiency to you, and will not suffer a meritorious act to go unrewarded. O how I daily experience the love of Christ towards me who am so vile, base, and unworthy! I pray God I may always be thankful, and both ready to do and suffer his most gracious will, which I trust through your prayers and God's grace I shall at all times submit to.

My father was with me last night, when I showed him your letter. I told him I utterly renounced the business of an attorney. He then asked what profession I chose; which I submitted to him, on condition it might prove agreeable to the will of God. He was pleased to say he thought me not mad, but very well in my senses, and would take me out on condition Dr Monro and the committee were of his opinion. Then he varied again, and thought it convenient for me to stay the summer, and to take medicine twice a week, fearing a relapse. I told him, as a father, he should be wholly obeyed; but when, at parting, he mentioned my leaving religion, I was somewhat stirred in my spirit, and told him, nothing should prevail upon me to leave Jesus Christ. This is the substance of what passed between us.

Upon the whole of the matter, sir, God gives me perfect resignation, and I trust when he shall see fit he will discharge me: I find his love daily more and more shed abroad in my heart. All things will work together for my good. If opportunity will let you, I should be sincerely glad to see you before you set out for America. May Almighty God, in his infinite goodness, prosper, guide, and protect you through this transitory life and hereafter receive you triumphantly into the heavenly Jerusalem, there to converse with, and see the ever blessed Jesus!

Your loving and sincere friend,

Joseph Periam

Upon reading this, I felt touched with a fellow-feeling of his misery, and at my request Mr Seward and two more friends went to see the committee. But alas, they esteemed my friends as much mad as the young man, and frankly told them that both I and my followers, in their opinion, were really beside ourselves. My friend Seward urged the example of the young persons who called the prophet that was sent to anoint Jehu king, a mad fellow; of our Lord, whom his own relations and the scribes and Pharisees took to be mad, and beside himself; and Festus's opinion of St Paul. He further urged that when young people were first spiritually awakened they were usually tempted by the devil to run into some extremes; but all such language confirmed the gentlemen more and more that Mr Seward was mad also. To prove that the young man was certainly mad, they called one of the attendants, who said when Mr Periam first came into the place he stripped himself to his shirt and prayed. The reason of this, as Mr Periam said afterwards, was that he might inure himself to hardship at once; for being brought from Bethnal Green, where he was taken great care of, into a cold place without windows, and a damp cellar under him, he thought it best to season himself at first, that he might learn to endure hardness as a good soldier of Jesus Christ. In the midst of the conference, some way or other, they mentioned his going to Georgia, and said, if I would take him with me, they would engage that his father should give leave to have him released. A day or two after, Mr Seward went to see his father, who gave his son an excellent reference, and consented to his going abroad. After this, he went to see the doctor, who pronounced him well. Today he went to see the committee again, who behaved very civilly, and gave the man a discharge.

He is now with me, and I hope will be an instrument of doing good. The hardships he has endured at Bethlehem will, I hope, prepare him for what he must undergo abroad. Being now not ignorant of Satan's devices, he will be better qualified to prevent his getting an advantage over others.

Dined at Clapham with Mr B., a Quaker. Preached in the evening at Kennington Common to about 15,000 people, who were very attentive and moved. Afterwards, I spent two hours at Fetter Lane Society, where we had a most useful conference concerning the necessity of every Christian to have some particular calling, whereby he may be a useful member of the society to which he belongs. We all agreed to this unanimously. For my own part, I think if a man will not labour, neither ought he to eat. To be so intent on pursuing the one thing needful as to neglect providing for those of our own households, in my opinion, is to be over-righteous.

Sunday, May 20. Went with our brethren of Fetter Lane Society to St Paul's, and received the holy sacrament as a testimony that we adhered to the Church of England. Preached at Moorfields and Kennington Common and at both places collected very nearly £50 for the Orphan House. A visible alteration is made in the behaviour of the people, for, though there were about fifteen thousand in the morning, and double the number in the afternoon, yet they were as quiet during my sermon as though there had not been more than fifty persons present. I did not meet with a moment's interruption. I could say of the assembly, as Jacob did on another occasion, 'Surely God is in this place.'

Olney

Tuesday, May 22. Reached Olney about ten at night, where I had long since promised to come. Here also God had prepared a table for us; and here I was not a little comforted in meeting with the Rev. Mr Rogers of Bed-ford, who like me has recently been thrust out of the synagogues for speaking of justification by faith, and the new birth, and has commenced as a field preacher. Once he was shut in prison for a short time, but thousands flock to hear him, and God blesses him more and more. I believe we are the first professed ministers of the Church of Eng-land that were so soon, and without cause, excluded from every pulpit. Whether our reverend brethren can justify such conduct the last day will determine.

Northampton

Reached Northampton about five in the evening, and was most courteously received by Dr Doddridge, Master of the Academy there.

At seven, as arranged, I preached to about three thousand hearers on a common near the town, from the starting-post. I preached with wonderful pleasure, because I thought I had then actual possession of one of the devil's strongholds. Oh that we may all run so as to obtain the crown of life, which God, the righteous judge, will give at the last day to all who love our Lord Jesus in sincerity.

Thursday, May 24. Preached again in the same place, at about eight in the morning, but to a much larger audience. Breakfasted with some pious friends. Was greatly comforted by several choice children of God, who came to me from different parts, and left Northampton about eleven, rejoicing with my friends at the mighty things God had already done, and was yet about to do for us. Many righteous souls live in and about Northampton, and nothing confirms me more that God intends to work a great work upon the earth, than to find how his children of all denominations everywhere wrestle in prayer for me.

Olney

Being much solicited to go to Olney, after the sermon yesterday I hastened there in company with about a dozen friends, eight long miles from Northampton, and got there about ten o'clock. Great numbers were assembled together, but on account of it being a rainy day it was judged inconvenient to preach in the fields. I therefore stood on an eminence in the street, and preached from there with such power as I have not for some time experienced. Though it rained all the time, yet the people stood very attentive and patient. All, I really believe, *felt*, as well as *heard* the word, and one was so pricked to the heart and convinced of sin that I scarcely ever saw the like instance. The word of God is quick and powerful, and sharper than a two-edged sword.

Bedford

Hastened away as fast as possible from Olney to Bedford, where I had promised, God willing, to preach tonight. About eight, I preached from the stairs of a windmill (the pulpit of my dear brother and fellow-labourer, Mr Rogers) to about three thousand people; and God was pleased to give me such extraordinary assistance that I believe very few, if any, were able to resist the power with which God enabled me to speak. My heart was full of God. God caused me to renew my strength, and gave me such inward support that my journey did not affect me. As my day is, so shall my strength be.

Friday, May 25. Preached at seven in the morning, and had rather a larger congregation than before. Took an affectionate leave of many gracious souls, and reached Hitchin, ten miles from Bedford, about one o'clock. About two, I got up on a table in the market-place, near the church; but some people were pleased to ring the bells in order to disturb us. At this, not having begun, we removed into a most commodious place in the fields; but being a little fatigued with my ride, and the sun beating most intensely upon my head, I was obliged in a short time to break off, being exceedingly sick and weak. A kind gentlewoman offered me her house, where I went and lay down for about two hours, and then came and preached near the same place, and God was with us. It was surprising to see how the hearts of the people were joined to me. I could have stayed with them longer, but being booked to go to St Albans I hastened there, but could not preach on account of my coming in so late. Great numbers had been expecting me, and it grieved me to think how little I could do for Christ, for he is a gracious master, and had I a thousand lives they should be spent in his service.

St Albans and London

Saturday, May 26. Had a comfortable night's rest, which much refreshed me. Preached at seven in the morning to about fifteen hundred people in a field near the town, and got safe to London by two in the afternoon.

Received an excellent letter from the Rev. Mr Ebenezer Erskine of Scotland, brother to Mr Ralph Erskine, acquainting me of his preaching last week to fourteen-thousand people. Blessed be God, there are other field preachers in the world beside myself! The Lord furnish us all with spiritual food with which to feed such great multitudes.

Monday, May 28. Preached, after earnest and frequent invitation, at Hackney, in a field belonging to one Mr Rudge, to about ten thousand people. I insisted much upon the reasonableness of the doctrine of the new birth, and the necessity of our receiving the Holy Spirit in his sanctifying gifts and graces, as well now as formerly. God was pleased to impress it most deeply upon the hearers. Great numbers were in tears, and I could not help exposing the impiety of those letter-learned teachers who say we are not now to receive the Holy Spirit, and who count the doctrine of the new birth as 'enthusiasm'. Out of your own mouths will I condemn you. Did you not, at the time of ordination, tell the bishop that you were inwardly moved by the Holy Spirit to take upon you the administration of the church? Surely at that time you acted the crime of Ananias and Sapphira over again. You lied, not to man, but to God.

Friday, June 1. Dined at Old Ford, and gave a short exhortation to a few people in a field, and preached in the evening at a place called Mayfair, near Hyde Park Corner. The congregation, I believe, consisted of nearly eighty thousand people. It was by far the largest I ever preached to yet. In the time of my prayer, there was a little noise; but they kept a deep silence during my whole talk. A high and very commodious scaffold was erected for me to stand on, and though I was weak in myself, yet God strengthened me to speak so loud that most could hear, and so powerfully that most, I believe, could feel. All love, all glory be to God through Christ!

I now go, I trust, under the conduct of God's Holy Spirit, to Pennsylvania and Virginia, and from there to Georgia, knowing not what will happen to me save that the Holy Spirit witnesses in every place, that labours, afflictions, and trials of all kinds remain with me. Let me do or suffer just as seems good in his sight. Only, Lord, give me that wisdom which lives with prudence, that I may never suffer for my own misconduct, but only for righteousness' sake.

Fourth Journal

*A Continuation
of the Reverend Mr Whitefield's Journal
during the time he was detained in England
by the Embargo
(June 1739—August 1739)*

Blackheath

Monday, June 4, 1739. Took leave of my weeping friends, and went in company with many of them to Blackheath, where there was nearly as large a congregation as at Kennington on the last Lord's Day. I think I never was so much enlarged since I have preached in the fields. My talk lasted about two hours, and the people were so melted down, and wept so loud, that they almost drowned my voice. I could not but cry out, 'Come, you Pharisees, come and see the Lord Jesus getting himself the victory.' Afterwards went to an inn upon the Heath, where many came drowned in tears to take a last farewell.

Bexley and Charlton

Friday, June 8. Preached at Bexley in the morning, and at Charlton in the afternoon, where I was invited by the Earl and Countess of Egmont. Both before and after the sermon they entertained me with the utmost civility. My heart was much comforted by God, and at night I returned with my friends to my sweet retreat at Blendon. Oh the comforts of being all of one mind in a house! It begins our heaven upon earth. Were I left to my own choice, here would be my rest. But a necessity is laid upon me, and woe unto me if I do not preach the gospel!

Saturday, June 9. Was much pleased and edified in reading Bishop Hall's *Christ mystical*, and Erskine's *Sermons*, both whose works, with Boehme's *Sermons*, I would earnestly recommend to everyone.

Blendon, Bexley and Blackheath

Sunday, June 10. Hastened back to Blendon, where more of our brethren came last night to see me. Preached with more power than ever, and assisted in administering the sacrament to about two hundred communicants in Bexley church. Dined, gave thanks and sang hymns at Mr Delamotte's. Preached with great power in the evening on Blackheath, to over twenty thousand people, and collected £16 7s. for the orphans. After the sermon I went to the Green Man, near the place where I preached, and continued till midnight instant in prayer, praise, and thanksgiving, and Christian conversation. I believe there were about fifty or sixty of us in all. Numbers stood by as spectators. God enlarged my heart much in prayer and exhortation.

Many of them watched unto prayer and praise all night. I think it every Christian's duty to be particularly careful to honour and glorify God where he is most dishonoured. Some can sing the songs of the drunkards in public houses; others can spend whole nights in chambering and wantonness; why should Christians be ashamed to sing the songs of the lamb and spend nights, as their Lord did before them, in exercises of devotion?

Tuesday, June 12. Read prayers at Bexley church. Began (being pressed both in spirit and by my friends to do so) to put some of my extempore talks into writing. Preached at Blackheath in the evening to about twenty thousand people. Several people of different ranks stood by as before. Some, I hope, went away edified, for God gave me great enlargement of soul.

Thursday, June 14. Spent the whole day in my pleasant and profitable retreat at Blendon; and in the evening had the pleasure of introducing my honoured and reverend friend, Mr John Wesley, to preach at Blackheath. The Lord gave him ten thousand times more success than he has given me! After the sermon we spent the evening most agreeably together with many Christian friends at the Green Man. About ten we admitted all to come in who would; the room was soon filled—God gave me utterance. I exhorted and prayed for nearly an hour, and then went to bed, rejoicing that another fresh inroad had been made into Satan's territories, by Mr Wesley's following me in field preaching in London as well as in Bristol.

Sunday, June 17. Preached to over twenty thousand people at Blackheath; and afterwards supped again at the Green Man. There were nearly three hundred in the room. I continued in exhortation and prayer till eleven o'clock, and then retired to bed, much pleased to think that religion, which had long been skulking in corners, and was almost laughed out of the world, should now begin to appear abroad, and openly shew herself at noonday.

Hertford

Monday, June 18. An embargo being laid upon the shipping for some weeks, I had time to go to Hertford, where I was invited by several pressing letters, declaring how God had worked by my ministry when I was there last.

Tuesday, June 19. Preached this morning about seven o'clock to nearly three thousand people. Many came to me under strong convictions of their fallen estate, and their lack of a God-Man to be their mediator. Many I heard of besides who had been much worked on by my preaching; several Christian families, I find, had been strengthened, and such immediate effects produced that I could not help rejoicing exceedingly. Breakfasted, dined, prayed and sang hymns with Mr S., a dissenting minister; was visited by some Quakers, and in the afternoon went to see Mr T., a Baptist teacher who unknown to me had sent a horse to fetch me from London. Preached at seven o'clock in the evening to about five thousand souls, upon the faith of Abraham, in which God was pleased to give me great freedom, and the people great attention. I believe God has many people in and near Hertford.

Broad-Oaks

Wednesday, June 20. Set out about five o'clock in the morning, and hastened to Broad-Oaks, about twenty miles from Hertford. Mr Delamotte, a convert of Mr Ingham's, came from Cambridge to meet us. He is scandalously opposed at that university. The students make him a proverb of reproach, and abuse him in the rudest manner. He has been forbidden to come into one college; and two or three who associate with him have been threatened much by their tutors for keeping him company. And here I cannot but remark what wonderful mercies God has shown this Mr Delamotte's family. About three or four years ago, God was pleased to touch the heart of his brother Charles, who hearing that Mr Wesley was going to Georgia (though his father would have settled him in a very handsome way), offered to go abroad with him as a servant. His parents' consent was asked, but they, and almost all their relations, opposed it strenuously. However, the young man being resolute and convinced that God was calling him, they at length somewhat consented. He went abroad, lived with Mr Wesley, served under him as a son in the gospel, did much good, and endured great hardships for the sake of Jesus Christ. See how God rewarded him for leaving all. Whilst he was absent, God was pleased to make use of the ministry of Mr Ingham and Mr Charles Wesley in converting his mother, two sisters, and this young gentleman at Cambridge; who, I pray God, may stand as a barrier against the profaneness, debauchery, luke-warmness, and deism of that seat of learning, and prove both a Barnabas and Boanerges in the Church of England.

Thaxted and Bishop Stortford

Friday, June 22. Read part of Jenks' *Submission to the Right-eousness of Christ*, a most excellent book. Preached at 9 o'clock in the morning at Thaxted, about two miles from Broad-Oaks, to upwards of a thousand people, and with such sweetness and power as I have not felt since I came into Essex. All around me were melted into tears. After-wards went to Bishop Stortford, about twelve miles from Thaxted, where I promised, God willing, to preach at night. About five o'clock we got there, and at six God en-abled me to preach with power to nearly four thousand people. Blessed be God, this itinerant preaching brings me acquainted with numbers of his children which otherwise I might never have seen or heard of in this life.

Blackheath

Saturday, June 23. Set out in good time from Bishop Stortford, and reached Blackheath about three o'clock in the afternoon. Preached at seven o'clock in the evening to about a thousand people. The smallness of the congrega-tion was occasioned by a report that I was dead. Wherever I went I found the people much surprised and rejoiced to see me alive. God knows I long to depart and to be with Christ, but as I have scarcely begun my testimony, I believe I shall not yet die, but live, and declare the works of the Lord.

Bexley

Sunday, June 24. Read prayers and assisted in administer-ing the sacrament at Bexley church. Many came from afar and expected to hear me, but the diocesan had been pleased to insist on the vicar's denying me the pulpit. Whether for just cause God shall judge at the last day. If we have done anything worthy of the censures of the church, why do not the Right Reverend the Bishops call us to a public account? If not, why do not they confess and own us? It is well we can appeal to the great bishop of souls. They say it is not regular, our going out into the highways and hedges, and compelling poor sinners to come in. We ought not *so* to beseech them to be reconciled to God. They desire to know by what authority we preach, and ask, 'What sign can you show that you do these things?' But alas, what further sign would they require? We did not go into the fields till we were excluded from the churches; and has not God set his seal to our ministry in an extraordinary manner? Have not many that were spiritually blind received their sight? Many that have been lame strengthened to run the way of God's commandments? Have not the deaf heard? The lepers been cleansed? The dead raised? And the poor had the gospel preached to them? That these notable miracles have been wrought, not in our own names, or by our own power, but in the name and by the power of Jesus of Nazareth cannot be denied. And yet they require a sign.

Gloucester, Randwick and Chafford

Sunday, July 1. Preached at seven o'clock in the morning to a much increased audience in my brother's field. Breakfasted at Gloucester; preached at eleven in the morning, read prayers in the afternoon, and preached again in the afternoon at Randwick church, about seven miles from Gloucester. The church was quite full, and about two thousand were in the churchyard, who, by taking down the window that lay behind the pulpit, had the convenience of hearing. Many wept sorely.

Thursday, July 5. Preached about ten in the morning, as usual, to a numerous and exceedingly moved audience. My own heart was so full of love to my dear countrymen, and they sincerely sympathised with me. Many friends after this came to take leave of me and told me what God had done for their souls. Having written my journal and dispatched my private business, after joining in prayer and singing with many, I left Gloucester. About five in the evening I reached Chafford Common; at seven preached till it was nearly dark to upwards of ten thousand people—a glorious increase since I was there last.

Bristol

Saturday, July 7. Preached at Baptist Mills to near the same number of people as last night, and found that Bristol had great reason to bless God for the ministry of Mr John Wesley. The congregations I observed to be much more serious and moved than when I left them; and their loud and repeated Amens, which they put up to every petition, as well as the exemplariness of their conversation in common life, plainly show that they have not received the grace of God in vain.

Sunday, July 8. Preached at the bowling-green to about ten thousand people, greatly moved indeed. About eleven I preached again at Hannam Mount, to nearly as many hearers; and at seven in the evening to about twenty thousand at Rose Green. I find such a visible alteration in the congregation for the better since I was here last, that convinces me more and more that God is truly with us. As our opposition increases, I doubt not but the manifestations of God's presence amongst us will increase also.

Monday, July 9. On Thursday I received a letter from the Bishop of Gloucester, in which his lordship affectionately admonished me to exercise my authority I received in the manner it was given me; his lordship being of opinion that I ought to preach the gospel only in the congregation wherein I was lawfully appointed to do so.

Today I sent his lordship the following answer:

Bristol, July 9, 1739

My Lord,—I thank your lordship for your lordship's kind letter. My frequent removes from place to place prevented my answering it sooner.

I am greatly obliged to your lordship, in that you are pleased to watch over my soul, and to caution me against acting contrary to the commission given me at ordination. But if the commission we then receive obliges us to preach nowhere but in that parish which is committed to our care, then all persons act contrary to their commission when they preach occasionally in any strange place; and consequently, your lordship equally offends when you preach out of your own diocese.

As for inveighing against the clergy, without a cause, I deny the charge. What I say, I am ready to make good whenever your lordship pleases. Let those who bring reports to your lordship about my preaching be brought face to face, and I am ready to give them an answer. St Paul exhorts Timothy not to receive an accusation against an elder under two or three witnesses. And even Nicodemus could say the law suffered no man to be condemned unheard. I shall only add that I hope your lordship will inspect the lives of your other clergy, and censure them for being *over-remiss*, as much as you censure me for being *over-righteous*. It is their falling from their Articles and not preaching the truth as it is in Jesus, that has excited the present zeal of those whom they in derision call the *Methodist preachers*.

Dr Stebbing's sermon (for which I thank your lordship) confirms me more and more in my opinion that I ought to be instant in season and out of season; for to me he seems to know no more of the true nature of regeneration than Nicodemus did when he came to Jesus by night. Your lordship may observe that he does not speak a word of original sin, or the dreadful consequences of our fall in Adam, upon which the doctrine of the new birth is entirely founded. No; like other polite preachers he seems to think that St Paul's description of the wickedness of the heathen is only to be referred to them of past ages; whereas I affirm we are all included as much under the guilt and consequences of sin as they were.

Again, my lord, the doctor entirely mistakes us when we talk of the *sensible* operations of the Holy Spirit. He understands us just as those Jews understood Jesus Christ who, when our Lord talked of giving them that bread which came down from heaven, said, 'How can this man give us his flesh to eat?' I know not that we use the word *sensible* when we talk of the operations of the Spirit of God; but if we do, we do not mean that God's Spirit manifests itself to our *senses*, but that it may be perceived by the soul, as really as any sensible impression made upon the body. But to disprove this the doctor quotes our Lord's allusion to the wind in the third chapter of John, which is one of the best texts he could urge to prove it. For if the analogy of our Lord's discourse be carried on, we shall find it amounts to this much: that although the operations of the Spirit of God can no more be accounted for than how the wind cometh and where it goes, yet they may be as easily felt by the soul as the wind may be felt by the body.

'But', says the doctor, 'these men have no proof to offer for their *inward* manifestations.' What proof, my lord, does the doctor require? Would he have us raise dead bodies? Have we not done greater things than these? I speak with all humility. Has not God, by our ministry, raised many dead souls to a spiritual life? Verily, if men will not believe the evidence God has given that he sent us, neither would they believe though one rose from the dead.

Besides, my lord, the doctor charges us with things we are entire strangers to—such as denying men the use of God's creatures; and encouraging abstinence, prayer, etc., to the neglect of the duties of our station. Lord, lay not this sin to his charge!

Again, my lord, the doctor represents as my opinion concerning Quakers in general, that which I only meant of those I conversed with in particular. But the doctor, and the rest of my reverend brethren, are welcome to judge me as they please. A little while longer, and we shall all appear before the great shepherd of our souls. There, there, my lord, shall it be determined who are his true ministers, and who are only wolves in sheep's clothing. Our Lord, I believe, will not be ashamed to *confess us publicly in that day*. I pray God we may all approve ourselves such faithful ministers of the New Testament that we may be able to lift up our heads with boldness!

As for declining the work in which I am engaged, my blood runs chill at the very thoughts of it. I am as much convinced it is my duty to act as I do, as I am that the sun shines at noonday. I can foresee the consequences very well. They have already, in one sense, thrust us out of the synagogues. By and by they will think it is doing God service to kill us. But, my lord, if you and the rest of the bishops cast us out, our great and common master will take us up. Even if all men deny us, yet he will not. However you may censure us as evil-doers and disturbers of the peace, yet if we suffer for our present way of acting, your lordship, on the great day, will find that we suffer only for *righteousness' sake*. In patience, therefore, do I possess my soul. I will willingly tarry the Lord's leisure. In the meanwhile, I shall continually bear your lordship's favours upon my heart, and endeavour to behave so as to subscribe myself,

My Lord, your lordship's obedient son and obliged servant,

George Whitefield

Tuesday, July 10. Preached yesterday evening at the brick-yard to about eight thousand people. Dined today with my honoured fellow-labourer, Mr Wesley, and many other friends at Two Mile Hill, in Kingswood; and preached afterwards to several thousand people and colliers in the school-house, which has been carried on so successfully that the roof is ready to be put up. The design, I think, is good. Old as well as young are to be instructed. A great and visible alteration is seen in the behaviour of the colliers. Instead of cursing and swearing, they are heard to sing hymns about the woods; and the rising generation, I hope, will be a generation of Christians. They seem much moved by the word, and attend the churches and Societies when Mr Wesley is absent from them. The prospect of their future welfare filled me with joy. They took a most affectionate leave of me.

Heard today that the town clerk of Bristol did my brother Wesley and me the honour to desire the grand jury at their quarter sessions to prevent our meetings, and to have the Riot Act read; but they paid him no regard—indeed one who was called to serve on the petty jury offered to subscribe to any fine, rather than do anything against us, who he said were true servants of Jesus Christ.

Bath and Bristol

Wednesday, July 11. Preached at eleven in the morning to a larger audience than last night. Hastened to Bristol and preached in the evening at Baptist Mills to a large congregation. It rained much, but, blessed be God, the people's hearts are so far influenced by the gospel of Christ that they care little whether it rains or shines.

After this, my brother Wesley and I went to the women's and men's Societies, settled some affairs, and united the two leading Societies together. How can I be thankful enough to God for sending me here to see that the seed has been sown in good ground, and that by the ministry of Mr Wesley it has received great increase. May it still increase with all the increase of God.

London

Saturday, July 21. Settled my affairs, and preached in the evening to upwards of ten thousand at Kennington Common. The word sank deep into their hearts; great numbers melted into tears, and my own heart overflowed with love to them. Blessed be God for what has been done here since I left London, by my honoured friend and fellow-labourer, Mr Charles Wesley. Surely, we can see the fruits of our labours. All love, all glory be to God, for giving so great an increase!

Sunday, July 22. Received a letter from Mr Ralph Erskine of Scotland. Some may be offended at my corresponding with him, but I dare not but confess my Lord's disciples. Had a pressing invitation to come into Lincolnshire. Preached, at seven in the morning, to about twenty thousand at Moorfields. A greater power than ever was amongst us. Scoffers and curious persons daily drop off; most who come now, I hope, do not attend out of curiosity. Never were such souls more melted down by the power of God's words; never did people offer their mites more willingly. I collected £24 17s. for the school-house being erected at Kingswood, and all seemed solicitous to express their affection. You scoffers, you blind Pharisees, come and see, and then call these tumultuous, seditious assemblies, if you can. Would to God they behaved so decently in any church in London!

Went to St Paul's, and received the blessed sacrament; preached in the evening at Kennington Common, to about thirty thousand hearers, and collected £15 15s. 6d. for the colliers. God gave me great power, and I never opened my mouth so freely against the letter-learned clergymen of the Church of England. Every day do I see the necessity of speaking out more and more. God knows my heart, I do not speak out of resentment. I heartily wish all the Lord's servants were prophets; I wish the Church of England was the joy of the whole earth; but I cannot see her sinking into papistical ignorance, and refined deism, and not open my mouth against those who, by their sensual, lukewarm lives, and unscriptural superficial doctrines, thus cause her to err. O Lord, we beseech thee, send out your light and your truth.

Friday, August 3. Spent the day in completing my affairs and taking leave of my dear friends. Preached in the evening to nearly twenty thousand at Kennington Common. I chose to talk on St Paul's parting speech to the elders at Ephesus (Acts 20), at which the people were much moved, and almost prevented my making any application. Many tears were shed when I talked of leaving them. I concluded with a suitable hymn, but could scarcely get to the coach for the people thronging me, to take me by the hand and give me a parting blessing.

And here I cannot but finish this part of my journal with a word or two of exhortation to my dear brethren, whoever they are, whom God stirs up to go into the highways and hedges, into the lanes and streets, to compel poor sinners to come in. You see, my dear brethren, what great things God has already done. I do not know how many have come to me under strong convictions of their fallen state. O my brethren, have compassion on our Lord's church, which he has purchased with his own blood. Let none of them be as sheep having no shepherd, or with worse than none, those blind leaders of the blind, who let them perish for lack of knowledge, and are no better than wolves in sheep's clothing. If you are found faithful, you must undergo strong persecution.

Oh let us strive together in our prayers, that we may fight the good fight of faith, that we may have that wisdom which comes from above, that we never suffer for our own faults, but only for righteousness' sake. Then will the Spirit of Christ and of glory rest upon our souls, and being made perfect by suffering here, we shall be qualified to reign eternally with Jesus Christ hereafter. Amen. Amen.

FIFTH JOURNAL

A Continuation
of the Reverend Mr Whitefield's Journal
from his embarking after the Embargo
to his arrival at Savannah in Georgia
(August 1739—January 1740)

On board the Elizabeth, *Capt. Stevenson, commander: bound*
from England to Philadelphia

Wednesday, August 15. Began to put those of my family who, I thought, were prepared for it into bands. In all we are eight men, four women, one boy and two children, besides Mr Seward and myself. The conversion of one of the men was particularly remarkable. Not long ago, he was master of a ship which was lost near the Gulf of Florida. Providence was pleased to throw him and his crew on a sand-bank, where they continually expected the waters to overwhelm them. At the end of ten days they saw a ship, and made a signal of distress. The ship made towards them; the captain (now with me) went out with his boat, and begged for a passage for himself and men. It was granted him on condition he would leave some of his crew behind upon the sand-bank, but he would not consent. At length the other commander agreed to take all, but as soon as my friend put off his boat to fetch them, the commander of the ship made sail and left them.

All this seemed quite *against*, but in the end God showed it was intended *for* the good of my friend. After thirty days' continuance upon the sand-bank, having fitted up the boat with some planks they had taken out of the ship, which had been lost five months before, nine of them committed themselves to the providence of God (the others not caring to venture in so small a boat). They sailed about one hundred and forty leagues, and at length came to Tyby Island, ten miles off Savannah. An inhabitant being near that place saw them, and brought them home with him. Being then in Georgia, and informed of what had happened, I invited the captain to breakfast with me, and reminded him of the goodness of God. He then seemed serious, and coming very providentially in the same ship with me when I returned to England, God was pleased to work more effectually in his soul, and he is now returning with me to Georgia again. Many offers have been made him to go back into the world, but he chooses rather to suffer affliction with the people of God. Most of my other assistants have left good places, and are willing freely to spend and be spent for the good of the Orphan House. Several of them have *already found*, all I hope are *seeking* Christ.

Monday, August 20. Fair wind all night, by which our ship was carried to the Bay of Biscay, and went before the wind at the rate of six miles an hour, almost the whole day. The wind being brisk, and a great swell coming from the Bay, most of us grew sick, and could do little else but lie down. This rejoiced me much, for I had a glorious opportunity of spending many hours in close communion with God, to ask pardon for the defects of my public ministry, and to pray for strength to prepare me for future work and trials. A sense of my actual sins and natural deformity humbled me exceedingly; and then the freeness and riches of God's everlasting love broke in with such light and power upon my soul, that I was often awed into silence, and could not speak. A dear companion was with me, and helped me to lament, pray and give praise. Oh, the comforts of religious friendship! Sanctify it, O Lord, to me, for your dear Son's sake.

Saturday, August 25. Had but little regular sleep since Tuesday, the wind continuing contrary. Last night it blew a gale. Most of my family still continued sick. I waited on them as well as I could, and prayed to God to make me willing to become the servant of all. Had two or three conferences with the captain of the ship, and some of his men. Read Dr Guise's *Paraphrase on the Evangelist St Matthew*, and think it the best I ever met with. Endeavoured to keep close to God by watching unto prayer, for direction and help in time of need. I was frequently enlightened to see the pride and selfishness of my heart, and as frequently longed for that perfect liberty wherewith Jesus Christ sets his servants free. The sea was calmer today than before. My family grew better, and we spent nearly two hours this evening in talking of the inward state of our souls, and preparing for the reception of the blessed sacrament. Lord, grant that we all may have on the wedding garment.

Sunday, August 26. Administered the holy sacrament early in the morning. Spent the remainder of the day in reading, intercession, etc. The wind was still contrary, and the sea rough; but I had a great calm and joy in my own soul. How can I be thankful enough for the opportunities I now enjoy for improvement. Let all that is within me praise God's holy name.

Friday, August 31. Very light winds for the last two days, and an entire calm today. I had many inward strugglings, and could do nothing but lie down and offer my soul to God. At night, I prayed before all my family, for them and all those dear people who have recommended themselves to my prayers. Afterwards I received comfort. Oh that these inward conflicts may purge, humble and purify my polluted, proud and treacherous heart.

I notice these inward trials always follow inward communications. For these two days past I have been much assisted. Lest I should be puffed up, and that my mind may be prepared to receive greater degrees of light, God out of love has sent me a thorn in the flesh. Lord, grant this loving correction of yours may make me truly great. Amen.

Saturday, September 15. Was exceedingly strengthened in reading Professor Francke's account of the Orphan House at Halle, near Glauchau. It seems, in many circumstances, to be so exactly parallel to my present undertaking for the poor of Georgia, that I trust the Orphan House about to be erected there will be carried on and ended with the like faith and success. Amen. Amen.

Saturday, September 22. Underwent inexpressible agonies of soul for two or three days, at the remembrance of my sins, and the bitter consequences of them. All the while I was assured God had forgiven me; but I could not forgive myself for sinning against so much light and love. I felt something of that which Adam felt when turned out of Paradise; David, when he was convicted of adultery; and Peter, when with oaths and curses he had three times denied his master. At length, my Lord looked upon me, and with that look broke my rocky heart, and I wept most bitterly. When in this condition, I wondered not at Peter's running so slowly to the sepulchre, when loaded with the sense of his sin. Were I always to see myself such a sinner as I am, and as I did then, without seeing the saviour of sinners, I should not be able to look up.

This latter part of the week, blessed be the Lord, he has restored to me the light of his countenance, and enabled me to praise him with joyful lips.

Sunday, September 23. Had a sweet sacrament, and love-feast afterwards. Was much strengthened both in my morning and evening devotions; but at night, a sense of my sins weighed me down again. Alas, how mistaken are they who go out of the world to avoid temptations. I never am so much tempted as when confined on shipboard: a mercy this from God to keep me in action. Luther says he never undertook fresh work but that he was either visited with a fit of sickness or some strong temptation. Prayer, meditation, and temptation are necessary accomplishments, in his account, for every minister. May I follow him, as he did Christ.

Saturday, September 29. Administered the holy sacrament this morning. Had fair winds, and stayed on deck with my companions the greatest part of the week. This afternoon I was greatly strengthened by perusing some paragraphs out of a book called *The Preacher*, written by Dr Edwards of Cambridge, and extracted by Mr Jonathan Warn, in his books entitled *The Church of England-Man turned Dissenter* and *Arminianism the Backdoor to Popery*.

Sunday, September 30. Administered the holy sacrament, and had a love-feast. Expounded with power in the morning to the sailors, and lent my cabin to the Quaker preacher in the afternoon. He spoke with much earnestness, but in my opinion his foundation was wrong. He seemed to make the light of conscience and the Holy Spirit one and the same thing, and represented Christ *within*, and not Christ *without*, as the foundation of our faith; whereas, the outward righteousness of Jesus Christ imputed to us, I believe, is the sole fountain and cause of all the inward communications which we receive from the Spirit of God. Oh that all of the persuasion were convinced of this; till they are, they cannot preach the truth as it is in Jesus.

Tuesday, October 9. This morning, our whole ship's company was brought to an allowance of bread, two biscuits a day for each person; but, blessed be God, through the bounty of friends in England, as yet my family have enough provisions. The Lord, in return, feed our benefactors with that bread which comes down from heaven.

Saturday, October 13. Still God is pleased to send us contrary winds, but very warm and pleasant weather. The power of writing has been in a great measure taken from me, but God has been with me in reading, expounding, and other exercises of devotion. I have experienced some blessed teachings of his Holy Spirit, in convicting me of the pride, sensuality and blindness of my own heart, and of the advantages Satan has gained over me by working on them. I have also been more enlightened to see into the mystery of godliness, God manifest in the flesh, and behold more and more of God's goodness, in letting me have this time of retirement to search my spirit. I would not have lost this voyage for a thousand worlds; it has been sweet and profitable to my soul. Lord I want to know myself and you. Oh let not the hurry of business, which awaits me on shore, prevent my hearing the still small voice of your Holy Spirit.

Sunday, October 14. Felt God's power with us, both at sacrament and public worship, morning and evening. Was enlarged in intercession, and had reason to believe there was sweet communion kept up between us and our friends on shore. The assurance of their prayers often lifts up my hands when they hang down, and strengthens my feeble knees. The prospect of the many changes and trials which I must necessarily be exposed to and undergo sometimes fills me with fear and trembling; but when I reflect that God has stirred up the hearts of his servants to pray for me, my fears vanish.

Saturday, October 27. Came into soundings on Sunday last; saw land on Monday, and were within a few leagues of Cape Lopen, which opens into the Bay where we are bound; but providence was pleased to keep us back by contrary winds.

Pennsylvania: Lewis Town

Tuesday, October 30. Being near Cape Lopen, a pilot came on board, in whose boat brother Seward, myself, and another dear friend went to Lewis Town, in order that we might go to Philadelphia by land and get a house in readiness before the ship arrived at the place. When we reached Lewis Town about evening, I took the first opportunity of retiring, to vent my heart in praises and thanksgiving for his abundant mercies conferred on me and mine. Oh how can I be thankful enough for this blessed voyage! I have been on board just eleven weeks, but they have seemed to me only as so many days. My knowledge, I trust, in spiritual things has been increased, my understanding enlightened, and my heart much enlarged. The remembrance of my humiliations is sweet unto my soul, and the freedom which God has given me over some darling failings fills me with joy unspeakable and full of glory.

About five in the evening, we landed at Lewis Town, situated in the southern part of the province of Pennsylvania, and about one hundred and fifty measured English miles from Philadelphia. Most of the houses are built of wood; it is not more than half as big, but more plentiful in respect of provision, than Savannah in Georgia. We had not been long in the inn before God showed us that he had prepared our way, for news had been brought a fortnight ago that I was coming here, and two or three of the chief inhabitants having been told of my arrival came and spent the evening with us, and desired me to give them a sermon on the next day, which I promised to do. We supped together, and after prayers and singing with the family I and my dear companions went to rest, admiring more and more the goodness and providence of the all-wise God. He is the great householder of the whole world, and I look upon all places and persons as so many little parts of his great family. I pray to him before I go, and I find that in answer to my prayer he always commands some or other of his household to take care of and provide for me. As there is here the same sun, so there is here the same God—in America as in England. I bless God all places are equal to me, so that I am where God would have me to be.

Wednesday, October 31. Spent the morning in writing, and sent some provisions on board for my fellow-travellers. Wrote some letters, and preached at two in the afternoon to a serious and attentive congregation. Persons of different denominations were present; and the congregation was larger than might be expected in so small a place, and at so short notice. After the sermon, the High Sheriff, Collector, and chief men of the place came and took leave of me; and by their means we were provided with horses and a guide for our journey at a reasonable expense. About five in the evening we left Lewis Town, and rode very pleasantly about 27 miles through the woods. At ten, we called at what they call a tavern, which was not very commodious; but the host and hostess were plain, well-meaning people. They made us a cake of unleavened bread, let us have a little cider, and a few eggs, and we went to bed rejoicing in all the mercies of God.

Thursday, November 1. Set out from our little inn about eight; dined at Dover, a small town (19 miles distant from our lodging), from where (having left a few books), we rode as pleasantly and with as much ease as though we were riding through Hyde Park. About eight in the evening we came to a more convenient inn, nearly fifty miles distant from the place where we stopped last night. Our Lord was with us as we came on our way.

Friday, November 2. Rode nearly sixty miles without fatigue, and reached Philadelphia before 11 at night. As I travelled, I observed the country was more and more open, and many fruitful plantations lay on each side of the road; so that I frequently thought I was, as it were, in England. Going abroad, if we make good use of it, cannot but help to enlarge our ideas and give us exalted thoughts of the greatness and goodness of God.

Philadelphia

Saturday, November 3. Went on board the *Elizabeth* to see my family, who arrived last night. Visited the Proprietor, Commissary and some others, who received me very civilly. Met with some gracious souls who talked with me concerning the things which belong to the kingdom of

God. Hired a house at a very cheap rate, and was entirely settled in it before night.

Sunday, November 4. Went in the evening to the Quakers' meeting, and felt somewhat in sympathy with the man that spoke. But I heartily wish that they would talk of an outward as well as an inward Christ; for otherwise, we make our own holiness, and not the righteousness of Jesus Christ, the cause of our being accepted by God.

Monday, November 5. Read prayers and preached to a large audience. Dined with the other churchwarden, and had some private and edifying conversation about our justification by faith in Christ. I was visited in the afternoon by the Presbyterian minister, and went afterwards to see the Baptist teacher, who seems to be a spiritual man; and spent part of the evening most agreeably with two Quakers. Had remarkable instances of God's answering our prayers which we put up on board ship; and that in the minutest particulars. Oh that I may watch God's particular providence more and more! It comforts and builds up my soul. How unhappy must they be who would exclude it from the world. To live without a sense of God's particular providence is, in effect, to live without God in the world.

Tuesday, November 6. Read prayers and preached in the morning, having had the use of the pulpit granted me for the whole week. Went, at the invitation of its father, to the funeral of a Quaker's child; and thought it my duty, as there was a great concourse of people at the burying-place, and none of the Quakers spoke, to give a word of exhortation. I hope this will be a means of making them more free in coming to hear the word, though preached within church walls. Oh that bigotry and prejudice were banished from the Christian world: Lord, let it not be once named among us, as becomes saints. Amen.

Was visited again in the evening by the Presbyterian and Baptist preachers, who were much rejoiced to hear Jesus Christ preached in the church. Whilst I was conversing with them, some women came desiring to be admitted to prayers with my family. Looking on this as from providence, I called them up, and felt much enlargement of heart in exhorting them, and pouring out my heart before God in their behalf. Many came up afterwards whom I desired, if they thought proper, to come again every night. Who knows but the Lord may be about to open a yet more effectual door? O prepare me to do your will, O God.

Thursday, November 8. Read prayers and preached to a more numerous congregation than I have yet seen here. Dined with an honest, open-hearted, true Israelitish Quaker; and had a sweet opportunity with him and his family of talking about Jesus Christ *and him crucified*. Preached at six in the evening from the Court House stairs to about six thousand people. I find the number that came on Tuesday to my house greatly increased and multiplied. The inhabitants were very solicitous for me to preach in another place besides the church; for it is quite different here from what it is in England. There, the generality of people think a sermon cannot be preached well without; here, they do not like it so well if delivered within the church walls.

Friday, November 9. I was visited in a kind manner by the minister of the parish; and preached again at six in the evening from the Court House steps. I believe there were nearly two thousand more present tonight than last night. Even in London, I never noticed so profound a silence. Before I came, all was hushed exceedingly quiet.

Saturday, November 10. Before it was light, there came a young person whom I had observed much moved last night, desiring to join in prayer.

Soon after came a little maid about seven years of age, telling me she had heard I was taking little children to Georgia, and desired me to take her. Dined with the minister of the parish; and at my return home was much comforted by the coming of Mr Tennent, an old grey-headed disciple and soldier of Jesus Christ. He keeps an academy 20 miles from Philadelphia. He is a great friend of Mr

Erskine, of Scotland, and as far as I can find both he and his sons are secretly despised by the generality of the Synod, as Mr Erskine and his brethren are hated by the law courts of Edinburgh, and as the Methodist preachers are by their brethren in England. Though we are but few, and stand alone, as it were like Elijah, yet I doubt not but the Lord will appear for us, as he did for that prophet, and make us more than conquerors.

Sunday, November 11. Read prayers in the morning, and preached in the afternoon to a very thronged congregation. Visited one sick person, and administered the holy sacrament to another. For ever adored be the divine goodness, the gospel has taken root in many hearts. As soon as I come home, my house is generally filled with people desirous to join in psalms and prayers. They are so eager for the bread of life that they scarcely give me time to take bodily refreshment and proper retirement in my room. This afternoon I was much carried out in bearing my testimony against the unchristian principles and practices of our clergy. Three of my reverend brethren were present; I know not whether they were offended. I endeavoured to speak with meekness as well as zeal. Were I to convert papists, my business would be to show that they were misguided by their priests; and if I want to convince Church of England Protestants, I must prove that the generality of their teachers do not preach or live up to the truth as it is in Jesus. In vain do we hope to set people right till we demonstrate that the way which they have been taught is wrong.

Brunswick and New York

Tuesday, November 13. Reached Brunswick at one. Here we were much refreshed with the company of Mr Gilbert Tennent, an eminent Dissenting minister, about forty years of age, son of that good old man who came to see me on Saturday at Philadelphia. God, I find, has been pleased greatly to own his labours. He and his associates are now the burning and shining lights of this part of America. Finding there was a general expectation of hearing me, I read the church liturgy, and preached in the evening at Mr Tennent's meeting-house; for there is no place set apart for the worship of the Church of England, and it is common, I was told, in America, for the Dissenters and Conformists to worship at different times in the same place. Oh that the partition wall were broken down, and we all with one heart and one mind could glorify our common Lord and saviour Jesus Christ!

Wednesday, November 14. Set out from Brunswick, in company with my dear fellow travellers, and my worthy brother and fellow-labourer, Mr Tennent. As we passed along, we spent our time most agreeably in telling one another what God had done for our souls. He recounted to me many instances of God's striving with his heart, and how grace, at last, overcame all his fightings against God. About noon, we got to Elizabeth Town, 22 miles from Brunswick. Here we took boat, and at four reached New York, where we were most affectionately received by the family of Mr Noble. I went to see Mr Vessey, the Commissary, but he was not at home. Then I went to the meeting-house to hear Mr Gilbert Tennent preach, and never before heard such a searching sermon. He convinced me more and more that we can preach the gospel of Christ no further than we have experienced the power of it in our own hearts. Being deeply convicted of sin, by God's Holy Spirit, at his first conversion, he has learned by experience to dissect the heart of a natural man. Hypocrites must either soon be converted or enraged at his preaching.

Thursday, November 15. Several came to see me at my lodgings, who also gave me kind invitations to their houses. Went to see Mr Vessey; but wished, for his own sake, he had behaved in a more Christian manner. He seemed to be full of anger and resentment, and before I asked him for the use of his pulpit, denied it. He desired to see my letters of orders, and, when I told him they were left at Philadelphia, he asked me for a licence. I answered that I never heard that the Bishop of London gave any licence to anyone who went to preach the gospel in Georgia; but that I was presented to the living of Savannah by the trustees, and upon that presentation had letters dismissory from my lord of London, which I thought was sufficient authority. But this was by no means satisfactory to him; he charged me with breaking my oath, with breaking the Canon, which enjoins ministers and churchwardens not to admit persons into their pulpit without a licence. How can I break that, when I am neither a churchwarden, nor have any church hereabouts to admit anyone into?

At this, knowing that he was a frequenter of public houses, I reminded him of that Canon which forbids the clergy to go to any such places. This, though spoken in the spirit of meekness, stirred him up more. He charged me with making a disturbance in Philadelphia, and sowing and causing divisions in other places. 'But you', he said, 'have a necessity laid upon you to preach.' I told him I had, for the clergy and laity of our church seemed to be settled on their lees; but that my end in preaching was not to sow divisions, but to propagate the pure gospel of Jesus Christ. He said they did not want my assistance. Alas, alas, what manner of spirit are the generality of the clergy possessed with? Is this the spirit of the meek lamb of God? Are these the fruits of the Holy Spirit? It cannot be. Their bigotry, if it was nothing else, in time would destroy them. Lord, for your mercy's sake, lighten their darkness and grant that many of the priests also may be obedient to the faith.

Dined with Mr Pemberton, the Presbyterian minister. Preached in the fields, to upwards of two thousand, at three in the afternoon; and expounded at six in the evening to a very thronged and attentive audience in Mr Pemberton's meeting-house. At first, for the sake of my weak brethren, I was unwilling to preach there; but hearing that Mr Vessey, the Commissary, himself had preached in the

Dutch Calvinistic meeting-house, when there was no place of worship for the people of our own communion, and the Dutch meeting-house being denied me, as well as the church, I thought it my duty to accept the kind offer made me by Mr Pemberton and his friends. In the field, a few mocked, but after speaking to them they grew more serious.

Sunday, November 18. Preached this morning at eight o'clock to a very attentive audience. Went to the English church both morning and evening, and felt my heart almost bled within me to consider what blind guides were sent into her. If I have any regard for the honour of Christ, and good of souls, I must lift up my voice like a trumpet, and show how sadly our church ministers are fallen from the doctrines of the Reformation. Her prophets prophesy lies, and I fear many of the people love to have it so.

New Brunswick

Tuesday, November 20. Reached here about six last night; and preached today at noon, for about two hours, in worthy Mr Tennent's meeting-house to a large assembly gathered together from all parts; and amongst them, Mr Tennent told me, was a great number of solid Christians. About three in the afternoon, I preached again; and at seven I baptised two children, and preached a third time. Among others who came to hear the word were several ministers, whom the Lord has been pleased to honour in making them instruments of bringing many sons to glory. Mr Cross, minister of a congregation of Barking Bridge, about twenty miles from Brunswick, told me of many wonderful and sudden conversions that had been wrought by the Lord under his ministry. For some time, eight or nine used to come to him together, in deep distress of soul; and I think he said three hundred of his congregation, which is not a very large one, were brought home to Christ. They are now looked upon as enthusiasts and madmen, and treated as such by those who know not God, and are ignorant of the hidden life of Jesus Christ in their hearts. Another was a Mr Camel, who has been a preacher of the doctrines of grace for these four years; was a regular and moral liver, and accounted a very good man; but within these last few years being convinced of sin, and that he knew nothing in his own experience of Jesus Christ (though he had pretended to preach him so long), after many struggles with himself told the Synod he was unconverted, and therefore dare not preach until he was; accordingly, he has left off preaching these two months, and has laboured under unspeakable anguish and distress of soul. By some he is looked upon as melancholy, and beside himself; but I have had much discourse with him, and really believe these humiliations will prepare him for great and eminent services in the church of God.

His case reminds me of Professor Francke, who having agreed on Easter Day to preach on the nature of divine faith, and finding he had not that faith himself, was convicted by God of his unregenerate state; upon which he ran into the woods, was there deeply humbled, and at last became a most exalted instance of faith. At our persuasion, Mr Camel promised to preach next Sunday, and I believe will be instrumental in convicting many heart-hypocrites among the Dissenting ministers. For that there are many such is evident from this: though they hold, have been bred up in, and preach the doctrines of grace, yet whenever the power of God appear in any congregation, they cry it down as much as our ministers of the Church of England. Oh that the Lord may comfort poor Mr Camel, and cause him to detect these wolves in sheep's clothing.

Trent Town and Neshaminy

Thursday, November 22. Set out for Neshaminy (20 miles distant from Trent Town), where old Mr Tennent lives, and keeps an academy, and where I had arranged to preach today. We came there about 12, and found over three thousand people gathered together in the meeting-house yard, and Mr William Tennent preaching to them because we were after the appointed time. When I came up, he soon stopped, and sang a psalm, and then I began to speak. At first the people seemed unmoved, but in the middle of my discourse the hearers began to be melted down, and cried much. After I had finished, Mr Gilbert Tennent gave a word of exhortation. At the end of his discourse, we sang a psalm and then dismissed the people with a blessing. Oh that the Lord may say Amen to it!

After our exercises were over, we went to old Mr Tennent, who entertained us like one of the ancient patriarchs. His wife seemed to me like Elizabeth, and he like Zacharias; both, as far as I can find, walk in all the ordinances and commandments of the Lord blameless. We had sweet communion with each other, and spent the evening in concerting measures for promoting our Lord's kingdom. It happens very providentially that Mr Tennent and his brethren are appointed to be a Presbytery by the Synod, so that they intend breeding up gracious youths, and sending them out into our Lord's vineyard. The place where the young men study now is, in contempt, called *the College*. It is a log-house, about twenty feet long, and nearly as many broad; and, to me, it seemed to resemble the school of the old prophets. That their habitations were mean and that they did not seek great things for themselves is plain from that passage of scripture where we are told that at the feast of the sons of the prophets one of them put on the pot, whilst the others went to fetch some herbs out of the field. From this despised place, seven or eight worthy ministers of Jesus have recently been sent out; more are almost ready to be sent; and a foundation is now being laid for the instruction of many others. It is now increased to a large college, now being erected in the New Jerseys. May it increase with all the increase of God. The devil will certainly rage against them; but the work, I am persuaded, is of God, and will not come to nought.

Worldly ministers oppose them strongly; and, because people, when awakened by Mr Tennent, or his brethren, see through them, and therefore leave their ministry, the poor gentlemen are loaded with contempt, and looked upon as persons who turn the world upside-down.

Neshaminy, Abingdon and Philadelphia

Friday, November 23. Parted with dear Mr Tennent and his worthy fellow-labourers; but promised to remember each other *publicly* in our prayers. Rode to Abingdon, about ten miles from Neshaminy, and preached to over two thousand people from a porch window belonging to the meeting-house. It is surprising how such bodies of people, so scattered abroad, can be gathered at so short a warning. At Neshaminy, I believe there were nearly a thousand horses. The people, however, did not sit upon them to hear the sermon, as in England, but tied them to the hedges; and thereby much disorder was prevented. As soon as I had done, I had fresh invitations to go to several places, should time and business permit. Though it was cold, the people stood very patiently in the open air, and seemed in no hurry to return home after the discourses were ended.

Sunday, November 25. Had great travail of soul, and struggling within myself, about a text to preach on. At last I fixed on one for the morning, and trusted to God to direct me to one for the evening; but before I came from church God showed me what I should do, for after I had done preaching a young gentleman, once a minister of the Church of England, but now secretary to Mr Penn, stood up with a loud voice, and warned the people against the doctrine I had been delivering, urging that there was no such term as *imputed righteousness* in holy scripture; that such a doctrine put a stop to all goodness; that we were to be judged for our good works and obedience, and were commanded *to do and live*. When he had ended, I denied his first proposition, and brought a text to prove that 'imputed righteousness' was a scriptural expression; but, thinking the church an improper place for disputation, I said no more at that time. The portion of scripture appointed for the epistle was Jeremiah 23, in which are these words: 'The Lord Our Righteousness'. Upon these I discoursed in the afternoon, and showed how the Lord Jesus was to be *our whole righteousness*. I proved how the contrary doctrine overthrew all divine revelation, and answered all the objections. I produced the Articles of our church to illustrate it, and concluded with an exhortation to all to lay aside reasoning unbelief and to submit to Jesus Christ, who is the end of the law for *righteousness* to everyone that believes. The verses at the beginning of the chapter, from which the text was taken, are very remarkable (Jeremiah 23:1–4). God was pleased to fulfil that promise in me; for, blessed be his name, I was not dismayed. The church was thronged within and without; all were wonderfully attentive; and many, as I was informed, were convinced that the Lord Christ was *our Righteousness*. In the evening, the gentleman came to see me; but alas, was so very dark in all the fundamentals of Christianity, and such an entire stranger to inward feelings, that I was obliged to say to him, 'You are Israel's teacher, and do you not understand these things?' Lord, convict and convert him for your infinite mercy's sake.

Philadelphia and German Town

Tuesday, November 27. As arranged, I preached at German Town, seven miles from Philadelphia, from a balcony, to over six thousand people. God strengthened me to speak nearly two hours, with such demonstration of the Spirit that great numbers continued weeping for a considerable time. I have not seen a more gracious melting for a considerable time. After I had done, people came to shake me by the hand, and invited me to their houses, and fresh places. A German most kindly entertained me. I had sweet converse, and felt a blessed union and communion with many souls, though of different nations and beliefs. I think there are no less than fifteen different denominations of Christians in German Town, and yet all agree in one thing, that is, to hold Jesus Christ as their head, and to worship him in spirit and in truth. I talked with one who had been banished from Switzerland for preaching Christ. Numbers are scattered round about the town who were driven out of their native countries for the sake of their holy religion. About four in the afternoon, we went with many dear disciples of the Lord, to see one Conrad Mattheus, an aged hermit, who has lived a solitary life for nearly forty years. He was heir to a great estate, but chose voluntary poverty. He has worked hard, but always without wages. He is now unable to do much, but God sends somebody or other to feed him. A friend built him the little house where he lives; and Jesus, I am persuaded, dwells with him. He talked most feelingly of inward trials; and when I asked him whether he had not many such in so close a retirement, he answered, 'It is no wonder that a single tree that stands alone is more exposed to storms than one that grows among others.' After half an hour's conversation, we took our leave. He kissed me and my friends, and was rejoiced to hear what was being done in England. Our hearts were knit together, and the God of love was truly with us. The Germans, I find, are about to translate my *Journals* into High Dutch.

About eight in the evening we reached Philadelphia, and found great numbers waiting round my door to hear the word of life. After I had paid a visit, and talked privately to two people who were doubtful of the principles of the Quakers, I returned home, and though I was weak I could not bear to let so many go away without a spiritual morsel; I therefore gave them a word of exhortation, sang a hymn, and prayed and dismissed them with a blessing. Many wept bitterly, and the people's behaviour more and more convinces me that God has begun a good work in many souls. Were proper encouragement given, I am persuaded Georgia might soon be full of people. Many would gladly go there with me. I cannot but hope that it will be in time a fruitful soil for Christians. One great reason, I believe, why Pennsylvania flourishes above other provinces is the liberty of conscience which is given all to worship God in their own way; by this means, it has become as it were an asylum or place of refuge for all persecuted Christians.

Philadelphia

Wednesday, November 28. Wrote a letter or two to my dear friends in England. I have not had time before, since my return from New York. People are continually coming in, and enquiring with many tears how they must come to Christ. It grieves me to send them away with such short answers; but necessity compels me.

An opposer told me I had unhinged many *good sort* of people. I believe many that contented themselves with good desires are now convinced they must have good habits also, and be thoroughly born again before they can see the kingdom of God.

Philadelphia and Chester

Thursday, November 29. Had the satisfaction of settling all my family affairs; gained considerably by the goods that were sold for the poor, and had a sloop lent me, which Mr Seward bought and named *Savannah*, in which I left orders for my family to set sail, immediately after my leaving Philadelphia. My friend Gladman (the captain mentioned before at the beginning) has been a helpmeet to me, and done everything without giving me any (or but little) trouble. About eleven in the morning, having corrected two sermons for the press, I took an affectionate leave of my family and Philadelphia people.

Newcastle

Sunday, December 2. Returned last night to Newcastle, that I might see my dear family, who came there in the sloop just after I had left. Slept at the house of Mr Gladman, and this morning went on board, prayed, sang psalms, gave a word of exhortation and rejoiced much to see all things in such excellent order. My dear friend the captain told me how kind the people of Philadelphia had been to my family after my departure. One brought them butter, another beer, etc., and the collector would not take his perquisite for clearing the sloop. The two children the people were particularly fond of, and gave them so many things that I was obliged to desire them to desist.

Maryland: North East

Monday, December 3. Came to North East in Maryland, where I had arranged to preach today. Little notice having been given, there were not above fifteen hundred people; but God was with us, and many were deeply moved. Several repeated invitations were sent me to preach at other places. Immediately after the sermon we passed over Susquehannah Ferry, about a mile broad, and were received at a gentleman's house that lay on our way. Though we were eight in company, all things were carried on with great freedom and generosity; and I hope God sent us providentially there, for the gentleman told us he had been a little melancholy, and had therefore sent for some friends to help him to drive it away. The bottle and the bowl, I found, were the means to be employed; but, blessed be God, the design was, in a good measure, prevented by our coming; another turn was soon given to the conversation, whilst I endeavoured to talk of God as much as I could. All joined in family prayer; and I went to bed pitying the miserable condition of those who live a life of luxury and self-indulgence. They are afraid to look into themselves; and, if their consciences are at any time weakened, they must be lulled to sleep again by drinking and evil company. None but a sincere Christian can with pleasure practise the duty of self-examination.

Joppa

Tuesday, December 4. Set out about eight in the morning,

and took leave of two dear friends who parted from us with weeping eyes. Lunched at Joppa, a little town about fifteen miles from the place where we lay. I gave a word of exhortation to about forty people in the church. Oh that the Holy Spirit may fall on them who heard the word, in as real though not in so visibly miraculous a manner as it did once on Cornelius and his household! Maryland, as far as I can hear, seems to be a place as yet unwatered with the true gospel of Christ, and with no likelihood of much good being done in it, unless one could abide there for some time. There is scarcely any town worth mentioning, because almost every planter has a landing-place from which he exports his tobacco at his own house, which generally lies very near the river. By this means the people are much dispersed, and consequently cannot be gathered together without much previous notice, which, even so, is difficult to give, because there are many large ferries between place and place.

Annapolis

Thursday, December 6. Had an opportunity of writing some letters last night and this morning to England. Went to see Governor Ogle, and was received with much civility. Went to pay my respects to Mr Stirling, the minister of the parish, who happened not to be in; but whilst we were at dinner he came and offered me his pulpit, his house, or anything he could supply me with. About four, he came and introduced me and my friends to a gentleman's house, where we had some useful conversation. Our conversation ran chiefly on the new birth, and the folly and sinfulness of those amusements whereby the polite part of the world are so fatally diverted from the pursuit of the one thing needful. Some of those present, I believe, thought I was too strict, and were very strenuous in defence of what they called *innocent* diversions; but when I told them everything was sinful which was not done with a single eye to God's glory, and that such entertainments not only showed a levity of mind, but were contrary to the whole tenor of the gospel of Christ, they seemed somewhat convinced; at least, I trust it set them *doubting*, and I pray God they may *doubt* more and more, for cards, dancing and such like draw the soul from God, and lull it asleep as much as drunkenness and debauchery. Every minister of Christ ought, with the authority of an apostle, to declare and testify the dreadful snare of the devil, whereby he leads many captive at his will, by the falsely called *innocent* entertainments of the polite part of the world; for women are as much enslaved to their fashionable diversions as men are to their bottle and their hounds. Self-pleasing, self-seeking is the *ruling principle* in both; and therefore, such things are to be spoken against, not only as so many trifling amusements but as things which show that the heart is wholly alienated from the life of God. If I may speak from my own as well as others' experience, as soon as ever the soul is stirred up to seek after God, nothing but what leads towards God can delight it; and therefore, when in company, I love to lay the axe to the root of the tree, show the necessity of a thorough change of heart, and then all things fall to the ground at once.

Friday, December 7. A visible alteration has taken place in the behaviour of the people of the house. Preached in the morning and evening to small polite audiences. In the evening, two of the chief inhabitants favoured me with a visit. The minister seemed somewhat moved, and under convictions; but I fear a false politeness, and the pomps and vanities of the world, eat out the vitals of religion in this place. I bless God I did not spare telling my hearers of it in my talks, and the minister told me they took it kindly.

Piscataway, Port Tobacco, and Potomac

Monday, December 10. Lunched at Port Tobacco and reached Potomac by three in the afternoon. We attempted to go over it; but after we had rowed about a mile the wind blew so violently, and night was coming on so fast, that we were obliged to go back and stay in the person's house who kept the ferry, where they brought out such things as they had. God showed us the benefit of returning, for the wind was very boisterous, and the night snowy; so that without a miracle (which in such a case we had no right to expect) both we and our horses must have been lost. Lord, grant we may always keep between the two extremes of distrusting or tempting you.

Virginia: Seals Church

Tuesday, December 11. Had a short and delightful passage over the river this morning, which we could not pass last night. Observed the country to be much more open, and the roads better than in Maryland. By six at night, we got to a place called Seals Church, 29 miles from Potomac. Here we called at a person's house to whom we were recommended; but the mistress of it was not at home, and the overseer of the slaves, at first, was unwilling to receive us. However, finding we were wet and strangers, he was at last prevailed upon to let us abide there all night; and in a little time furnished us with a good fire, with some meat, milk, and a cake baked on the hearth, which was exceedingly refreshing and afforded us no small matter for praise and thanksgiving. Oh that we may abound in that duty more and more.

Wednesday, December 12. Went on, having pleasant roads and a warm day, till we came to Piscataway ferry, 18 miles from Seals Church, where the man of the house spared us some corn and sheaves for our horses, but had neither milk nor bread in the house for ourselves. However, I endeavoured to feed him with spiritual bread; but he seriously asked one of us if I was not a Quaker, because (as I supposed) he heard me talk of the necessity of being born again of the Spirit. If I talk of the Spirit, I am a Quaker! If I say grace at breakfast, and behave seriously, I am a Presbyterian! Alas, what must I do to be accounted a member of the Church of England? About one we set out, and before four in the afternoon reached an inn. Here we were most opportunely refreshed with what meat they had in the house. There being no other public-house for some miles, and being wearied more than common for want of usual sustenance, we tarried all night. In the evening some gentlemen came the worse for drink; but the woman of the house kept them from us, so we slept very comfortably on the bed that she made us in the kitchen. I talked to her of religion, and told her that we must be born again. She said that was true, but it was to be done *after* death; also she thought God was very merciful, and that it would be no harm to swear by her faith. I could not help noticing how the devil loves to represent God as *all mercy*, or *all justice*. When persons are awakened, he would if possible tempt them *to despair*; when dead in trespasses and sins he tempts them *to presume*. Lord, preserve us from making shipwreck against either of these rocks. Give us such a sense of your justice as to convince us that we cannot be saved if we continue in sin, and such a sense of your mercy as may keep us from despair, through a living faith in your dear Son who is the saviour of sinners!

Thursday, December 13. Set out just as the sun rose; got to an inn by noon; ate what was set before us with some degree of thankfulness; and reached the house of Colonel Whiting, father of my dear friend Captain Whiting, long before night. Here God spread a plentiful table before us and, what was more desirable, sent us a well-inclined person to whom, I trust, my conversation was blessed. That passage in St John, where it is said that our Lord had to go through Samaria (when the poor woman was to be converted) has often stirred me. The same good providence, I trust, led me through these parts for the sake of the person before mentioned. Oh that, like the woman at the well, he may have Christ revealed in his heart, and be filled with a holy zeal to go and invite his neighbours to him. Amen.

Williamsburgh

Saturday, December 15. Went to see, and afterwards (at

his invitation) dined with, the Governor, who received me with joy, asked me to preach, and wished my stay was to be longer. He has been chiefly instrumental in raising a beautiful college at Williamsburgh, in which is a foundation for about eight scholars, a president, two masters, and professors in the different sciences. Here the gentlemen of Virginia send their children, and as far as I could learn by enquiry they are under about the same regulation and discipline as in our universities at home. The present masters came from Oxford. Two of them, I find, were my contemporaries there. I rejoiced in seeing such a place in America. It may be of excellent use if learning Christ be made one end of their studies, and arts and sciences only introduced and pursued as subservient to that. For want of this, most of our English schools and universities have sunk into mere seminaries of paganism. Young men's heads are stuffed with heathen mythology, and Christ or Christianity is scarcely so much as named amongst them; so that when they come to be converted, they are obliged to undo what they have been doing for many years. Revive, O Lord, a radical spirit, and then we may hope for some radical schools to be erected and encouraged amongst us.

North Carolina

Wednesday, December 19. A little while after our coming in, I begged leave to lie down to rest my weary limbs. In some way or other, in my absence, my friends acquainted our host who I was; at which he was so rejoiced that he could not tell how to express his satisfaction. His wife also seemed most anxious to oblige, and they were only concerned that they could do no more for us. The honest old man told us that his son-in-law, who lived about three miles off, ever since he heard of me in the *News*, wished that I would come there. This is not the first time, by a long way, that I have found the advantage of the things my adversaries have inserted in the public papers: they only excite people's curiosity, and serve to catch their attention, while men of seriousness and candour naturally infer that some good must be doing where such stories and falsities are invented. It often gives me unspeakable comfort to see how wisely God overrules everything for the good of his church.

Eden Town

Thursday, December 20. God was pleased to humble my body by weakness, and my soul by conviction of past sin, yet before we went to rest he was pleased to refresh me with exceeding peace, and in the midst of my humiliations exalted me by giving me a more lively sense of his favour and loving kindness, which is better than life itself. I think I often feel what our Lord meant, when he said the tax collector went down to his house justified rather than the Pharisee. I do not doubt that while he was pouring out his soul and beating his breast, the Holy Spirit overshadowed him and assured him of his pardon. It is a dreadful mistake to deny the doctrine of assurance or to think it is confined to a time of persecution or to the early ages of the church. Not only righteousness and peace but joy in the Holy Spirit, which is the consequence of assurance, is a necessary part of the kingdom of God within us; and though all are not to be condemned who have not an immediate assurance, yet all ought to labour after it. I really believe one great reason why so many go mourning all their life long, is owing to ignorance of their Christian privileges. They do not have assurance, because they do not ask for it; they do not ask because they are taught that it does not belong to Christians of these days; whereas I know numbers whose salvation is written upon their hearts as it were with a sunbeam. They can rejoice in God their saviour, and give men and devils the challenge to separate them, if they can, from the love of God in Christ Jesus their Lord. Dear redeemer, enlighten all your followers to see their privileges, and never let them cease wrestling with you till you bless them, by assuring them of their eternal salvation.

Bath Town

Sunday, December 23. Sent to the minister of the place and had some conversation with him last night. Preached about noon to about a hundred people, which I found was an extraordinary congregation, there being seldom more than twenty at church. I felt the divine presence, and did not spare to tell my hearers that I thought God was angry with them because he had sent a famine of the word among them for a long while, and not given them a teaching priest. All seemed attentive to what was spoken. After the sermon, one poor woman came with a full heart, desiring my prayers. I asked her whether she had been convicted by the sermon, or whether she knew Christ; she answered that she had been seeking him for some time, but wanted to find a minister who had understanding in divine things. This case is not uncommon.

Newborn Town

Tuesday, December 25. Went to public worship, and received the holy sacrament, which was celebrated in the Court House; but mourned much in spirit to see in what an indifferent manner everything was carried on. I cried mightily to the Lord in my secret devotions, and in the afternoon when I read prayers and preached he was pleased to show that he had heard me, for I scarcely know when we have had a more visible manifestation of the divine presence since our coming to America. The people were uncommonly attentive, and most were melted into tears. After the sermon, a poor woman with a heart full of concern ran to me desiring that I would come and preach where she lived, and another told me I had given him a home stroke. The woman where we lodged would take nothing for our Christmas dinner, and wished we could stay with them longer.

Soon after the evening service I and my friends took horse, rode about eight miles and were entertained by a German who kept an inn, and who had been one of my hearers. The people of that nation (as far as I can tell) are the most industrious as well as serious people that ever came into America. Wrote this morning to the minister of Newborn, who I heard countenanced a dancing master, by allowing his own son to be one of his learners. Several of the inhabitants, I was informed, had subscribed to his assemblies, and they were generally attended with ill consequences, which made me the more desirous to leave my testimony against them. It grieves me to find that in every little town there is a settled dancing master, but scarcely anywhere a settled minister to be met with; such a proceeding must be of dreadful consequence to *any*, especially a *newly settled* province. All Governors, if it were only from a human policy, ought to put a stop to it; for such entertainments altogether enervate the minds of people, imperceptibly leading them into effeminacy, and unfitting them to endure those hardships and fatigues which must necessarily be undergone to bring any province to perfection. True religion alone exalts a nation; such sinful entertainments are a reproach, and will in time be the ruin of any people.

Thursday, December 27. A young man welcomed me to America who, upon enquiry, I found had been one of my parishioners at Savannah; this gave me an immediate opportunity of falling into religious conversation, and afterwards I went, as my usual custom is, among the negroes belonging to the house. One man was sick in bed, and two of his children said their prayers after me very well. This more and more convinces me that negro children, if early brought up in the nurture and admonition of the Lord, would become as proficient as any white people's children. I do not despair, if God spares my life, of seeing a school of young negroes singing the praises of him who made them, in a psalm of thanksgiving. Lord, you have put into my heart a good design to educate them; I do not doubt you will enable me to bring it to good effect.

South Carolina

Tuesday, January 1, 1740. About sunset, we came to a tavern five miles within the province of South Carolina. Here I immediately perceived the people were more polite than those we generally met with; but I believe the people of the house wished I had not come to be their guest that night; for, it being New Year's Day, several of the neighbours were met together to divert themselves by dancing country dances. By the advice of my companions, I went in amongst them whilst a woman was dancing a jig. When I first went in I endeavoured to show the folly of such entertainments, and to convince her how well pleased the devil was at every step she took. For some time she endeavoured to outbrave me; neither the fiddler nor she desisted; but at last she gave over, and the musician laid aside his instrument. It would have made anyone smile to see how the rest of the company, one by one, attacked me and brought, as they thought, arguments to support their wantonness; but Christ triumphed over Satan. All were soon put to silence, and were for some time so overawed that after I had talked with them on the nature of baptism and the necessity of being born again in order to enjoy the kingdom of heaven, I baptised, at their entreaty, one of their children, and prayed afterwards as I was enabled, and as the circumstances of the company required. I and my companions then took a little refreshment; but the people were so bent on their pleasure that notwithstanding all that had been said, after I had gone to bed I heard their music and dancing, which made me look back upon my own past follies with shame and confusion of face; for such a one, not long since, was I myself. Lord, for your mercies' sake, show all unhappy formalists the same favour, and do not allow them to go in such an unspiritual complacency till they lift up their eyes in torment! Draw them O draw them from feeding upon such husks. Let them know what it is to feast upon the fatted calf, even the comforts of the blessed Spirit. Amen.

Wednesday, January 2. Rose very early, prayed, sang a hymn, and gave a sharp reproof to the dancers, who were very attentive and took it in good part. At break of day, we mounted our horses and, I think, never had a more pleasant journey. For nearly twenty miles we rode over a beautiful bay as plain as a terrace walk, and as we passed along were wonderfully delighted to see the porpoises taking their pastime, and hear, as it were, shore resounding to shore with the praises of him who has set bounds to the sea that it cannot pass, and has said, 'Here your proud waves will be held back.' At night we intended to call at a gentleman's house, where we had been recommended, about forty miles distant from our last night's lodging; but the moon being totally eclipsed, we missed the path that turned out of the road and then thought it most advisable, as we were on the main road, to go on our way, trusting to the Almighty to strengthen both our beasts and us. We had not gone far when we saw a light. Two of my friends went up to it, and found a hut full of negroes; they enquired after the gentleman's house to which we had been directed, but the negroes seemed surprised, and said they knew no such man, and that they were newcomers. From these circumstances, one of my friends inferred that these negroes might be some of those who had recently made an insurrection in the province, and had run away from their masters. When he returned, we were all of his mind, and therefore thought it best to mend our pace. Soon after, we saw another great fire near the roadside, and imagining there was another nest of such negroes, we made a circuit into the woods, and one of my friends at a distance observed them dancing round the fire. The moon shining brightly, we soon found our way onto the main road again; and after we had gone about a dozen miles (expecting to find negroes in every place) we came to a great plantation, the master of which gave us lodging, and our beasts provender. Upon our relating the circumstances of our travels, he satisfied us concerning the negroes, informed us whose they were, and upon what occasion they were in those places in which we found them. This afforded us much comfort, after we had ridden nearly sixty miles, and as we thought in great peril of our lives. Blessed be your name, O Lord, for this and all your other mercies, through Jesus Christ!

Charleston

Sunday, January 6. Went to public service in the morning, but did not preach, because the curate had no authority to lend the pulpit unless the Commissary (then out of town) were present. Most of the town, however, being eager to hear me, I preached in the afternoon in one of the Dissenting meeting-houses, but was grieved to find so little concern in the congregation. The audience was large, but very polite. I question whether the court-end of London could exceed them in affected finery, gaiety of dress, and a deportment ill becoming persons who have had such divine judgements recently sent amongst them. I reminded them of this in my sermon; but I seemed to them as one that mocked. This made me more importunate in secret prayer, and I hoped God would let me see that he intended to visit the inhabitants with mercy as well as with judgements; for nothing is a greater sign of a people's being hardened, than their continuing unreformed under divine visitations.

Monday, January 7. Finding the inhabitants desirous to hear me a second time, I preached at the French church at 11 in the morning, and blessed be God I saw a glorious alteration in the audience, which was so large that many stood outside the door. I felt much more freedom than I did yesterday. Many were melted into tears. One of the town, most remarkably gay, was observed to weep. Instead of the people going out (as they did yesterday) in a light, unthinking manner, a visible concern was put in most of their faces.

Beaufort in Port Royal

Tuesday, January 8. Got up a good while before day, left our horses in Charleston, and set out for Georgia in an open canoe (having five negroes to row and steer us), God being pleased to give us, for the most part, fair weather. The poor slaves were very civil, diligent and hard-working. We slept one night on the water; and about five on Wednesday evening arrived at Beaufort in Port Royal (100 miles from Charleston), within the province of South Carolina. We drank a little tea at our inn, and then went to see the Rev. Mr Jones, the minister of the place, who received us with great civility, and was very desirous that I should take a bed at his house, as I did when I passed through the place after I left Georgia last. But intending to set out by two in the morning, we thought it best to sleep at our inn.

Wednesday, January 9. The wind being very high, and sailing impracticable, we stayed at Beaufort all the morning, and dined with kind Mr Jones. Afterwards, the weather being fair, we took boat, and refreshed ourselves at a plantation on the way. In the night we made a fire on the shore and slept round it for about four hours. A little after midnight we prayed with the negroes, took boat again, and reached Savannah before noon the next day, where I had a joyful meeting with my dear friends.

Here I would stop, but I think it may not be amiss to put down some remarks which I have made on the state of religion in those provinces which I have recently passed through. And here I cannot but give Pennsylvania the preference. To me it seems to be the garden of America. Their oxen are strong to labour, and there seems to be no complaining in their streets. What is best of all, I believe they have left the Lord for their God. This I infer from their having so many faithful ministers sent out amongst them, and except Northampton in New England the work of conversion has not been carried on with so much power in any part of America, that I can hear of, as under the ministry of Messrs Tennents, Cross and the other labourers before mentioned. The constitution is far from being arbitrary; the soil is good, the land exceedingly fruitful, and there is a greater equality between the poor and rich than perhaps can be found in any other place in the known world. For my part, I like it so well that, God willing, I purpose taking up some land to erect a school for negroes, and settle some of my English friends, whose hearts God shall stir up or whom the fury of their enemies obliges to depart from their native land.

Philadelphia is one of the most regular planned towns I ever saw. Above seventy new houses were built in it last year, and it is likely to increase in inhabitants every day. It is rightly called Philadelphia, i.e. brotherly love, for by the charter all are permitted to worship God in their own way, without being branded as schismatics, dissenters, or disturbers of the established constitution. The Quakers have the pre-eminence in the government. The Assembly is made up of them, with the exception of about four, which prevents all preparations for military defence, it being one of their principles not to fight at all. Much of the simplicity of dress and manners which may be observed among the inhabitants is, I think, in great measure owing to them. I saw less of the pride of life in Pennsylvania than elsewhere. But it has happened to them as it will to all other religious societies when they flourish and have the upper hand. I mean that many, for profit's sake, have been known to dissemble with them. I fear numbers amongst them, as amongst us, can give no other reason why they are Quakers than that their fathers were so before them. I say this because I find little of divine power stirring amongst them; and most of them are too stiff and rigid about external things, I was credibly informed. One of their own preachers warned them lately of their backsliding, and told them that without a reformation God would remove the candlestick from them and work no more by their hands. In the city of Philadelphia they have two large meeting-houses, where they assemble frequently together; and all things considered are the most regular society of men I have seen or heard of. Besides this, there are Baptist and Presbyterian meetings. I had the pleasure of conversing with the ministers of both, and found there were some in their congregations, particularly in the Baptist, who loved the Lord Jesus in sincerity. The Church of England is at a low ebb in the province in general, and in Philadelphia in particular. In all the places that I passed through, the Presbyterians and Quakers had larger congregations than any of our missionaries; and we may guess that the love of many of the Church of England in Philadelphia must have grown cold, for the church, which was begun if I mistake not some years ago, is now far from being finished inside. Many of late, however, have been convinced what true Christianity is; and I hope a church of Jesus Christ will before long be selected out of the members of our own communion.

The little time I was in New York would not permit me to make as many observations of the situation of affairs of religion in the province as otherwise I might have done. A great complaint was made to me by some of the most religious inhabitants of it, that it was a very complacent place, and that a work of God had never been carried on in it since its first settlement. The heads of the Church of England seemed resolved to shut out the kingdom of God from amongst them; but our Lord Jesus has been pleased to get himself the victory; for though I was mostly opposed in New York, yet if I may judge of what I saw myself, and have heard since my departure, as much if not more good has been done there than in any other place in so short a time.

In Maryland religion seems to be at a very low ebb. There are Roman Catholics in some parts, four congregations of Presbyterians, and a few Quakers; but by far the greatest part call themselves Church of England, which might no doubt greatly flourish were her ministers found faithful. But the government, I fear, spoils them by giving them too much tobacco; for some, I hear, have thirty thousand, others fifty thousand, and others sixty thousand pounds of tobacco a year. It is gathered by the High Sheriff of the county, and every person taxable is obliged to pay forty pounds of tobacco yearly to the ministers, though great numbers never hear or see them.

In Virginia matters are not so bad. The ministers' stipends are not so large; the Commissary seems to have more power, and to exercise more discipline; but almost all are quite settled upon their lees. In Virginia there are no Dissenters from the established church except one or two meetings of Quakers. The importation of so many negroes and convicts is one great reason why there is so little religion to be seen; but the main cause of irreligion, both in Virginia and Maryland, I take to be their not incorporating into towns; for round here people living at a distance from the church are apt to make every little thing serve as an excuse to keep them from public worship. Whilst in this condition, religious societies cannot well be settled, and without control wicked men may more easily revel and get drunk. Ministers, even if they wanted to, cannot visit from house to house; and, what is as bad as anything, schools for the education of children cannot be so conveniently erected when the houses are so far apart. The greatest probability of doing good in Virginia is among the Scots-Irish who have recently settled in the mountainous parts of that province. They raise little or no tobacco, but things that are useful for common life. I hear the Governor has given leave for a minister of their own religious persuasion to come whenever he can be procured.

In North Carolina there is scarcely so much as the form of religion. Two churches were begun some time ago, but neither is finished. There are several dancing masters, but scarcely one regular settled minister; so that in most places they have readers who read a sermon every Sunday to the people for which they pay five shillings a quarter of their currency, which is ten shillings sterling for one. However, the Governor, I hear, has made proposals to the Society for Propagating the Gospel in Foreign Parts to send missionaries. But I should rather that people had no minister than see such as are generally sent over; and I cannot see the charity of contributing towards sending out missionaries, unless greater care be taken in the choice of those who are sent. All the account most of them have given for some time is that they have baptised so many, and that so many have received the sacrament; and, on the whole, if it be asked why there is so little religion in the Church of England, it may be answered that the missionaries for the most part set very bad examples. In South Carolina they have many ministers, both of our own and other persuasions; but I hear of no stirring among the dry bones. Mr Garden, the present Commissary, is strict in the outward discipline of the church.

And now I am come to Georgia, what shall I say? Many of the inhabitants have left it since we were here last; but I hope these blessings are in reserve. Oh that all who remain would acquaint themselves with God, and be at peace with him; then would they be more than conquerors over all their enemies.

Thus have I put down a few thoughts that have occurred to my mind. May God enlighten me where I am in the dark, correct me wherever I am wrong, and bless this further account of his dealings with me to all who shall read it. Amen.

Sixth Journal

*A Continuation
of the Reverend Mr Whitefield's Journal
after his arrival at Georgia
to a few days after his second return there from
Philadelphia
(January 1740—June 1740)*

Savannah

Friday, January 11, 1740. Went this morning with some friends to view a tract of land consisting of five hundred acres which Mr Habersham, whom I left schoolmaster of Savannah, was directed, I hope by providence, to choose for the Orphan House. It is situated on the northern part of the colony, about ten miles from Savannah, and has various kinds of soil in it; a part of it very good. Some acres, through the diligence of my friend, are cleared. He has also stocked it with cattle and poultry. He has begun the fence, and built a hut, which will greatly forward the work. I choose to have it so far off the town, because the children will be more free from bad examples, and can more conveniently go up on the land to work. For it is my design to have each of the children taught to labour, so as to be qualified to get their own living. Lord, teach and excite them to labour also for that meat which endures to everlasting life!

Thursday, January 24. Went this morning and took possession of my lot. I called it Bethesda, that is, the House of Mercy, for I hope many acts of mercy will be shown there, and that many will thereby be stirred up to praise the Lord, as a God whose mercy endures for ever.

Tuesday, January 29. Took in three German orphans, the most pitiful objects, I think, I ever saw. No new negroes could look more despicable, or require more pains to instruct them. They have been used to exceedingly hard labour, and though supplied with provisions from trustees, were treated in a manner unbecoming even heathens. Were all the money I have collected to be spent in freeing these three children from slavery, it would be well laid out. I have also in my house about twenty more who, in all probability, if not taken in, would be as ignorant of God and Christ as the Indians. Blessed be God, they begin to live in order. Continue this, and all other blessings to them, for your mercies' sake, O Lord.

Today I began the cotton manufacture, and agreed with a woman to teach the little ones to spin and card. I find annual cotton grows fairly well in Georgia; and to encourage the people, I bought today three hundred pounds weight, and have agreed to take all the cotton, hemp and flax that is produced the following year through the whole province. Though there are fewer inhabitants in Savannah, yet I think they are in a better situation than when I was here last. They now live independent of any public store. Provisions (flour especially) are much cheaper, cattle more plentiful; and if any manufacturer can be raised among themselves, to prevent them exporting so much money, they may yet do well.

Wednesday, January 30. Went with the carpenter and surveyor, and laid out the ground on which the Orphan House is to be built. It is to be sixty feet long and forty wide. The foundation is to be brick, and is to be sunk four feet within, and raised three feet above the ground. The house is to be two storeys high, with a hip roof: the first ten, the second nine feet high. In all, there will be about twenty commodious rooms. Behind are to be two small houses, one for an infirmary, the other for a work-house. There is also to be a still-house for the apothecary; and, I trust, before my return to England I shall see the children and family quite settled. I find it will be an expensive work; but it is for the Lord Christ. He will take care to defray all charges. The money that will be spent, on this occasion, will keep many families from leaving the colony, and in all probability bring many others over. There are nearly thirty working at the plantation already, and I would employ as many more, if they were to be had. Whatever is done for God ought to be done speedily, as well as with all our might.

Monday, February 11. Took in four fresh orphans, and set out with two friends to Frederica in order to fetch the orphans in the southern parts of the colony.

Frederica

Monday, February 18. Got up this morning by one o'clock. Took boat in order to go to St Andrews; but the rudder breaking, we were obliged to go back and desist from our intended voyage. Went to bed and slept for a few hours. Spent a good part of the day with the General. Received from him a bill of exchange for £150, which he advanced me in order to begin a church at Savannah. About seven o'clock, set off for Darien, where I had promised to return to take Mr MacLeod and the orphans with me to Savannah. The passage to that place takes generally about four hours; but the wind being contrary, we were obliged to come to a grappling, near an open reach, and did not get to Darien till the next day at noon. Mr MacLeod and his friends received us with joy, and finding me ill, advised me to lie down; by which I was much refreshed. Oh who can express the loving kindness of the Lord, or show all his praise!

Savannah

Thursday, February 28. Preached on Monday, and on

Tuesday settled a school both for grown persons and children at Darien, to the great satisfaction of the inhabitants. Set out with my friends and four orphans on Tuesday evening. Had pleasant weather. Slept two nights in the woods. Reached Bethesda about noon; and was pleased with the improvements that had been made there in my absence. Took horse and came home to my family at Savannah, who received me with love and joy. The people of the parish also rejoiced at my coming. They flocked to and seemed very attentive at public worship.

Charleston

Friday, March 14. Arrived last night at Charleston, being called there to see my brother, who has recently come from England and had brought a packet of letters from my dear friends. Blessed be God, his work goes on amongst them! Went to see the Commissary, with my brother and other companions, but met with a cool reception. After I had been there a little while, I told him I was informed he had some questions to propose to me, and that I had now come to give him all the satisfaction I could in answering them.

At this, I immediately perceived passion to arise in his heart. 'Yes, Sir,' he said, 'I have several questions to put to you. But', he added, 'you have got above us,' or something to that effect. Then he charged me with enthusiasm and pride, for speaking against the generality of the clergy, and desired I would make my charge good. I told him I thought I had already; though as yet I had scarcely begun with them. He then asked me wherein the clergy were so much to blame. I answered that they did not preach justification by faith alone; and upon talking with the Commissary I found he was as ignorant as the rest. He then sneered me with telling me of my modesty, expressed in my letter to the Bishop of Gloucester; charged me with breaking the Canons and ordination vow; and, even though I informed him I was ordained by letters dismissory from the Bishop of London, in a great rage he told me if I preached in any public church in that province he would suspend me. I replied I should take as much notice of that as I would of a Pope's bull. 'But Sir,' I said, 'why should you be offended at my speaking against the generality of the clergy? I always spoke well of you.'

'I might as well be offended', added my brother, 'at you saying the generality of people were notorious sinners, and come and accuse you of speaking evil of me because I was one of the people.' I further added, 'You did not behave thus when I was with you last.'

'No,' he said, 'but you did not speak against the clergy then.' I then said to him, 'If you will make an application to yourself, be pleased to let me ask you one question: Have you delivered your soul by exclaiming against the assemblies and balls here?'

'What,' said he, 'must you come to catechise me? No, I have not exclaimed against them; I think there is no harm in them.'

'Then, Sir,' I replied, 'I shall think it my duty to exclaim against you.'

'Then, Sir,' he said in a very great rage, 'get you out of my house.'

I and my friends took our leave, pitying the Commissary, who I really thought was more noble than to give such treatment. After this we went to public prayer, dined at a friend's house, drank tea with the Independent minister, and preached at four in the afternoon to a large audience in his meeting-house.

Saturday, March 15. Breakfasted, sang a hymn, and had some religious conversation on board my brother's ship. Preached in the Baptist meeting-house; and was much pleased when I heard afterwards that from the same pulpit a person not long ago had preached, who denied the doctrine of original sin, the divinity and righteousness of our Lord, and the operation of God's blessed Spirit upon the soul. I was led to show the utter inability of man to save himself, and absolute necessity of his dependence on the rich mercies and free grace of God in Christ Jesus for his restoration. Some, I observed, were put under concern; and most seemed willing to know whether those things were so. In the evening, I preached again in the Independent meeting-house to a more attentive audience than ever; and had the pleasure afterwards of finding that a gentlewoman whose whole family had been carried away for some time with deistical principles began now to be dislodged, and to see that there was no rest in such a scheme for a fallen creature to rely on. Lord Jesus, for your mercies' sake, reveal yourself in her heart, and make her willing to know the faith as it is in you. Amen.

Sunday, March 16. Preached at eight in the morning in the Scots' meeting-house, to a large congregation. Visited a sick person. Went to church and heard the Commissary represent me as the Pharisee who came to the temple saying, 'God, I thank you that I am not as other men are'; but whether I do what I do out of a principle of pride or duty, the searchers of hearts will discover before long, in front of men and angels. I was very sick and weak at dinner. Went to church again in the afternoon; and about five preached in the Independent meeting-house yard, the house being not capacious enough to hold the audience.

Monday, March 17. Preached in the morning in the Independent meeting-house, and was more explicit than ever in exclaiming against balls and assemblies. Preached again in the evening, and, being encouraged to do so by some of the inhabitants, I spoke on behalf of my poor orphans, and collected upwards of £70 sterling, the largest collection I have ever yet taken for that cause: a further sign to me that we shall yet see greater things in America, and that God will carry on and finish the work begun in his name at Georgia.

Savannah

Tuesday, March 25. Went to Bethesda, and with full

assurance of faith laid the first brick of the great house. The workmen attended, and with me kneeled down and prayed. After we had sung a hymn suitable to the occasion I gave a word of exhortation to the labourers, and bid them remember to work heartily, knowing that they worked for God. Much satisfaction seemed to be amongst them and, blessed be God's holy name, his work prospers much in our hands. Nearly twenty acres of land are cleared, and almost ready for planting. Two houses are already raised, and one nearly finished. All the timber of the great house is sawn, and most of it brought to the place where it is to be built. A good part of the foundation is dug, and many thousands of bricks ready for use. Nearly forty children are now under my care, and nearly a hundred mouths are daily supplied with food from our store. The expense is great, but our great and good God, I am persuaded, will enable me to defray it. As yet, I am kept from the least doubting. The more my family increases, the more enlargement and comfort I feel. And though what has been done hitherto, comparatively speaking, may be only like a grain of mustard seed, yet I believe it will in God's time take root and fill the land, and many poor distressed souls will come and lodge under the branches of it.

Sunday, March 30. Found myself very sick and weak in body, but was strengthened to go through most of the duties of the day, and to take an affectionate leave of my parishioners, because it appeared that providence called me northward. One woman, who had been a constant attender on the means of grace, and thought herself a Christian for many years, came to me acknowledging that she had been a self-deceiver, and knew nothing of the righteousness of, or true living faith in, Jesus Christ. A tradesman, of the same stamp, having felt the power of the doctrines of grace, sent me 17 volumes of Archbishop Tillotson's *Sermons*, of which he had been a great admirer, to do what I would with them. A captain of a ship, who had been a strong opposer of the truth, wrote and came to me under great convictions, confessing his sin, and desirous of being a true Christian.

Philadelphia

Tuesday, April 15. Paid my respects to the Governor and Proprietor. Went to the Commissary's house, who was not at home; but afterwards, speaking to him in the street, he told me that he could lend me his church no more because I had not treated the Bishop of London well, in my *Answer* to his late Pastoral Letter; and also, because I had misquoted and misrepresented Archbishop Tillotson, in a letter published in the last week's *Gazette*. I told him he had best show that in public. He replied that the printers would not publish anything for them, and that the press was shut against them. I answered that it was without my knowledge. Upon this we parted. In the afternoon I was much pressed in spirit to preach upon the blind beggar, to whom the scribes and Pharisees said, 'How dare you lecture us!' I stood upon a balcony on Society Hill, from which I preached my farewell sermon last fall. Towards the conclusion of my discourse I read to the people some extracts I had taken from Dr Edwards against Archbishop Tillotson's writings; and then appealed to them, where was the presumption in pretending to teach even *him*.

Abingdon and Philadelphia

Thursday, April 17. Rode last night after the sermon about eight miles. Slept at a friend's house, and preached this morning to about three or four thousand people at Abingdon, a district under the care of Mr Treat, a Presbyterian minister to whom God has been pleased recently to show mercy. He has been a preacher of the doctrines of grace for some years; but was deeply convinced when I was here last that he had not experienced them in his heart. Soon after I went away, he attempted to preach, but could not; he therefore told his congregation how miserably he had deceived both himself and them, and desired those who were gifted to pray for him. Ever since, he has continued to seek Jesus Christ, sorrowing, and is now under deep convictions, and a very humbling sense of sin. He preaches as usual, though he has not a full assurance of faith; because he said it was best to be found in the way of duty. I believe God is preparing him for great services, and I hope he will also be a means of awakening some dead, false-hearted preachers among the Dissenters, who hold the form of sound words but have never felt the power of them in their own souls.

German Town and Whitemarsh

Friday, April 18. Was employed for two hours this morning in giving answers to several who came to me under strong convictions; amongst whom was a negro or two, and a young girl of about fourteen years of age who was turned out of the house where she boarded because she wanted to hear me and would not learn to dance.

Philadelphia

Saturday, April 19. Was still much engaged in giving answers and praying with various persons who applied to me under deep convictions. Preached this morning and evening to seven or eight thousand people each time; and I was much rejoiced to see with what order and devotion they constantly attend. Scoffers seem to be at a stand what to say. They mutter in coffee houses, give a curse, drink a bowl of punch, and then cry out against me for not preaching up more morality. Poor men! where is the morality they so much boast of? If God judges them, as he certainly will do, by their morality, on which they so much rely, out of their own mouths will he condemn them. They say, but do not; and how can they, since they are ignorant of a living faith in Jesus Christ, which alone can enable us to do anything acceptable in the sight of God.

Sunday, April 20. Preached at seven o'clock, with much

freedom, to about ten thousand people, and collected
£110 sterling for my poor orphans. The people threw in
their mites willingly, and thereby reminded me much of
what God had done for me at Moorfields and Kennington
Common, when I was last in England. Went to church
morning and evening, and heard the Commissary preach
a sermon on justification by works, from James 2:18. Many
people seeing me go in, followed; and numbers of them
told me afterwards that the Commissary (though uninten-
tionally) had confirmed them in the truths which I had
delivered. In the evening, I preached from the same words
to about fifteen thousand people, and confuted the false
doctrines and many fundamental errors contained in the
Commissary's talk; for he all along took faith to be only an
assent to the truths of the gospel. He said, St Paul and St
James spoke of the same kind of justification; that works
mentioned by St Paul were only the works of the ceremo-
nial law; that the doctrine of an imputed righteousness
had done much harm, and hindered the conversion of the
heathen; and that we were to be justified by our works at
the last day, and consequently were to be justified in the
same manner now. To all these things I endeavoured to
answer distinctly.

Philadelphia

Tuesday, April 22. Preached both morning and evening to
rather larger congregations than I have yet seen on a
weekday. There were not less than ten thousand people.
When I came to take my farewell, being about to depart
for New York on the morrow, a great number wept sorely.
Many of the negroes were also much moved. Today I
bought five thousand acres of land on the forks of the
Delaware, and ordered a large house to be built thereon
for the instruction of these poor creatures. The land, I
hear, is exceedingly rich. It is a manor, and pays only a
white rose yearly for chief rent. I took up so much because
I intend settling some English friends there, when I come

next from England. I have called it Nazareth; and I trust in a few years the Lord will let us see much good come out of it. Amen, Lord Jesus, Amen.

Went in the evening to visit a young woman under deep convictions. She was struck down by the power of God's word on Sunday, and has continued, as Paul did, ever since sick in body, and under great agony of soul. I talked and prayed with her, and with about twenty more that came into the room.

Neshaminy

Wednesday, April 23. Reached Neshaminy near three in the afternoon, and preached to upwards of five thousand people in old Mr Tennent's meeting-house yard. When I got there, my body, through heat and labour, was so weak and faint that my knees were knocking, my face changed, and I was ready to drop down as soon as I had finished my prayer. But God was pleased to revive me. Great numbers were melted; and one in particular, who after the sermon came to me with tears, saying, 'You have brought me under deep convictions; what shall I do to be saved?' Upwards of fifty, I hear, have been lately convicted about this place. The Lord grant his arrows may stick fast in them till they have got a closing interest with Jesus Christ; for many, I find, receive the word with joy for a season, but having no root in themselves soon fall away. Lord, if it be your will, have mercy on these and such-like unhappy apostates, and let them be renewed again to repentance. Amen and Amen.

Montgomery and Shippack

Thursday, April 24. Was hospitably entertained with my friends last night at Montgomery, where the Dutch people live. It was seemingly a very wilderness part of the country but there were not less, I believe, than two thousand hearers. When I had done, Peter Bohler, a deacon of the Moravian church, a dear lover of our Lord Jesus Christ, preached to his countrymen in Dutch. Travelling and preaching in the sun again weakened me much and made me very sick; but by the divine assistance I took horse, rode 12 miles, and preached in the evening to about three thousand people at a Dutchman's plantations, who seemed to have drunk deeply of God's Holy Spirit. The German Brethren were exceedingly loving to me, and I spent the evening with many of them in a most agreeable manner. The order, seriousness, and devotion of these people in common life is most worthy of imitation. They prayed and sang in *their* language, but then God enlarged my heart to pray in *ours*.

Brunswick, Woodbridge, Elizabeth Town and New York

Monday, April 28. Underwent great conflicts in my soul last night and this morning. Wrote some letters to my dear English friends, who are continually upon my heart. Took a sorrowful leave of Captain Gladman, and my dear brother and fellow-traveller Mr Seward, whom I have despatched to England to bring me over a fellow-labourer, and to transact several affairs of importance. Captain Gladman has had the command of our sloop; but being obliged to despatch him on business to England, I have now committed the care of it to his mate, whom God was pleased to bring home to himself when I was last at Philadelphia. Not long since he was an abandoned prodigal, and ringleader in vice; but God struck him to the heart. Captain Gladman had prayed that God would send him a mate. This young man was strongly drawn to come and offer himself; the captain hired him; and now, I believe, he is a child of God.

Set out about eight in the morning, and reached Woodbridge by ten, where I preached to about two thousand people. Here again, my bodily strength was small; but God enabled me to speak home to many hearts, for many were moved. After the sermon I and my friends dined at the Dissenting minister's house, who invited me to preach; and then we hastened to Elizabeth Town, where the people had been waiting for some hours. I preached in the meeting-house, as when I was there last. It was full, and was supposed to contain two thousand people. Ten Dissenting ministers were present, and two church ministers; but they did not tarry very long. God gave me much freedom of speech. I dealt very plainly with the Presbyterian clergy, many of whom, I am persuaded, preach the doctrines of grace to others without being converted themselves. No doubt, some were offended: but I care not for any sect or party of men. As I love all who love the Lord Jesus, of whatever communion, so I reprove all, whether Dissenters or not Dissenters, who take his word into their mouths but never felt him dwelling in their hearts.

New York

Tuesday, April 29. I met with Mr William Tennent, who refreshed my heart by telling me what the Lord was doing for numbers of souls in the Highlands, where he has recently been. Surely Jesus Christ is getting himself the victory indeed! About five in the evening I preached on the common to five or six thousand people, but observed no scoffers, as there were when I was here last. The people were still and quiet after I began; and though I did not perceive much power in the congregation, yet God enabled me to speak with all boldness. Oh that I may never be ashamed of Christ or of his gospel; for it has been the power of God to my salvation. O grace! grace!

Wednesday, April 30. Preached this morning from a scaffold erected for that purpose, to a somewhat less congregation than last night, but with much greater power; for towards the conclusion of my talk God's Spirit came upon the preacher and the people, so that they were melted down exceedingly. Afterwards I began to collect money from private hands for my orphans, and met with success. Blessed be God, who has the hearts of all men in his hands. Dined at Mr P.'s, but was obliged to retire as soon as dinner was over, for my body was weak, and my soul was in an unspeakable agony for near an hour. At length I dropped asleep, but rose about five in the evening and preached to upwards of seven thousand people on our Lord's temptations.

Thursday, May 1. I received another packet of letters from Charleston and Savannah, amongst which were two or three from my little orphans. I preached in the evening at New York to as large a congregation as ever; but my spirits being exhausted, I preached, as I thought, only heavily. But I have been too apt to build on my frame of mind, and think I do no good or do not please God only because I do not please myself; for I have often found that my seemingly less powerful talks have been much owned by God. I find it absolutely necessary that gospel ministers and hearers may know themselves to be but men.

Friday, May 2. Preached twice in the field, and once in the meeting-house; and was agreeably refreshed in the evening with one Mr Davenport whom God has recently highly honoured by making use of his ministry for the conversion of many at the east end of Long Island. He is looked upon as an enthusiast and a madman by many of his reverend pharisaical brethren; and as far as I can tell there is as great an enmity against the work of God in the hearts of most even of the Dissenters (though they preach the doctrines of grace) as there is in our clergy, who for the generality entirely disown them.

Philadelphia

Thursday, May 8. Had what my body much wanted, a thorough night's repose. Was called up early in the morning, as I always am, to speak to poor souls under convictions. The first who came was an Indian trader whom God was pleased to bring home by my preaching when here last. He is just come from the Indian nation, where he had been praying with and exhorting all he met who were willing to hear. He has hopes of some of the Indians, but his fellow traders endeavoured to prejudice them against him. However, he proposes to visit them again in the autumn, and I humbly hope the Lord will open a door amongst the poor heathen. The conversion of one of their traders I take to be one great step towards it.

I conversed also with a poor negro woman who has been visited in a very remarkable manner. God was pleased to convert her by my preaching last autumn; but suffering dejection on Sunday morning she prayed that salvation might come to her heart, and that the Lord would be pleased to reveal himself to her that day. Whilst she was at meeting, hearing Mr M., a Baptist preacher, the word came with such power to her heart that at last she was obliged to cry out, and a great concern fell upon many in the congregation. The minister stopped, and several persuaded her to hold her peace; but she could not help praising and blessing God. Many since this have called her mad, and said she was full of new wine; but the account she gave me was rational and solid, and I believe in that hour the Lord Jesus took a great possession of her soul. Such cases, indeed, have not been very common, but when an extraordinary work is being carried on, God generally reveals himself to some souls in this extraordinary manner. I do not doubt that when the poor negroes are to be called God will highly favour them to wipe off their reproach and show that he is no respecter of persons, but that whoever believes in him will be saved.

Friday, May 9. Agreed to build my Negro Schools on the land which I have recently purchased. Preached in the evening, and afterwards began a Society of young men, many of whom I trust will prove good soldiers of Jesus Christ. Amen.

Saturday, May 10. Though God has shown me great things already in this place, yet today I have seen greater. I preached twice, and to larger congregations than ever. In the evening I went to settle a Society of young women who, I hope, will prove wise virgins. As soon as I entered the room and heard them singing, my soul was delighted. When the hymn was over I desired to pray before I began to converse; but my soul was so carried out that I had no time to talk at all. A wonderful power was in the room, and with one accord they began to cry out and weep most bitterly for half an hour. They seemed to be under the strongest convictions, and did indeed seek Jesus sorrowing. Their cries might be heard a great way off. When I had done, I thought it right to leave them at their devotions. They continued in prayer for over an hour, confessing their most secret faults; and at length the agonies of some were so strong that five of them seemed affected as those who are in fits. The present captain of our sloop going near the waterside was called in to a group almost in the same circumstances, and at midnight I was desired to come to one who was in strong agonies of body and mind but felt something of joy and peace, after I had prayed with her several times. Her case reminded me of the young man whom the devil tore when he was coming to Jesus. Such-like bodily agonies, I believe, are from the devil; and now the work of God is going on he will, no doubt, endeavour by *these* to bring an evil report upon it. O Lord, for your mercy's sake rebuke him; and though he may be permitted to bite your people's heel, fulfil your promise and let the seed of the woman bruise his head! Amen, Amen!

Sunday, May 11. Preached to about fifteen thousand people in the morning. Went twice to church, and heard myself taken to task by the Commissary, who preached from these words: 'I bear them record, they have a zeal for God, but not according to knowledge.' I could have wished he had considered the next words: 'For they being ignorant of God's righteousness, have not submitted themselves to the righteousness of God.' Had he considered these words, I might justly have said, 'Does Mr Commissary speak of this false zeal in reference to himself, or of some other man?' He exclaimed loudly against me in the pulpit, and, I soon found, obliged many of his hearers to do what they were before inclined to do, namely, resolve to leave me entirely. I bear him record that experience will soon convince him that whatever mine may be, his own zeal is by no means according to knowledge. After he had done, I preached my farewell sermon to very near twenty thousand hearers. Though the Commissary's sermon was chiefly of personal reflections, I thought it not right to render railing for railing. However, I considered it my duty in an especial manner to commend the Messrs Tennents and their associates, being most worthy preachers of our Lord Jesus.

About fifty negroes came to give me thanks for what God had done to their souls. How heartily did those poor creatures throw in their mites for my poor orphans! Some of them have been effectually wrought upon, and in an uncommon manner. Many of them have begun to learn to read. One, who was free, said she would give me her two children, whenever I settle my school. I believe masters and mistresses will shortly see that Christianity will not make their negroes worse slaves. I intended, had time permitted, to have settled a Society for negro men and negro women, but that must be deferred till it shall please God to bring me to Philadelphia again. I never saw a more general awakening in any place. Religion is all the talk; and I think I can say the Lord Jesus has got himself the victory in many hearts. I have scarcely had time to eat bread from morning to evening; someone or other was generally applying to me under deep soul-concern, and others continually pressing upon me to baptise their infants. I did comply with as many as I could, but I was obliged sometimes to say, 'The Lord sent me not to baptise, but to preach the gospel.'

Many of the Quakers have been convinced of the righteousness of Jesus Christ, and openly confess the truth as it is in Jesus; for which, I believe, they will shortly be put out of their synagogues. Some of their head men are zealous against me, and are much afraid their foundation will be sadly shaken. Great numbers of the inhabitants would have built me instantly a very large church, if I had consented; but the Lord, I am persuaded, would have his gospel preached in the fields, and building a church would, I fear, imperceptibly lead the people into bigotry and make them place the church again, as they have done for a long time, in the church walls. For these reasons I declined it; though even so, I believe they will build some place. What I mostly fear is, now there is such a general awakening, the people will not know where to go for proper food, and thereby fall into different sects and parties.

With preaching, and praying, and conversing, I was truly weary by eight at night, but I went and baptised two children; took my leave of both the Societies; and I had not prayed long in the women's Society before two of them fell down in violent fits, so that I was obliged to leave them.

Derby, Chester, and Wilmington

Monday, May 12. Got up early to answer those who came for private advice. Visited three persons, one of whom was under such deep convictions that she had taken scarcely anything to eat for a fortnight. Another had a prospect of hell set before her last night in the most terrifying colours; but before morning received comfort. When I came to my lodgings, many friends were waiting to accompany me on horseback, and great numbers of the common people were crowding about the door. About nine I left Philadelphia, and when I came to the ferry was told that people had been crossing over as fast as two boats could carry them ever since three in the morning. After we had waited some time, I and my friends got over, and I preached at Derby, seven miles from Philadelphia, to about four thousand, and collected there and at Derby upwards of £40 for my orphans. Here I parted with more friends; but several went with me to Wilmington, fifteen miles from Chester. We got in about 11 at night. My body was weak; but God strengthened me to pray, to sing psalms and to exhort a roomful of people for about an hour. At this place I stayed at a Quaker's house for the night.

Wilmington and Whiteclay Creek

Tuesday, May 13. In the morning, preached at Wilmington to five thousand; and at Whiteclay Creek, about ten miles distant, in the evening to three thousand. The word, I believe, was both like a fire and a hammer; for many were melted, and one cried out most bitterly, as in great agonies of soul. At both places we collected about £24 for the Orphan House, and the people were very solicitous for me to bring our sloop up their Creek the next time I came, that they might put in provisions. Never did I see a more plentiful country than Pennsylvania. I have seen but very few poor objects since my arrival. Almost everyone enjoys peace and plenty. The rich do not swallow up the poor, as in other provinces; but there seems to be a proper balance.

Nottingham

Wednesday, May 14. Preached at Nottingham, both morning and evening, with such demonstration of the Spirit and such a wonderful movement amongst the hearers as few ever saw before. It surprised me to see such a multitude gathered together at so short a notice, and in such a desert place. I believe there were about twelve thousand. I had not spoken long before I perceived numbers melting. As I proceeded, the influence increased till at last (both in the morning and the afternoon) thousands cried out, so that they almost drowned my voice. Never did I see a more glorious sight. Oh what tears were shed and poured out after the Lord Jesus. Some fainted; and when they had got a little strength they would hear and faint again. Others cried out in a manner as if they were in the sharpest agonies of death. Oh what thoughts and words did God put into my heart!

Fagg's Manor

Thursday, May 15. Preached at Fagg's Manor, three miles
from Mr Blair's house, where he had earnestly invited me
to come. The congregation was about as large as that at
Nottingham. As great, if not a greater commotion was in
the hearts of the people. Most were drowned in tears. The
word was sharper than a two-edged sword. The bitter cries
and groans were enough to pierce the hardest heart. Some
of the people were as pale as death; others were wringing
their hands; others lying on the ground; others sinking into
the arms of friends; and most lifting up their eyes to heaven
and crying to God for mercy. I could think of nothing,
when I looked upon them, so much as the Great Day. They
seemed like people awakened by the last trump, and coming out of their graves to judgement. One would imagine
none could have withstood the power, or avoided crying
out, 'Surely God is in this place'; yet Mr E., a Dissenting
minister, a virulent opposer of Mr Tennent and his brethren, after the sermon was over, whilst thousands were
under the deepest distress of soul, came desiring to have a
public disputation. I told him I was going to Newcastle, and
that the place we were now in was not proper to dispute in.
But he thinking that was only to evade the trial, I desired
him to begin, and I would answer such questions as he
should propose. He then charged me with saying that those
who only had a faith of adherence were in a damnable condition. I answered that such a thing never entered my
thoughts. I only said that a faith of adherence was not to be
rested in, but that all should ask for, and labour after, a
full assurance of faith. He then quoted a passage from
Isaiah 1:10 to prove that a person might be in Christ, and
yet not know it. I told him that if he were a spiritual person
he would have known that there was a time when God
withdraws his felt presence from a believer's soul, and yet
that soul may even then be kept from doubting of his
interest in Christ. He was about to quote some other

passage of scripture, but by this time the people were exasperated, and one cried out in haste that he would take Mr E. out of the place. For this I rebuked him, telling him that was not the Spirit of Christ, and at the same time blamed Mr E. for coming at such an inappropriate time to dispute, when he saw the power of God so obviously amongst us. I also told him that if he had any objections to make, I would answer them as I rode to Newcastle, or in a letter, if he would send them on to me. At this he seemed somewhat aware of his fault, and said he thought it was best to withdraw.

On board the Savannah

Friday, May 16. Got up by break of day, parted with two more friends, and put my things and little family in order as soon as I could. Was pleasantly surprised to see the variety and quantity of provisions and sea-stores which had been sent on board by Philadelphia people. I found that in goods and money I had received about £500 sterling. Blessed be the Lord God of Israel, who alone brings mighty things to pass. I am now going to make one addition to my family, of half a dozen persons, a bricklayer, a tailor, two maidservants, two little girls whose father kept a dancing school, assembly and concert room in Philadelphia. Their mother, I believe, had a work of grace in her heart, was well-bred, and much concerned for some time at the business in which her husband was engaged. When last at Philadelphia, I did what I could, but now God opened Mr Seward's heart to relieve the parents. I took these two children, and an end will entirely be put to the assembly, etc., at least in that house. It is a shame they should be permitted in any Christian country. They enervate people's minds, unfit them for business, as well as religion, and grieve the Holy Spirit exceedingly.

Monday, May 19. Was much refreshed today by reading the *Journal* of an Indian trader, mentioned a little before, and could not help thinking that God would open a door for preaching the gospel among the Alleghanian Indians. Being much pressed in spirit to do so, I wrote them a letter in which I laid down the principles of our holy religion, told them the promises of the gospel that had especial reference to them, and cautioned them against such things as I thought might be a hindrance to their embracing Christianity. The Head or Chief of them is well inclined, and the white people thereabouts have heard of me and have got my sermons. Who knows but God may now begin to give his Son the heathen for his inheritance, and the uttermost parts of the earth for his possession. This trader, I really believe, is called of God, and God never sends any of his servants on a needless errand.

Lewis Town

Friday, May 23. Came this morning to Old Kilroad, and dropped anchor, the wind being contrary. Went ashore at Lewis Town, read prayers and preached in the church to a small and unmoved congregation. The minister hearing our sloop was coming, stayed to give me the meeting. I quickly found he was one of those who subscribed to the Articles of the Church of England in his own sense. He inveighed bitterly against the doctrines of grace in private, but seemed struck dumb after he heard me speak in public, for he did not open his lips about the doctrines afterwards. Oh how divine truths make their own way, when attended by divine power! They either convict or confound gain-sayers. I think the Church of England is by no means beholden to Bishop Burnet for his *Exposition* of her Articles. He has opened a door for the most detestable equivocation; and, were it possible for the compilers of our Articles to rise again from the dead, I am persuaded they would insist on their being taken in the grammatical sense. They cannot, in my opinion, admit of a two-fold interpretation.

Sunday, May 25. Preached twice from a balcony to about two thousand, the church not being capable of holding them. In the evening, talking about Abraham's faith, a great many, and some even of the most polite, wept much; but alas, when I came to turn from the creature to the Creator, and to talk of God's love in sacrificing his only begotten Son Jesus Christ, their tears, I observed, dried up. I told them of it. We can weep at the sufferings of a martyr, a man like ourselves; but when are we moved by the relation of the sufferings of the Son of God? Pascal, I have been informed, always wept when he read of our dear Lord's passion. Though weeping may not always be a sign of grace, yet I think it is an evidence of the hardness of our hearts and a lack of a due sense of sin, when we can remain unmoved at the account of the sufferings of a dying saviour.

Savannah

Friday, June 6. Blessed be the God of all grace, who continues to do for me marvellous things. Today I hope salvation is come to many in my house. Long have I interceded for poor Savannah. Strong wrestlings have I had with God, time after time, both in public and private, on behalf of the inhabitants; and tonight God has most remarkably answered my requests. About four, I prayed earnestly, and particularly for my friends, who were in the room with me. Many came into the passage near us and wept much before the Lord, deeply labouring in their souls. After this, I went up and prayed for half an hour with some of the women of the house, and three girls who seemed to be weary with the weight of their sins. But when we came to public prayer, the Holy Spirit seemed to come into the congregation like a mighty rushing wind, carrying all before it. I had not long begun before several young men and maidens, old men and children, were all dissolved in tears, and mourning after Jesus. I believe there were scarcely half a dozen in the whole congregation who were not deeply affected. I never saw the like before. Being come home, I laid myself upon the bed, weak in body, and astonished at the power of God; but finding so many people came up in such a condition, I rose from bed and betook myself to prayer again. This continued for nearly an hour, till at last, finding their concern rather increase than abate, I desired all to retire. I was delighted afterwards, to hear some praying most earnestly to God in every corner of the house, and it surprised me to hear what a spirit of supplication was put into the hearts of some of the boys and girls.

Our affairs are now carried on with decency and order, and I believe Savannah will yet become the joy of the earth. Before long, I trust, the Lord will take it into his own hands, and then the curse which has hitherto been lying on it will be taken off. I am beginning to build a church, and when matters are brought to a sufficient extremity, then, I believe, will be the Lord's opportunity to save and deliver us. He seems to be purging the province apace. The children are industrious. We have now in the house about one hundred yards of cloth spun and woven. We have several tradesmen belonging to the House, many cattle on our plantation, and I hope before long we shall live amongst ourselves. There are several masters set over the children, who watch over them, both in and after school hours. Generally once a day, if I do not, they walk with their respective charges, tell them of the glory of God in creation, and praise him by singing a hymn.

Seventh Journal

*A Continuation
of the Reverend Mr Whitefield's Journal
from a few days after his return to Georgia
to his arrival at Falmouth
on the 11th of March, 1741
containing an account of the work of God at
Georgia, Rhode Island, New England, New York,
Pennsylvania, and South Carolina*

Ebenezer

Wednesday, June 25, 1740. Went on Monday to, and
returned this evening from, Ebenezer, which I have seen
with no small satisfaction. Surely there is a difference, even
in this life, between those that serve the Lord and those
that do not. All other places of the colony seem to be like
Egypt, where was darkness, but Ebenezer, like the land of
Goshen, where there was great light. For about four miles
I walked in one almost continuous field, with a most plentiful crop of corn, pease, potatoes, etc., growing upon it, all
the product of a few months' labour. But God blesses the
labourers; they are unanimous; the strong help the weak,
and all seem hearty for the common good. In a few years I
believe the people from Salzburg will be a flourishing
people. Their land is good, and lies very near the river.

They already provide food, and before long will be capable of providing clothing for themselves. I shall send them up cotton, spinning wheels, and a loom to begin a manufactory for themselves; and next year they hope their own land will produce enough flax, cotton, etc., to carry it on. I had communication with their ministers. Our sister Orphan House there is blessed by their means.

Beaufort in Port Royal

Tuesday, July 1. Went, as soon as it was light, to a relation of our fellow-travellers', and afterwards had some conversation with Mr Jones, the minister of the parish, about the great doctrines of the gospel. He received us with much tenderness and respect, but thought I went too far in condemning Archbishop Tillotson. I think the arguments I brought were conclusive, and the account my new convert (one of his parishioners) gave of God's dealing with his soul, rational and, as he confessed, satisfactory; but he could not see clearly into the doctrine of *free justification* without regard to anything foreseen in the creature. However, being more noble than most of his brethren, he was candid, courteous, and, even though he was in danger of incurring the Commissary's displeasure thereby, he read prayers and requested me to preach in the evening at his church. I preached, but to a small audience, there being but little notice given of it. After the sermon, Mr J. thanked me and, having promised to preach again, God willing, as I went back to Savannah, I took my leave.

Charleston and Ashley Ferry

Sunday, July 6. Preached twice yesterday and twice today, and had great reason to believe our Lord got himself the victory in some hearts. Went to church in the morning and afternoon, and heard the Commissary preach as virulent, unorthodox, and inconsistent a discourse as ever I heard in my life. His heart seemed full of choler and resentment; and, out of the abundance thereof, he poured out so many bitter words against the Methodists (as he called them) in general, and me in particular, that several who intended to receive the sacrament at his hands withdrew. Never, I believe, was such a preparation sermon preached before. I could not help thinking the preacher was of the same spirit as Bishop Gardiner in Queen Mary's days. After the sermon, he sent his clerk to desire me not to come to the sacrament till he had spoken with me. I immediately retired to my lodgings, rejoicing that I was accounted worthy to suffer this further degree of contempt for my dear Lord's sake. Blessed Jesus, lay it not to the Commissary's charge! Amen and Amen!

Wednesday, July 9. Found myself still weaker, but was strengthened to preach under a tree near Mr C.'s meeting-house, at ten in the morning, it being now too small to contain the congregation. People seemed to come from all parts, and the word came with convincing power. Having changed my linen (which I am obliged to do after every sermon, by reason of my prodigious sweating), I hastened to Charleston; but my body was so exceeding weak, and the sun shone so intensely hot, that five miles before I reached town I called in at a public house, and lay for a considerable time, almost breathless and dead. But God comforted me, and being strengthened in the inner man I once more set forward with my fellow-travellers, reached town about four, and preached at six in the usual place, with more freedom and power than could have been expected, considering the great weakness of my body. But I can do all things through Christ strengthening me. I thank you, holy Father, that I have so often the sentence of death within myself. Oh, let me be daily taught by it not to trust to myself in the least, but in you, the ever-living God.

Sunday, July 13. In the morning I went to church and heard the Commissary preach. Had some infernal spirit been sent to draw my picture, I think it scarcely possible that he could have painted me in more horrid colours. I think, if ever, then was the time that all manner of evil was spoken against me falsely for Christ's sake. The Commissary seemed to ransack church history for instances of enthusiasm and abused grace. He drew a parallel between me and all the Oliverians, Ranters, Quakers, French Prophets, till he came down to a family of the Dutarts, who lived not many years ago in South Carolina and were guilty of the most notorious incests and murders. To the honour of God's free grace be it spoken, whilst the Commissary was representing me thus I felt the blessed Spirit strengthening and refreshing my soul. God, at the same time, gave me to see what I was by nature, and how I had deserved his eternal wrath; and therefore I did not feel the least resentment against the preacher. No; I pitied, I prayed for him; and wished, from my soul, that the Lord would convert him as he once did the persecutor Saul, and let him know that it is Jesus whom he persecutes. In the evening many came, I was informed, to hear what I would say, but as the Commissary himself hinted that his sermons would be printed, and as they were full of invidious falsehood, I held my tongue and made little or no reply.

Saturday, July 19. Preached twice every day this week at Charleston, except on Wednesday and Thursday evening, the last of which days I was called upon to preach at the house of Madame W. This gentlewoman, as she informed me herself, was at one time much prejudiced against me, so much so that she thought it dangerous to come and hear me; but, having read my sermons, she changed her mind, and coming to hear me preach was, with her daughter and another gentlewoman, much melted down. Being given to hospitality, she provided food sufficient for a great multitude. People came from town and the neighbouring places. Her barn was put into proper order, and I read prayers and preached in it. A lovely melting was visible in several parts of the audience. After the sermon, God enabled me to speak many gospel truths amidst a polite set of people. At the request of Madame W., I stayed all night, which gave me an opportunity of teaching her family the way of God more perfectly, and also of resting my body, which seems to be declining more every day. Blessed be God, I hope it will not be long before worms destroy it, and my soul carried to see God.

Sunday, July 20. Preached in the morning as usual, and went afterwards to church to hear the Commissary. His text was, 'Consider carefully how you listen.' At first, I thought we should have a peaceable sermon, especially since we had conversed the night before so amicably; but the gall soon began to flow from his tongue, though not with such bitterness as last Sunday. He endeavoured to defend his legal proceedings, condemned all that followed me, and gave hopes of heaven to *all* who adhered to him and the church. In the evening (though I got up from my bed to do it, and was carried in a chaise) the Lord Jesus strengthened me to take my last farewell of the people of Charleston. Many seemed to sympathise with me.

Two or three Dissenting ministers, by my advice, agreed to set up a weekly lecture. I advised the people, since the gospel was not preached in the church, to go and hear it in the meeting-houses. May the Lord be with both ministers and people, and cause them to preach and hear as becomes the gospel of Christ. At my first coming, the people of Charleston seemed to be wholly devoted to pleasure. One person, well acquainted with their manners and circumstances, told me that they spent more on their polite entertainments than the amount raised by their rates for the poor. But now the jewellers and dancing-masters begin to cry out that their craft is in danger. A vast alteration is discernible in ladies' dresses; and some, while I have been speaking, have been so convinced of the sin of wearing jewels that I have seen them, with blushes, put their hands to their ears and cover them with their fans. But the reformation has gone further than externals. Several of the negroes did their work in less time than usual so that they might come to hear me, and many of the owners who have been awakened have resolved to teach them

Christianity. Had I time and proper schoolmasters, I might immediately erect a negro school in South Carolina, as well as in Pennsylvania. Almost every day something was sent for my orphans at Georgia. The people were very solicitous about my health, when they saw me so weak, and sent me many small presents. I sometimes feared they would be too hot against the Commissary, but I endeavoured to stop their resentment as much as possible, and recommended peace and moderation to them in most of my talks.

Savannah

Sunday, August 3. Last night, through weakness of body, just as I began family prayer, I was struck, as I thought, with death. I put up a few broken accents and breathed out, 'Lord Jesus, receive my spirit.' Though exceedingly weak, and I had almost laid aside thoughts of officiating today, yet, at Mr J.'s intimating that friends came expecting to hear me, I promised if I could to preach, and begged him to read prayers. He did, but I found myself so ill that I would fain have persuaded Mr T. to preach for me. He refused, urging that God would strengthen me if I began. Before I had prayed long, Mr B. dropped down as though shot with a gun. Afterwards he got up, and sat attentively to hear the sermon. The influence spread. The greatest part of the congregation were under great concern. Tears trickled down apace, and God manifested himself much amongst us at the sacrament.

Monday, August 4. Was sent for at noon to see Mr Jonathan B. At my coming, I found him under great concern and strong convictions of sin. He reflected much on his misspent life and blessed God for bringing him now to Savannah, and hoped that he might be found in Christ before he returned home. His wife sat by, weeping. Mr B. lay on a bed groaning in bitterness of soul, under a sense of guilt, and crying out for an interest in Jesus. I asked what caused him to fall down yesterday. He answered,

'The power of God's word.' After half an hour's conversation on the nature of the new birth, and the necessity of closing with Christ, I kneeled down, prayed with them, and took my leave, hoping the Lord would pluck them as brands from the burning. Amen and Amen.

Sunday, August 10. In the evening, when my friends were sitting together, I began to speak to them of the things of God. Their concern increased till many burst into tears, and one fell on the ground. Before I had done, some of my parishioners came up, and the rest of my family. When I had finished speaking to them from God, I spoke in prayer to God for them. My soul was carried, as it were, out of the body, and I wrestled with our Lord in prayer on their behalf. He did not let us go without a blessing. The room was filled with the cries of those around me, and many at that time sought Jesus sorrowing. The concern continued after the duty was over. A Cherokee Indian trader who was present desired to speak with me, saying, 'I never saw or felt anything like it before.'

Saturday, August 16. Parted with Mr B. and Mr B., on Tuesday, who, I hope, could say, 'Lord now let your servants depart in peace; for our eyes have seen, our hearts have felt, your salvation.' Several times this week I was obliged to come out through weakness of body, in the midst of our public worship. But, as troubles abounded, consolations abounded also.

Charleston

Monday, August 25. Being weak in body, I have preached only once each day (except on Sundays); but, I think, with greater success. I scarcely knew the time when I did not see a considerable melting in some part of the congregation, and after it spreads over the whole of it. Several times I was so weak before I began to preach that I thought it almost impossible for me to get through half the discourse; but the Lord brought life and light and supported me above measure. Out of weakness, I became strong. The audiences were more numerous than ever, and it was supposed that not less than four thousand were in and about the meeting-house when I preached my farewell sermon. The Commissary, having run his utmost length, thought it best to say no more. Finding, when I was here last, that Jesus Christ was not preached in the church, my conscience would not allow me to attend on those that preached there any more. I therefore went to the Baptist and Independent meeting-houses, where Jesus Christ was preached. I have administered the sacrament three times in a private house. Never did I see anything more solemn. The room was large, and most were in tears, as though they were weeping at their saviour's cross. Surely Christ crucified was set out before them. Many who were not receiving stood by, at their request, and they wept bitterly. I prayed for them all, and I hope the Lord will clothe them with the wedding garment. What was best, Baptists, church folks and Presbyterians all joined together and received according to the Church of England rite, except two who desired to have it sitting: I willingly complied, knowing that it was a thing quite immaterial.

Great, a very great alteration is made in the life and manners of several of the polite ladies. The rooms that were usually employed for balls and assemblies are now turned into society rooms. Every night, where I was invited to supper it became customary to have the house filled with company, with whom the Lord enabled me to pray and exhort.

Newport in Rhode Island

Sunday, September 14. Several gentlemen of the town soon came to pay their respects to me, amongst whom was Mr Clap, an aged Dissenting minister, and the most venerable man I ever saw in my life. He looked like a good old puritan, and gave me an idea of what stamp those men were who first settled in New England. His countenance was very heavenly, and he prayed most movingly for a blessing on my coming to Rhode Island.

In the evening, with him and some more friends, I went to see Mr H., the minister of the Church of England, and desired the use of his pulpit. At first he seemed a little unwilling, and wished to know what extraordinary call I had to preach on weekdays, which he said was 'disorderly'. At last, after he had withdrawn and consulted with the gentlemen, he said if my preaching would promote the glory of God and good of souls, I was welcome to his church as often as I would during my stay in town. We then agreed to make use of it at ten in the morning, and three in the afternoon. After this I went to see the Governor, who seemed to be a very plain man, and had a plain house. In belief he is a Seventh Day Baptist, and he is a man of good report as to his conduct and dealing with the world.

Monday, September 15. Breakfasted this morning with old Mr Clap, and was much edified with his conversation. I could not but think, whilst at his table, that I was sitting with one of the patriarchs. He is full of days; a bachelor, and has been minister of a congregation in Rhode Island upwards of forty years. People of all denominations respect him. He abounds in good works; gives all away, and is wonderfully tender of little children; many of different persuasions come to be instructed by him. At ten in the morning I read prayers and preached in the church. It is very commodious, and will contain three thousand people. It was more than filled in the afternoon, people of all denominations attending. God assisted me much.

Tuesday, September 16. When I came home to my lodgings, the woman of the house greeted me with 'Blessed are you of the Lord'. I looked round to see the reason of such a greeting, and found it on the couch, where there lay a young woman under great distress of soul. After a little conversation, I found she had a gracious discovery of the Lord Jesus made to her soul, when I was speaking from these words, 'Come, see a man who told me everything that I ever did.' She told me she had often grieved the Spirit of God, but now she believed the Lord was calling her home effectually. 'The word,' she added, 'came with such power that I was obliged to go out of the church, otherwise I would have disturbed the congregation. When I left home, contrary to my parents' inclinations, I insisted, I knew not why, on staying at Newport for six weeks. They wanted me to stay only a month, but at last consented that I should stay my own time. Tomorrow is the last day of the six weeks, and, oh, the goodness of God in sending you just now, before my time was up,' or words to that effect.

Afterwards, one or two more came under similar circumstances, crying out in the bitterness of their souls after the Lord Jesus. I prayed with each of them, and exhorted them not to rest till they found rest in Jesus Christ. In the evening I went, privately as I thought, to a friend's house; but the people were so eager to hear the word that in a short time, I believe, more than a thousand were at the door, besides those that were indoors, and filled every room in the house. I therefore stood upon the threshold, and spoke for about an hour on these words: 'Blessed are those who hunger and thirst for righteousness, for they will be filled.' It was a very solemn meeting. Glory be to God's great name! At my return to my lodgings, good old Mr Clap went with me into a private room, gave me something for my orphans and spoke many kind things to me. Although very old, yet he followed me from one end of the town to another, so that people said I had made old Mr Clap young again. Oh what a crown of glory is a hoary head, when found in the way of righteousness!

They are very plain people in general; though I observed there were some foolish virgins at church, covered all over with the pride of life. I find they are sadly divided amongst themselves as to outward things. I think there are no less than four different congregations of Baptists, two of the Independents and one of the Quakers. Dean Berkeley's name is much respected amongst them.

The established church is in excellent order as to externals; but many of the chief members were bigots. They seemed very fearful lest I should preach in Mr Clap's meeting-house, and gloried much in my bringing the good old man to church. Nor is there less bigotry amongst those of other communions. All, I fear, place the Kingdom of God too much in meats and drinks, and have an ill name round about for smuggling goods. One day, when I said in my sermon, 'What will become of you who cheat the king of his taxes?', the whole congregation seemed surprised, and looked at one another as though to say, 'We are guilty.' Lord Jesus, give them to know you, and the power of your resurrection, and teach them to live soberly, righteously and godly in this present evil world. Amen and Amen.

Boston

Friday, September 19. It being a day on which the clergy of the established church met, I had an opportunity of conversing with five of them together. I think one of them began with me for calling 'that Tennent and his brethren *faithful* ministers of Jesus Christ'. I answered that I believed they were. They then questioned me about the validity of the Presbyterian ordination. I replied that I believed it was valid.

'And is Mr Wesley altered in his sentiments?' said one; 'for he was very strenuous for the church, and rigorous against all other forms of government when he was at Boston.' I answered that he was then a great bigot; but God had since enlarged his heart, and I believed he was now like-minded with me in this matter. I then urged that a catholic spirit was best, and that a Baptist minister had recently taken communion with me at Savannah.

'I suppose', said another, 'you would do him as good a turn, and would take communion with him.' I answered that I would, and urged that it was best to preach the new birth, and the power of godliness, and not to insist so much on the form: for people would never be brought to one mind as to that; nor did Jesus Christ ever intend it. I added further, that I saw regenerate souls among the Baptists, among the Presbyterians, among the Independents, and among the church folks—all children of God, and yet all born again in a different way of worship: and who can tell which is the most evangelical?

'What, can you see regeneration with your eyes?' said the Commissary, or words to that effect.

Soon after, we began to talk of the righteousness of Christ, and the Commissary said Christ was to make up for the defects of our righteousness. I asked him whether conversion was not instantaneous. He was unwilling to confess it, but he having just before baptised an infant at public worship, I asked him whether he believed that very instant in which he sprinkled the child with water, the Holy Spirit fell upon the child. He answered, 'Yes.'

'Then,' said I, 'according to your own principles, regeneration is instantaneous, and since you will judge of the new birth by the fruits, pray watch that child, and see if it brings forth the fruits of the Spirit.' I also said that if every child was really born again in baptism, then every baptised infant would be saved. 'And so they are,' said Dr Cutler.

'How do you prove that?'

'Because the rubric says that all infants dying after baptism before they have committed actual sin are undoubtedly saved.'

I asked what text of scripture there was to prove it. 'Here,' said he (holding a prayer book in his hand), 'the church says so.'

We then just hinted at predestination. I said I subscribed to the seventeenth Article of the Church in its literal sense with all my heart. We then talked a little about falling away finally from grace. I said a true child of God, though he might fall foully, yet could never fall finally.

'But', said he, 'the Article says, "Men may fall away from grace given."'

I answered, 'But then observe what follows: "and by the

grace of God they may rise again."'

Several other things of less consequence passed between us. Finding how inconsistent they were, I took my leave, resolving they should not have an opportunity of denying me the use of their pulpits. However, they treated me with more civility than any of our own clergymen have done for a long while.

Saturday, September 20. Was refreshed with several packages of letters sent to me from different parts of England and America, giving me an account of the success of the gospel. Yet I was a little cast down to find some English friends had thrown aside the use of means, and others were disputing for *sinless perfection* and *universal redemption*. I know no such things asserted in the gospel, if explained aright. Lord, cause even this to work for good, and give me grace to oppose such errors without respect of person, but with meekness, humility and love. Amen.

Preached in the morning to about six thousand hearers, in the Rev. Dr Sewall's meeting-house; and afterwards on the common to about eight thousand; and again at night to a thronged company at my lodgings. I spent the remainder of the evening with a few friends in preparing for the Sabbath. The Sabbath in New England begins on Saturday evening, and perhaps is kept better by the ministers and people than in any other place in the known world. Oh that we may be always in the Spirit on the Lord's Day!

Sunday, September 21. Went in the morning, and heard Dr Colman preach. Dined with his colleague, the Rev. Mr Cooper. Preached in the afternoon to a crowded audience at the Rev. Mr Foxcroft's meeting-house; immediately after, on the common, to about fifteen thousand; and again at my lodgings to a greater company than before. Some afterwards came up into my room; and though hoarse, I was enabled to speak, and could have spoken, I believe, till midnight. To see people ready to hear makes me forget myself.

Wednesday, September 24. Went this morning to see

and preach at Cambridge, the chief college for training the sons of the prophets in New England. It has one president, four tutors, and about a hundred students. The college is scarcely as big as one of our least colleges at Oxford, and as far as I could gather from some who knew the state of it, not far superior to our universities in piety. Discipline is at a low ebb. Bad books are become fashionable among the tutors and students. Tillotson and Clark are read, instead of Shepard, Stoddard and such-like evangelical writers; and therefore I chose to preach from these words: 'We are not as many, who corrupt the word of God.' A great number of neighbouring ministers attended. God gave me great boldness and freedom of speech. The President of the college and minister of the parish treated me very civilly. In the afternoon I preached again, in the court, when, I believe, there were about seven thousand hearers. The Holy Spirit melted many hearts. A minister soon after wrote me word that one of his daughters was savingly wrought upon at that time. Lord, add daily to the church those who are to be saved!

Roxbury

Sunday, September 28. Preached in the morning at Dr Sewall's meeting-house, to a very crowded audience, and £555 currency was collected for the Orphan House. Was taken ill after dinner with a vomiting fit, but was enabled to preach in the afternoon at Dr Colman's, to as great if not a greater congregation than in the morning. Here £470 was collected. In both places, all things were carried on with great decency and order. People went slowly out, as though they had not a mind to escape giving; and Dr Colman said it was the most pleasant time he had enjoyed in that meeting-house through the whole course of his life. After the sermon I had the honour of a private visit from the Governor, who came to take his leave of me for the present. At their request I then went and preached to a great number of negroes on the conversion of the Ethiopian (Acts 8);

and, at my return, gave a word of exhortation to a crowd of people who were waiting at my lodgings. My spirits were almost exhausted, and my legs ready to sink under me, but the Lord visited my soul, and I went to bed greatly refreshed with divine consolations.

Hampton

Tuesday, September 30. Took ferry, immediately after the sermon, and with the Rev. Mr Cotton, minister of the place, who came to fetch me, went in a chaise to Hampton. I was pleased to see more plainness in Mr Cotton's house than I had seen in any minister's house since my arrival. His wife was as one who serves. Oh that all ministers' wives were so! Nothing gives me more offence than to see clergymen's wives dressed out in the pride of life. By this they bring a reproach upon religion. They generally live up to the utmost of their income; and being above working, after their husband's decease they are of all women most miserable. From such a wife, good Lord, of your infinite mercy, deliver me!

Marble Head, Maulden and Boston

Monday, October 6. Preached at Marble Head about 11; and the Lord attended his word with such mighty power that I trust it will be a day much to be remembered by many souls. I was upon the mount myself. The two ministers presented me with £70 for the Orphan House, which they had voluntarily collected yesterday in their own private meetings. Had the satisfaction of hearing that brother Seward had arrived safely in England. The Lord prosper the work of his hands! My health has much improved since I left Boston. Though I had ridden 178 miles, and preached 16 times, yet I was not in the least wearied. I went to rest full of peace, and desiring to be thankful to the Lord for causing me thus to renew my strength. Oh what a good master is Jesus Christ!

Wednesday, October 8. I think I never was so drawn out

to pray for little children, and invite little children to Jesus Christ, as I was this morning. I had just heard of a child who, after hearing me preach, was immediately taken sick and said, 'I will go to Mr Whitefield's God.' In a short time he died. This encouraged me to speak to little ones; but oh, how the old people were moved when I said, 'Little children, if your parents will not come to Christ, come yourselves, and go to heaven without them.' There seemed to be but few dry eyes.

Thursday, October 9. Every morning since my return I have been applied to by many souls under deep distress, and was grieved that I could not have more time with them. Gave, this morning, the public lecture at Dr Sewall's meeting-house, which was very crowded. When I came near the meeting-house, I found it much impressed upon my heart that I should preach upon our Lord's conference with Nicodemus. When I got into the pulpit, I saw a great number of ministers sitting around and before me. Coming to these words, 'you are Israel's teacher, and do you not understand these things?' the Lord enabled me to open my mouth boldly against unconverted ministers; for, I am persuaded, the generality of preachers talk of an unknown and unfelt Christ. The reason why congregations have been so dead is because they had dead men preaching to them. O that the Lord may quicken and revive them! How can dead men beget living children? It is true, indeed, that God may convert people by the devil, if he chooses; and he may by unconverted ministers; but I believe he seldom makes use of either of them for this purpose. No: he chooses vessels made fit by the operations of his blessed Spirit. For my own part, I would not ordain an unconverted man for ten thousand worlds. Unspeakable freedom God gave me while treating this subject.

Went to a funeral of one belonging to the Council; but do not like the custom at Boston of not speaking at the grave. When can ministers' prayers and exhortations be more suitable than when the corpse before them silently assists them, as it were; and, with a kind of dumb oratory, bids the spectators consider their latter end?

Cambridge and Boston

Saturday, October 11. Was weak in body, having taken cold. But preaching, I find, is a constant remedy against all indispositions. Went again to Cambridge, four miles from Mystick, and preached at the meeting-house door to a great body of people, who stood very attentively (though it rained), and were much moved. It being a university town, I talked on the words: 'Noah, the eighth person, a preacher of righteousness'; and endeavoured to show the qualifications for a true evangelical preacher of Christ's righteousness. I spoke very plainly to tutors and pupils.

Sunday, October 12. Went with the Governor, in his coach, to the common, where I preached my farewell sermon to about twenty thousand people—a sight I have not seen since I left Blackheath—and a sight perhaps never seen before in America.

The remainder of the evening was almost entirely spent in speaking to persons under great distress of soul. I believe the poor girl that followed me from Roxbury got a saving knowledge of Christ this morning, for when I preached on these words, 'The Lord our righteousness,' she was enabled to say 'The Lord *my* righteousness', and that she was not afraid to die.

Boston is a large, populous place, and very wealthy. It has the form of religion kept up, but has lost much of its power. I have not heard of any remarkable stir for many years. Ministers and people are obliged to confess that the love of many is grown cold. Both seem to be too much conformed to the world. There is much of the pride of life to be seen in their assemblies. Jewels, patches, and gay apparel are commonly worn by the female sex. The little infants who were brought to baptism were wrapped up in such fine things and so much pains taken to dress them, that one would think they were brought there to be initiated into, rather than to renounce, the pomps and vanities of this wicked world. There are nine meeting-houses of the Congregational persuasion, one Baptist, one French, and one belonging to the Scots-Irish. There are two monthly, and one weekly lectures; and those, too, only poorly attended. I mentioned it in my sermons, and I trust God will stir up the people to tread more frequently in the courts of his house. One thing Boston is very remarkable for, namely the external observance of the sabbath. Men in civil offices have a regard for religion. The Governor encourages them; and the ministers and magistrates seem to be more united than in any other place where I have been. Both were exceedingly civil during my stay. I never saw so little scoffing, and never had so little opposition. Still, I fear many rest in a head-knowledge, are privately Pharisees, and have only a reputation for being alive. It must needs be so, when the power of godliness is dwindled away, where only the form of religion is become fashionable amongst people. However, there are 'a few people in Sardis who have not soiled their clothes'. Many letters came to me from pious people, in which they complained of the degeneracy of the times, and hoped that God was about to revive his work in their midst.

Worcester and Leicester

Wednesday, October 15. Perceived Governor Belcher to be more affectionate than ever. After morning prayer, he took me by myself, and exhorted me to go on stirring up the ministers; for, said he, 'reformation must begin at the house of God'. As we were going along to meeting, he said, 'Mr Whitefield, do not spare rulers any more than ministers, no, not the chief of them.' I preached in the open air to some thousands. The word fell with weight; it carried all before it. After the sermon, the Governor remarked, 'I pray God I may apply what has been said to my own heart. Pray, Mr Whitefield, that I may hunger and thirst after righteousness.'

Northampton

Friday, October 17. We crossed the ferry to Northampton, where no less than three hundred souls were saved about five years ago. Their pastor's name is Edwards, successor and grandson to the great Stoddard, whose memory will be always precious to my soul, and whose books entitled *A Guide to Christ* and *Safety of appearing in Christ's Righteousness* I would recommend to all. Mr Edwards is a solid, excellent Christian, but, at present, weak in body. I think I have not seen his like in all New England. When I came into his pulpit, I found my heart drawn out to talk of scarcely anything besides the consolations and privileges of saints, and the plentiful effusion of the Spirit upon believers. When I came to remind them of their former experiences, and how zealous and lively they were at that time, both minister and people wept much. In the evening I gave a word of exhortation to several who came to Mr Edwards' house.

Sunday, October 19. Felt great satisfaction in being at the house of Mr Edwards. A sweeter couple I have not yet seen. Their children were not dressed in silks and satins, but plain, as becomes the children of those who in all things ought to be examples of Christian simplicity. Mrs Edwards is adorned with a meek and quiet spirit; she talked solidly of the things of God, and seemed to be such a helpmeet for her husband that she caused me to renew those prayers which, for some months, I have put up to God, that he would be pleased to send me a daughter of Abraham to be my wife. Lord, I desire to have no choice of my own. You know my circumstances; you know I only desire to marry in and for you. You chose Rebecca for Isaac; choose one to be a helpmeet for me in carrying on that great work which is committed to my charge. Preached this morning, and good Mr Edwards wept during the whole time of exercise. The people were equally moved; and in the afternoon the power increased yet more. Our Lord seems to keep the good wine till the last.

Suffield and Windsor

Tuesday, October 21. Set out for Suffield, which is about eight miles from the place where I slept. Reached there and preached at 11 o'clock to several thousands of people. Meeting with a minister on the way who said it was not absolutely necessary for a gospel minister to be converted, I insisted much in my discourse upon the doctrine of the new birth, and also the necessity of a minister being converted before he could preach Christ aright. As I was riding to Windsor, after dinner, an old man came up to me saying he knew what I had preached in the morning was true, for he had felt it. 'I was under the spirit of bondage twenty years,' he said, 'and have received the spirit of adoption twenty-three years'. The people of God seemed much revived at Windsor, where a converted man is minister. As soon as the sermon was over, I rode a mile and a half and preached to a thronged congregation belonging to old Mr Edwards, father of Mr Edwards of Northampton. After exercise, we supped at the house of old Mr Edwards. His wife was as aged, I believe, as himself, and I fancied that I was sitting in the house of a Zacharias and Elizabeth. I parted from him and his son (who came with me thus far) with regret; but, blessed be God, we shall meet in eternity!

New Haven

Saturday, October 25. Was refreshed this morning by the sight of Mr Jedediah Mills, the minister at Ripton near Stratford. He wrote to me some time ago. I felt his letter, and now also felt the man. I could not help thinking God would do great things by him. He had a remarkable work in his parish some time ago, and talked like one who was no novice in divine things. With him I dined at the Rev. Mr Clap's, Rector of New Haven College, about one-third as big as that of Cambridge. It has one Rector, three Tutors, and about a hundred students. I hear of no remarkable concern amongst them regarding religion. I preached twice, and there were sweet meltings discernible both times. I spoke very closely to the students, and showed the dreadful ill consequences of an unconverted ministry.

Stanford and Rye

Wednesday, October 29. Came here last night in safety, though dark and rainy. Was somewhat dejected before I went from my lodgings, and distressed for a text after I got up into the pulpit. But the Lord directed me to one, and before I had preached half an hour the blessed Spirit began to move the hearers' hearts in a very awesome manner. Young, and especially many old people were surprisingly moved. At dinner I spoke with such vigour against sending unconverted ministers into the ministry that two ministers with tears in their eyes publicly confessed that they had laid hands on two young men without so much as asking them whether they were born again of God or not. After dinner, I prayed, and one old minister was so deeply convicted that, calling Mr Noble and me out, with great difficulty (because of his weeping) he desired our prayers, 'for', said he, 'I have been a scholar, and have preached the doctrines of grace for a long time, but I believe I have never felt the power of them in my own soul.' Oh that all unconverted ministers were brought to make the same confession!

On many accounts, New England certainly excels all other provinces in America, and for the establishment of religion perhaps all other parts of the world. The towns all through Connecticut and eastward toward York, in the province of Massachusetts, near the riverside, are large and well peopled. Every five miles or perhaps less, you have a meeting-house; and I believe there is no such thing as a pluralist or non-resident minister in both provinces. Many, nay most that preach, I fear, do not know Christ in their own experience; yet I cannot see much worldly advantage to tempt them to take up the sacred function.

I think the ministers preaching almost universally from notes is a mark that they have, in a great measure, lost the old spirit of preaching. Though all are not to be condemned who use notes, yet it is a symptom of the decay of religion when reading sermons becomes fashionable where extempore preaching did once almost universally prevail. When the spirit of prayer began to be lost, then forms of prayer were invented, and I believe the same observation will hold good as to preaching. The civil government of New England seems to be well regulated; and I think at the opening of all their courts, either the judge or a minister begins with a prayer. Family worship, I believe, is generally kept up; and the negroes are better treated than in any other province I have yet seen. In short, I like New England exceeding well. Send out, O Lord, your light and your truth, and for your infinite mercy's sake show you have a particular delight in these habitable parts of the earth! Amen.

Staten Island

Tuesday, November 4. I was much refreshed with the sight of Mr Gilbert Tennent and Mr Cross. The former has recently lost his wife, and though dear unto him, yet he was enabled with great calmness to preach her funeral sermon, whilst the corpse was lying before him. This reminded me of Melanchthon, who, at the news of his wife's death, said, 'My Kate, I'll come after you before long.' Since his wife's decease, Mr Tennent has been in the West Jerseys and Maryland, and told me how remarkably God had worked by his ministry in many places. Mr Cross has also seen great and wonderful things in his congregations, so great that when I came to desire a detailed account, he said it directly answered the account given by Mr Edwards of the work of God in Northampton.

Baskinridge

Wednesday, November 5. I found Mr Davenport had been preaching to the congregation, as arranged. It consisted of about three thousand people. I had not spoken long before, in every part of the congregation, someone or other began to cry out, and almost all were melted to tears. A little boy, about eight years of age, wept as though his heart would break. Mr Cross took him up into the waggon, which so moved me that I broke from my discourse and told the people that, since old believers were not concerned, God, out of an infant's mouth, was perfecting praise; and the little boy should preach to them. As I was going away, I asked the little boy what he was crying for. He answered, his sins. I then asked what he wanted. He answered, 'Christ.' After the sermon, Mr Cross gave notice of an evening lecture in his barn, two miles off. There we went, and a great multitude followed. Mr Gilbert Tennent preached first; and I then began to pray and gave an exhortation. In about six minutes, one cried out, 'He is come! He is come!' and could scarcely sustain the manifestation of Jesus to his soul. The eager crying of others, for a similar favour, obliged me to stop; and I prayed over them as I saw their agonies and distress increase. At length we sang a hymn, and then retired to the house where the man that received Christ continued praising and speaking of him till near midnight. My own soul was so full that I retired, and wept before the Lord, under a deep sense of my own vileness and the sovereignty and greatness of God's everlasting love. Most of the people spent the remainder of the night in prayer and praises. It was a night much to be remembered.

Baskinridge and New Brunswick

Thursday, November 6. After breakfast this morning, at the desire of Mr Cross, I went and gave the word of exhortation to, and sang and prayed with, a few people in the barn. Before I mounted my horse, many came to me under great concern of soul. A lad about 13 years old told me he never felt sin till yesterday. A poor negro woman said she was 'filled with a love of Christ', and, being too fond of the instrument of her awakening, wanted to go with me. Her master consented, but I bid her go home and with a thankful heart serve her present master. When I was upon my horse several women came to shake me by the hand. I asked one whether she knew Christ. She said, 'Yes.' 'How long?' 'Three years the third Sunday in next March,' she answered. I asked another the same question. She replied, 'Yes, but I am waiting for a fresh breathing from the blessed Spirit.' I took my leave of them, and rode in company with many children of God to New Brunswick, 23 miles from Baskinridge. Here letters awaited me from Savannah, acquainting me that there had been a great mortality among the people of that place, though the orphans continued very healthy; and that a minister was coming over to supply my place at Savannah. This last much rejoiced me, having resolved to give up the Savannah living as soon as I arrived at Georgia. A parish and the Orphan House together are too much for me; besides, God seems to show me it is my duty to evangelise, and not to fix in any particular place. In the evening I preached in Mr Gilbert Tennent's meeting-house. A little after, Mr B. (a young minister, who I hope will hereafter come fairly out for God) preached for about an hour, and then, at the desire of Mr Tennent, I concluded with a word of exhortation.

Philadelphia

Sunday, November 9. Several came to see me, with whom I prayed. Preached at eleven in the morning to several thousands in a house built for that purpose since my departure from Philadelphia. It is a hundred feet long and seventy feet broad. A large gallery is to be erected all round it. Both in the morning and the evening God's glory filled the house. It was never preached in before. The roof is not yet up, but the people raised a convenient pulpit, and boarded the bottom. Great was the joy of most of the hearers when they saw me; but some still mocked. Between the services I received a packet of letters from England, dated in March last. May the Lord heal, and bring good out of the divisions which at present seem to be among the brethren there. Many friends being in the room, I kneeled down, prayed, and exhorted them all. I was greatly rejoiced to look round them, because there were some who had been marvellous offenders against God. I shall mention two only. The first is a Mr Brockden, recorder of deeds, etc., a man eminent in his profession, but for many years a notorious deist. In his younger days, he told me, he had some religious impressions, but coming into business, the cares of the world so choked the good seed that he not only forgot God but at length began to doubt of, and to dispute his very being. In this state he continued many years, and has been very zealous to propagate his deistical, I could almost say atheistical, principles among moral men; but he told me he never endeavoured to make proselytes of vicious, debauched people. When I came to Philadelphia this time last year, he had no curiosity to hear me. But a brother deist, his choicest companion, pressing him to come and hear me, to satisfy his curiosity he at length complied with his request. It was night. I was preaching at the Court House stairs, upon the conference which our Lord had with Nicodemus. I had not spoken much before God struck his heart, 'for,' said he, 'I saw your doctrine tended to make people good.' His family did not know that he had been to hear me. After he came home, his wife, who had been at the sermon, came in also, and wished heartily that he had heard me. He said nothing. After this, another of his family came in, repeating the same wish; and, if I mistake not, after that another, till at last being unable to refrain any longer, with tears in his eyes, he told them that he had been hearing me; and expressed his approbation. Ever since, he has followed on to know the Lord. Though upwards of threescore years old, he is now, I believe, born again of God.

The other is Captain H., formerly as great a reprobate as ever I heard of; almost a scandal and reproach to human nature. He used to swear to ease his stomach, and was so fond of new oaths that he used to go on board the transport ships, and offer a guinea for a new oath, that he might have the honour of coining it. By God's grace he is now, I believe, a Christian. Not only reformed, but renewed. Whatever men's reasoning may suggest, if the children of God fairly examine their own experiences—if they do God justice, they must acknowledge that they did not choose God, but God chose them. And if he chose them at all, it must be from eternity, and that too without anything foreseen in them. Unless they acknowledge this, man's salvation must be in part owing to the free-will of man; and if so, unless men descend from other parents than I did, Christ Jesus might have died, and never have seen the travail of his soul in the salvation of one of his creatures. But I would be tender on this point, and leave persons to be taught it by God. I am of the martyr Bradford's mind. Let a man go to the grammar school of faith and repentance, before he goes to the university of election and predestination. A bare head-knowledge of sound words avails nothing. I am quite tired of Christless talkers. From such may I ever turn away. Amen.

Saturday, November 15. Preached twice every day this week, in the new house, one morning excepted, when I preached in Mr C.'s meeting-house on account of the snow. On that occasion the word seemed to smite the congregation like so many pointed arrows. Many afterwards told me what they felt; and, in the evening I was sent for to a young woman who was carried home from the meeting and had continued almost speechless. I prayed with her, and heard afterwards she was in a more comfortable state. I cannot say we had one dry meeting. The least moving, I think, was one afternoon, when I was unaccountably carried out to talk against reasoning unbelievers. At dinner I had not fixed on a text. When I was going to preach, I was so ill that some of my friends advised me to go home. I thought it best to trust in God. I went on, began preaching, and found my heart somewhat refreshed; but, all on a sudden, my soul was so carried out to talk against relying on our natural reason, that my friends were astonished, and so was I too; for I felt the Holy Spirit come upon me, and had never spoken like that before. As I was going home, I said to a friend, 'Surely some reasoners were in the congregation.' Upon enquiry, I found a number of them were present, and then I knew why I was so assisted. Oh who would but trust in God! One of these reasoners a little later, meeting Mr B., said, 'What! Mr Whitefield could not make the people cry this afternoon.' 'A good reason for it,' said Mr B., 'he was preaching against deists, and you know they are a hardened generation.' Lord, take from them a heart of stone, and give them a heart of flesh!

Another afternoon, there was such a universal commotion in the congregation as I never saw in Philadelphia before. Numbers wept so sorely that I broke off prayer after the sermon sooner than otherwise I would have done. I preached on these words, 'What shall I do to be saved?'— and, as I afterwards found, was providentially directed to that subject: for a Mrs P., as I have it in a paper taken down verbatim, went to Mr Cummins to know why I should not preach in the church. He, after several invectives against me, said he could not answer his oath to the Bishop of London if he did give me leave, and cautioned her against going to hear me, adding that if she followed or adhered to what I said she was in a woeful condition. 'Nay,' said he, 'you are damned if you do.' He also told her he was distressed in his soul for her, because she was a good liver, and had been brought up under pious parents. Mrs P. asked if she, by God's assistance, lived up to the doctrine and example of our saviour and the apostles, as laid down in the New Testament, would she not do well? He answered, 'Yes.'

'Then, sir,' she replied, 'I must believe in Mr Whitefield's doctrine.'

'There now,' he said, 'you are running on again; I tell you, you are mad. Go home and hear him no more, and you'll do well enough.'

'No, sir,' said Mrs P., 'I cannot stay away; and seeing so many people admire Mr Whitefield's doctrine, and you so bitter against him, "What must I do to be saved?" for you are enough to distract me between you.'

'You are good enough,' replied Mr Cummins, 'and may dance or play at cards, and be in a far better way than Whitefield or his followers. For my part, I will wash my hands of your blood, and will leave you.'

'No,' said Mrs P., 'you love money too well, sir, to leave this place.'

After a great deal more conversation, Mrs P. left him, in great distress of mind, and often repeating to herself, 'Lord, what must I do to be saved?' Contrary to Mr Cummins' advice, she went in the afternoon, says the paper before me, to hear Mr Whitefield, and he providentially preached on the trembling jailor's words, 'What must I do to be saved?'—which gave the gentlewoman so much comfort that she is thankful to God for having an opportunity of hearing that text explained, is much strengthened, and will by God's grace follow his commandments. Lord, for your mercy's sake, work in her both to will and to do, after your good pleasure! Amen.

It would be almost endless to recount all the particular instances of God's grace which I have seen this week past. Many who before were only convicted now plainly proved that they were converted. My chief business was now to build up and to exhort them to continue in the grace of God. Even so, many were convicted, almost every day, and came to me under the greatest distress and anguish of soul. Several Societies are now in the town, not only of men and women but of little boys and little girls. Being so engaged, I could not visit them as I would, but I hope the Lord will raise me up some fellow-labourers, and that elders will be ordained in every place; then we shall see a glorious church settled and established in Philadelphia. Hasten that time, O Lord.

I cannot leave off giving an account of this week's work without mentioning another instance of God's grace. About the middle of last week I was called to visit one Mrs D., then lying on a sick bed, who had been brought home to God when I was at Philadelphia last spring. Her husband was then at sea, and on his return home greatly persecuted his wife, denying her spiritual friends leave to visit her. God now inclined his heart to let me come and pray with her, according to her desire. When I went the first time, he was not called up to join us. The next day he himself met me in the street, and gave me an invitation. I complied, and visited his wife several times. Never before did I see a soul so exult in God, or talk so touchingly of the love of Jesus, though sometimes in extremity of pain. Sometimes she was so full of God that she could not speak; and at other times, when she could not speak, and I bid her lift her hands if all was well, she stretched them with great earnestness. As soon as she recovered breath, she would talk of Jesus, saying that his love was above her pain, that she longed to depart, but was willing to tarry the Lord's leisure. When I told her that I wanted to be gone too, she said, 'No, you must stay longer, and bring home some more souls to Christ.'

Bohemia in Maryland, and St George's in Pennsylvania

Monday, November 24. Got here about eleven last night, and was most kindly received by old Mrs B., a true mother in Israel. Read my English letters, and thought it was the will of God that I should embark for my native country next spring. Rode with my friends about ten miles to a place called St George's, where a kind and courteous Quaker received us into his house. Here God showed me more clearly the way I should go. Lord guide me with your counsel till you bring me to everlasting glory.

Bethesda in Georgia

Monday, December 29. Enjoyed a very comfortable Christmas at Bethesda, having God often with us in my public ministrations amongst the family and labourers. One woman received Christ in a glorious manner; and several others were brought under strong convictions. On Christmas Day I married Mr Periam to one of the schoolmistresses whom I brought with me from Philadelphia, and who was converted some time ago at Savannah. Both times the bridegroom of the church was present with us; and many, I hope, felt a union between Jesus Christ and their souls. Having appointed Mr Barber to take care of the spiritual, and Mr Habersham to superintend the outward affairs of the Orphan House, and settled all things to my satisfaction, finding my call clear to England I last night took a sorrowful and affectionate leave of my family.

In the evening I preached at Savannah, and took my final leave of the people, it being inconsistent with my other affairs to act as their pastor any more. Another minister is not yet come, but is expected daily. I gave the Trustees notice in January last of my plan to give up the parsonage. Blessed be God! I am now free to evangelise and go wherever the Lord is pleased to call me. I still hope well of Georgia, though, at present, it is in a very declining and piteous state. It will flourish, I believe, when settled upon a religious foundation. Till then, God will bring the counsels of men to nought. It was so with New England: I am persuaded it will be so with New Georgia. Glory be to God! I leave behind me some who love the Lord Jesus in sincerity.

Mr Jonathan Bryan's plantation near Port Royal in South Carolina

Thursday, January 1, 1741. Left Savannah on Tuesday, in the afternoon. Arrived here this morning about two o'clock, with some more friends in Mr Jonathan Bryan's boat, who with some others came to Bethesda in the hope of my returning with them. I trust he and two or three more since our last meeting have accepted Christ. In the afternoon I preached at his house to several of the neighbouring people. The Lord made it a Bethel. In the evening came Mr Hugh Bryan, his brother, recently converted at Savannah. His wife died some time ago; in what frame, the following letter, which he sent to a niece of his now at Bethesda, will testify.

Dear Child,—Under written are the dying words of your aunt, which I send for your satisfaction and information. She died October 7, between the hours of nine and ten in the morning, being filled with the full assurance of faith in Christ, and a joyful hope of eternal salvation through his merits and mediation.

As your aunt and I were praying to our Lord Jesus to give her the comforts of his Holy Spirit to support her under the agonies of death, she replied, 'I see him! I see him! Now I see light.' After this, she continued in prayer about half an hour; but her speech failing her, we could not during that time understand what she spake, only we could hear the name of Jesus often, and 'Come Jesus! Come Jesus!' Then again she spoke out plainly and said, 'Who would die without God? Now I see light.' Then she lay in an agony about half an hour, and again spoke out and said, 'God has let me see great and glorious things which would not be believed if they were told.' Then your uncle R. coming into the room, spoke to your aunt S., and your dying aunt hearing his voice called him to her, and when he was come she spoke to us and said, 'Mind what I say to you; for hereafter you must all give an account of what I now say to you. God has enabled me to speak to you before I go (for I am just going).' Then she said, 'God is a just God as well as merciful. Be diligent in searching your hearts. Brother, tell Mr — he is in the wrong. My pain is great, but Christ is sufficient for me.' And she repeated that 'God had let her see great things that would not be believed if they were told.' She said also, 'Follow Whitefield, God will bless him, wherever he goes. Don't speak lightly of him. Bless him. Bless him. God has enabled me to speak to you before I go. I am just going. Farewell, Farewell. God be with you!' Then she composed herself, and lay about half an hour, and neither moved nor groaned, except her lips and tongue, and the heaving of her breast in breathing, seeming to be in her perfect senses till about a minute before she died. She looked round at each of us that were about her bed, and then departed in quietness.

Thus far Mr Bryan. I shall only add, O death, where is your sting! O grave, where is your victory over true believers! What fools are they who count their lives madness.

Charleston

Saturday, January 10. Preached twice every day this week, and expounded frequently in the evening, to a great company at Mr F.'s. The Holy Spirit applied the word with power. Several had acquainted me what God had done for their souls; and one was so filled when Christ manifested himself to her soul, that she continued a whole night praying and praising God. Some have fallen away, but, blessed be God, the greatest part continue steadfast. Enemies are more enraged. As a proof of it, take the following instance. When Mr Jonathan Bryan came to Georgia, he showed me a letter written by his brother, Mr Hugh Bryan, in which it was hinted that the clergy break their canons, and this he desired me to correct for the press. I did. It was published this week. Immediately, Mr Bryan was apprehended and bound over; and, being asked, frankly confessed that I corrected and made some alterations in it. This evening a constable came to me.

I went before the C.J., confessed that I had revised and corrected Mr B.'s letter for the press, and gave security to appear, by his attorney, at the next general quarter sessions, under the penalty of £100 proclamation money. Blessed be God for this further honour! My soul rejoices in it. I think this may be called persecution. I think it is for righteousness' sake. Oh how gently does the Lord deal with me, and by these little trials forewarn and, I trust, prepare me for greater ones!

Sunday, January 11. Preached this morning upon Herod's sending the wise men to find out Christ, under a pretence that he intended to come and *worship* him, when in reality he intended to *kill* him. I endeavoured to show how dreadful it was to persecute under a pretence of *religion*. Mr W. telling me that what he did was out of a *sense of duty*, and that binding me over to the Sessions was *no persecution*, led my thoughts this way. In the afternoon, preached from these words: 'They proclaimed a fast and seated Naboth in a prominent place among the people. Then two scoundrels came and sat opposite him and brought charges against Naboth before the people, saying, "Naboth has cursed both God and the king." So they took him outside the city and stoned him to death.' (1 Kings 21:12–13.) My hearers, as well as myself, made the application. It was pretty close. I especially directed my discourse to *men in authority*, and showed them the heinous sin of *abusing the power* which God had put into their hands.

Thursday, January 15. Received several encouraging letters from my friends at Boston. The Rev. Mr Cooper writes thus:

> I can inform you that there are many abiding proofs that you did not labour in vain amongst us in this place. I could much more than fill this paper with the accounts I have received from the persons who have been impressed under the word preached by you. But I can only now say in general, some have been awakened who were before quite complacent, and, I hope, a good work begun in them. Others, who have been under religious impressions, are now more earnestly pressing into the kingdom of heaven; and many of the children of God stirred up to give diligence for the full assurance of faith. There is a great flocking to all the lectures in the town; and the people show such a disposition to the new Tuesday evening lecture that our large capacious house cannot receive all who come.

Mr Welch, a pious merchant, writes thus:

I fear I am tedious, but I can't break off till I just mention, to the glory of the grace of God, and for your comfort and encouragement, the success your ministry of late has had among us. The impressions made seem to be abiding on the minds of many. The doctrines of grace seem to be more the topic of conversation than ever I knew them. Nay, religious conversation seems to be almost fashionable, and almost every one seems disposed to hear or speak of the things of God. Multitudes flock to the evening lecture, though it has sometimes been the worst of weather. Ministers seem to preach with more *life*, and the great audiences seem to hear with solemn attention; and, I hope, our Lord Jesus is getting himself the victory over the hearts of many sinners.

Others write to the same effect. All love, all glory be to God!

Friday, January 16. Preached twice every day this week, and expounded in the evening as usual. Congregations much increased since Saturday night last; and I never received such generous tokens of love from any people as from some in Charleston. They so loaded me with sea-stores that I sent many of them to Savannah. Having now all things finished according to my mind, I preached my farewell sermon last night, and spoke at the burial of a Quaker woman, at the desire of her surviving friends. Today I went on board the *Minerva*, Captain Meredith, in which I took passage for myself and some others to England. O God of the sea and the dry land, be with us on our voyage, and prepare me for the many perils and mercies that await me amongst my own countrymen! Amen and Amen.

On board the 'Minerva'

Sailed over Charleston bar, January 24, and arrived at Falmouth on March 11. In the beginning of the voyage, my body was weak, and my spirits low; but afterwards God was pleased to strengthen me both in body and soul. The books of Genesis and Exodus, which I expounded in course, morning and evening, were much blessed to my spiritual comfort; and the Lord has been pleased to give me freedom to write down some of my extempore discourses, which I hope he will bless for his own name's sake. In short, this voyage has been a profitable voyage to my soul, because of my having had many opportunities for reading, meditation, and prayer. I cannot but adore the providence of God in favouring me with such blessed retirements I have frequently enjoyed on the great waters. I dared not expect to meet with such success as he has been pleased to give me abroad; and I do not doubt I shall yet see greater things there, as well as at home. I never had such a variety of trials and changes of life lying before me as at this time, but I throw myself into the hands of the blessed Jesus.